BEHIND THE PEACOCK THRONE

BEHIND THE PEACOCK THRONE

Minou Reeves

SIDGWICK & JACKSON
LONDON

First published in 1986 in Great Britain
by Sidgwick and Jackson Limited

ISBN 0–283–99275–1

Typeset by Falcon Graphic Art Ltd
Wallington, Surrey
Printed in Great Britain by
The Garden City Press
Letchworth, Hertfordshire
for Sidgwick and Jackson Limited
1 Tavistock Chambers, Bloomsbury Way
London WC1A 2SG

Contents

Acknowledgements

This book could not have been completed without the help of many friends and colleagues. I wish to express my particular gratitude to Dr Siegfried Unseld, the director of the German publishers, Suhrkamp, who read what was to become the first chapter and encouraged me to persist at a very early and uncertain stage. I was greatly assisted during its writing by Rüdiger Görner, Wilja Sepasgozarian and Renate Senft, who suggested many improvements. Although the book is largely based on personal experience I found the rich statistical and historical material supplied by Robert Graham, Sir Roger Stevens and Ehsan Tabari invaluable. Johannes Gewiess assisted me with important archival information. I am also indebted to Ingeborg Fruin and Linda Robson for their prompt and efficient support in typing the script. Ruth Liepman and Herta Ryder were a source of unflagging encouragement in the publishing process, while I wish to record an especial debt to Susan Hill and Esther Jagger for their wise and acute judgement in the editing of the book. Lastly I must thank my husband, Nigel Reeves, who remained a constant source of inspiration.

London, November 1985

To the memory of my parents

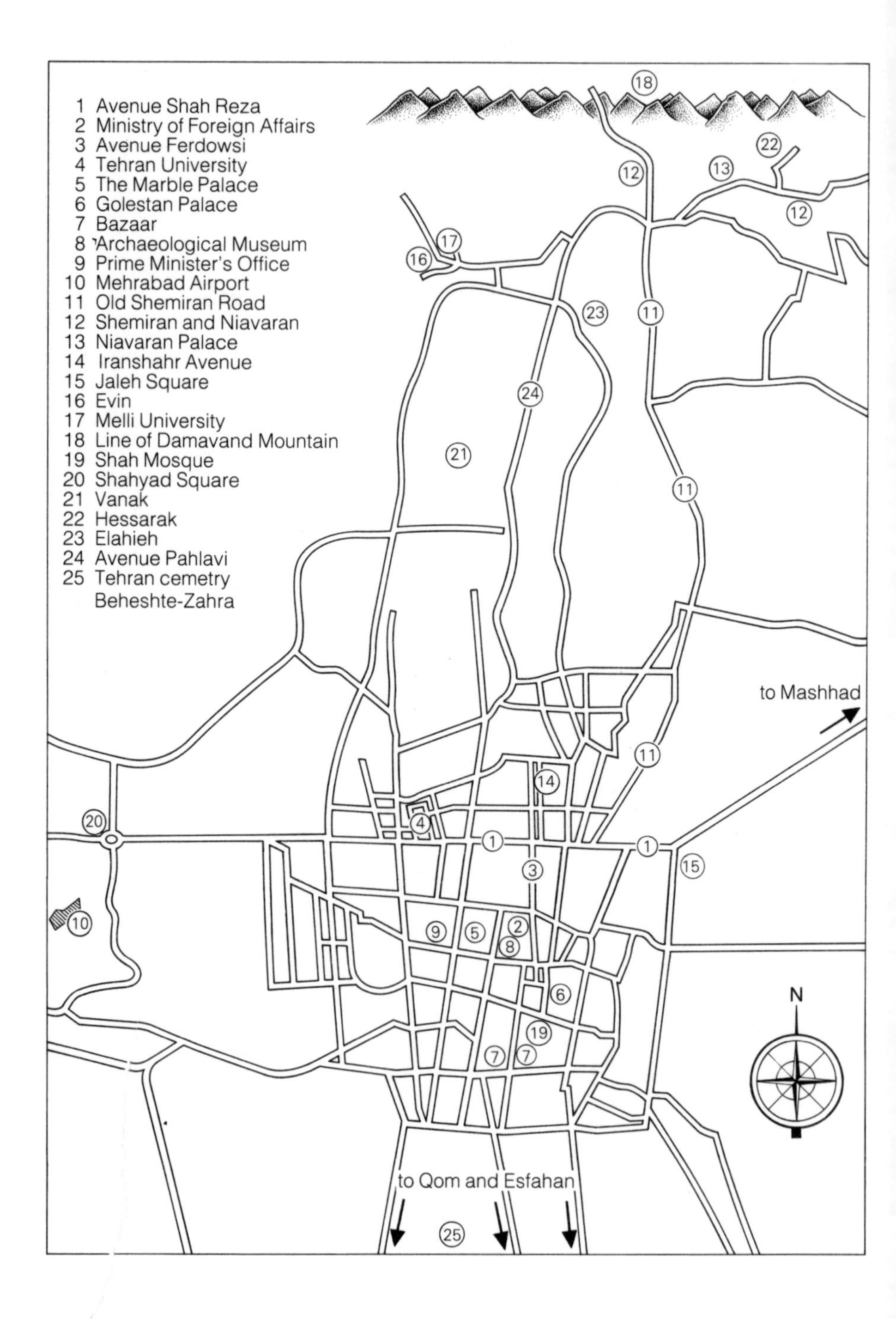

1 Avenue Shah Reza
2 Ministry of Foreign Affairs
3 Avenue Ferdowsi
4 Tehran University
5 The Marble Palace
6 Golestan Palace
7 Bazaar
8 Archaeological Museum
9 Prime Minister's Office
10 Mehrabad Airport
11 Old Shemiran Road
12 Shemiran and Niavaran
13 Niavaran Palace
14 Iranshahr Avenue
15 Jaleh Square
16 Evin
17 Melli University
18 Line of Damavand Mountain
19 Shah Mosque
20 Shahyad Square
21 Vanak
22 Hessarak
23 Elahieh
24 Avenue Pahlavi
25 Tehran cemetry Beheshte-Zahra
to Mashhad
N
to Qom and Esfahan

TURKEY
AZARBAIJAN
Tabriz
CASPIAN SEA
U.S.S.R
GILAN
Rasht
KORDESTAN
MAZANDARAN
Mashdad
IRAQ
Karaj
TEHRAN
Qom
LORESTAN
KHORASHAN
Esfahan
AFGHANISTAN
I R A N
Ahvaz
Yazd
Khorramshahr
KHUZESTAN
Abadan
Pasargadae
Kerman
N
Persepolis
Shiraz
F A R S
PAKISTAN
SEISTAN
BALUCHESTAN
PERSIAN GULF
0
200 mls
0
200 km

His promises were, as he then was, mighty;
But his performance, as he is now, nothing.

William Shakespeare, *Henry VIII*, Act IV, Scene II

1

The Escape

On a strange, unforgettable day in the spring of 1979 I was sitting in a taxi taking me to Tehran airport. The air stank of death. The ravages of the revolution stared at me from all sides. It was almost unbelievable that the face of a city, my city, could have been so utterly destroyed in such a short time.

The taxi drove me through the chaotic sites of the most recent street battles. Bearded young men in military green, calling themselves 'Guardians of the Revolution', kept watch. I prayed that they would not stop and question us. We drove on past the burnt-out shells of banks, government buildings, factories, cinemas and department stores, past the demolished memorials and beheaded statues of the Shah and the Crown Prince. Remains of revolutionary slogans on the walls were still legible. Now and again we heard shots, but could not tell from which quarter of the city they came. Destruction and confusion reigned everywhere.

My country had experienced a violent revolution. It had annihilated the monarchy, a political system of 2500 years' standing in Iran, and an Islamic Republic was to be created in its place. It was difficult to recall the chronological sequence of the events which had finally led to the 'Great Revolution'; but one thing was certain: after unprecedented mass demonstrations, general strikes and appalling bloodshed, the Iranian people had succeeded in driving out of the country its monarch, Shah Mohammed Reza Pahlavi, and his family. Most Iranians of the middle and lower classes had been unanimous in their demand for the abdication of the Shah and in favour of the return of the exiled religious leader, Ayatollah Khomeini. The Ayatollah's sensational homecoming and the hysteria it triggered had turned the eyes of the world towards Iran. I remembered the banner headlines in the Tehran daily newspaper *Keyhan* – 'THE SHAH IS GONE' – and the subsequent jubilation among the people on the streets which now seemed so lifeless and deserted.

Now I was on my way to Mehrabad airport, where these two historic events had taken place. It was here that the final farewell of the Shah to a country which he had ruled for thirty-eight years had occurred, and here again that his rival, Ayatollah Khomeini, returning to replace him after sixteen years in exile, had been welcomed.

The taxi driver turned on the radio. We heard the strains of a revolutionary song: 'Spring is here . . . Spring is here . . . . Red tulips have grown from the blood shed by our countrymen . . . .'

Yes, it was spring, but I was sad; not for the fall of the Pahlavi dynasty, but for an ancient and proud country – the cradle of Oriental art, poetry and philosophy. It now lay in ruins. What were the real causes of this seemingly swift upheaval? Why had it been necessary for so many people to lose their lives? Had my compatriots been misguided when they sacrificed their lives for the sacred cause, for freedom, democracy and social justice, as the song said – in short, for a better future? Was the new regime capable of offering the Iranian people these ideals? Profoundly disturbed by this and by many other questions, I cast my mind back to the springtimes of my childhood.

Spring, the most beautiful season of the year in Iran, has a special meaning for Persians, who observe a number of ancient customs and traditions at this time. Before New Year people clean their houses thoroughly and buy new clothes and shoes. Everything is intended to look just as fresh and new as nature, the spirit waking from its long winter sleep. So before the turn of the year Persian families gather for the Haft-Sin, which means seven S's. In each home the table is set with seven articles whose names begin with S. These are *Sabseh* – usually lentils or grains of wheat, wrapped in a damp cloth and left to germinate, then placed on a plate to form a dense, green cluster; *Serkeh* – vinegar; *Sib* – apples; *Sonbol* – hyacinths; *Senjed* – whitebeam berries; *Somagh* – a lemon-flavoured spice; and *Samanou* – a sweet dish made from malt. In addition a mirror – symbol of light – and a glass bowl of water containing a pair of goldfish – symbol of movement and of life – adorn the table. In every house the air is filled with the fragrance of the hyacinths. On New Year's Day it is traditional to visit other members of one's family. The samovar simmers all day long, and small glasses of Persian tea are served along with various delicacies. As a parting present the children are given gold coins by the oldest member of the family. I remember as a child looking forward immensely to returning home and counting the gold coins I had accumulated. Back home, the festivities continued with a celebration meal of rice with fresh herbs and fried white salmon.

But this spring was different. Haft-Sin is possibly the only relic of an earlier religion, based on pantheistic beliefs, to have survived the thirteen centuries of Islamic domination in Iran. The festival had therefore been banned, because it was regarded as heathen in the eyes of our new strict Islamic rulers. What was there for Persian families to celebrate this spring, anyway? Nearly every family had far more reason to mourn: many mothers had lost their sons in the revolution, many children no longer had a father. Most people were wearing black. Was this the country of legendary rose gardens, which, along with the springtime fragrance of narcissi and the song of the nightingale, had enchanted our poets from time immemorial? Alas, today they belonged only to the realm of the imagination.

The taxi driver simply turned off the radio and shook his head as if to express his scepticism about the situation; he was probably too scared to voice his opinions. When we reached the airport he helped me with my one small suitcase and then drove quickly away.

For some time I just stood there, feeling faint. Then I took a deep breath and strode, as if on automatic pilot, to the desk where I checked in my case. Next I had to report to the passport office. Now my heart began to pound and I felt cold sweat on my back. What would happen if they told me that there was no passport in my name? All passports had to be handed in to the Islamic authorities by the airline concerned for a final check forty-eight hours before departure, and only thus could one's exit permit be confirmed. It seemed to take them forever at the counter . . .

but at last an arm reached out and handed me my passport.

That passport had already cost me several sleepless nights. I believe in fate, in a chain of coincidences which can change the whole direction of a person's life; and it is impossible to imagine how different everything would have been for me if I had not earlier met a certain young man.

My name was on the long list of those who had been linked with the *ancien régime*, or who had held important posts during its time. Everyone on this blacklist had either already been executed, was in prison awaiting trial, was under house arrest, or simply could not leave the country. I had never been involved in Iranian politics, nor had I ever acted against the interests of the people during my twelve years of service in the Iranian Embassy in Berne and in the Empress's private office in Tehran. But the leaders of the Revolution were quite determined to divide the nation into two groups: the privileged and the needy. The group branded as 'privileged' was under suspicion and had to answer for its conduct in the past.

At the end of February I went to the passport office with my brother Mehrdad, an electronics engineer educated in Britain. Like many Iranians who had received technological training in Europe or America, he had returned to his country to meet the needs of its rapid industrial development in the sixties and seventies. However, the new Islamic leaders were hostile to Western technology and intended to halt all the existing development projects. What was to become of my brother and his expertise? He could do nothing but leave the country again – so he was planning to return to Britain. As we waited our turn in the long queue I noticed a young police lieutenant who was talking to an elderly man a few yards away from us, but was unaccountably staring at me. 'Why is that policeman looking at me like that?' I fretted. Then he came over and introduced himself, explaining to my relief that he had met me when we were selling the contents of my brother's house.

Now I remembered the green-eyed visitor who had rung the doorbell early one morning at my brother's flat, where I was staying at the time, and wanted to look at the things we had for sale. He was not wearing his uniform that day. I was struck immediately by the colour of his eyes, since most Iranians have dark ones; his politeness had equally impressed me. He apologised repeatedly for having disturbed us at such an inconvenient time, and he only stayed for a few minutes because he did not find anything that suited him.

Before leaving Iran, my brother had decided to sell the entire contents of his home. That provided me with an opportunity to dispose of my wardrobe, since, due to the Islamic government's increasingly stringent regulations concerning women's public dress, I could see no chance of being able to wear Western clothing again. At the beginning, just after the Revolution, it had been possible to get by with an ordinary headscarf. But as time went on the rules became stricter and stricter, so that no Iranian woman dared leave home without a full black veil or without covering her head and legs. The propaganda of the Islamic rulers had influenced public opinion to such an extent that women without veils were subjected to verbal insults or even physical assault by passers-by in the street. Yet to our astonishment, the demand for the things we were selling was enormous. We never believed it would be possible under the circumstances to sell our possessions, but some women still liked to wear Western clothes in the privacy of their homes and it was as if people needed a respite from the violence of the preceding months. For a few weeks, there was a kind of ceasefire, and people felt more at ease. Simple, veiled women and bearded men from the bazaar quarter came and bought furniture, electrical appliances, paintings, crockery, clothes, shoes, handbags and many other items.

Now the friendly policeman asked us, as we stood in the passport queue, if he could help in any way. I did not know what to say. Of course I needed assistance. After the Islamic clergy had seized power I had been placed under surveillance, since I had been an employee of Empress Farah's. In the Niavaran Palace, the residence of the imperial couple until their departure, a revolutionary committee controlled by an old mullah had been set up. My personal data were on file there and I had to report twice a week to have my identity card stamped. So there was no question of my leaving the country. Was I to trust this man? It soon became clear that he worked in the security section of the passport office – in the department which held the list of those prohibited from leaving the country.

My brother had got his passport back and I persuaded him to book the first available flight and not to worry about me. I am not sure how many days and nights went by before I made up my mind to go and see the police lieutenant again on my own behalf.

What kind of a person was he? What was his true function within the new administration? Why did he want to help me? I spent many sleepless hours working out hypothetical answers to these questions. He might belong to the group of officers who had completely accepted the Islamic seizure of power and carried out the orders of their new superiors without demur; in other words, he could be extremely dangerous. Yet he did not look dangerous. Alternatively, he could simply be a poor, unsuspecting soul who would do his daily duty under any regime and never question his situation. Yet he seemed too intelligent for that. Or perhaps he worked for them because he had no other prospects – to him it might simply have been a means of earning a living, even though he was basically dissatisfied with the new state of affairs. His behaviour seemed to me to make this the most likely possibility. However, I was only too aware that I would have to follow all my instincts to avoid making irrevocable mistakes.

So one morning, at last, I went to see him. He greeted me courteously and I sensed that my visit did not surprise him. I told him that I had worked for the Empress, that I had been interrogated by Islamic judges and that I still had to report to an Islamic committee twice a week. He stood up calmly, lit a cigarette and rapidly enumerated on his fingers the steps that had to be taken to get me safely out of Iran.

'You need a passport. I shall have to delete your name from the blacklist. You will also need an exit permit and you'll have to consider how you wish to leave the country. I'll do my best to help you. . . . Please leave now, and don't come here again.' He took my address and telephone number, and assured me that he would keep in touch. Then we said goodbye.

To be on the safe side I was wearing a long black veil which enveloped me from head to toe and made it difficult to walk. With trembling steps I made my way to my car and drove home. Was it a trap? This worrying thought hammered incessantly in my head and I knew that I would have no more peace of mind. A whole month passed. I felt like a convicted murderer on Death Row. One evening, a maid came and told me that there was a gentleman at the door who wanted to speak to me. I was filled with foreboding, yet there was no alternative but to go to the door and find out who he was. I at once recognized my green-eyed rescuer, looking very pale and holding an envelope.

'Have you read the evening paper?' he asked me in a hushed voice.

'No,' I answered. I had long since stopped reading the newspapers, since they had nothing to report but executions, deaths and occasions for mourning.

I was appalled to hear that his name was on a list of officers who, on the Shah's orders, had suppressed an armed rebellion in the north of Iran a few years previously. I knew exactly what that meant: the charge, corruption on earth; the punishment, execution. His helpless, innocent face looked like that of an abandoned child. Yet with infinite politeness he handed me the envelope that contained my passport.

'Leave this blood-soaked country!' he said, and added emphatically, 'They'll never forgive you for having worked at the Imperial Court.'

'And what's going to happen to you?' I asked him in alarm.

'I shall have to stay in hiding from now on,' he said. 'My life is hopeless anyway. You, on the other hand, have good prospects abroad. I can at least die with a good conscience when I remember that I have saved your life.'

I embraced him and then burst into tears – I had him to thank for my life, but I could do nothing in return for him. He stepped backwards in some embarrassment, wished me good fortune and left hurriedly.

Now I was waiting at the airport for my plane. I had my passport in my pocket and I thought of him, wondering if he was still alive.

Soon I was high over my homeland, flying towards an uncertain future in the West. Beyond exhaustion, I pressed my face to the window and caught my last glimpse of that mountainous country with its vast brown plateaux, its deserts and rocky ranges – a land with an ancient culture which had produced such figures as Hafez, Saadi and Omar Khayyam. I knew I would never see Iran again, and suddenly I became aware of how much I love my country – not for nationalistic reasons, for I am not a nationalist, but because of the many memories, some beautiful, some painful, which link me with it.

The other passengers were predominantly non-Iranians who were obviously leaving because of the political uncertainty. One of the few Iranians on board attempted to get into conversation with me. I soon found out that he was one of those businessmen who had accumulated enormous profits during the 1970s. The consequence of that economic boom was a corruption that spread everywhere. As a result of Iran's growth conscienceless profiteers made huge fortunes, especially in the construction industry and through land speculation. Since there was nothing more to be squeezed from Iran, these people had pulled out and were now relaxing after all their efforts with the aid of their Swiss and American bank accounts. It is impossible to put a figure on the damage done to my country by such people.

Many confused thoughts passed through my mind. Who was responsible for the decline of the 'Iranian Empire'? What could explain the fall of the Shah, the king of kings, and its tragic consequences? Was this total collapse of an ancient monarchical system a result of his personal failure or of deep-rooted historical circumstances? Of one thing I was sure – I had been witness to a decisive moment in history.

2

A Persian Childhood

Iran, or Persia as it was known until 1935, is a vast country of over 600,000 square miles, bordered on the north by the Caspian Sea and the USSR, on the east by Afghanistan and Pakistan, on the south by the Persian Gulf, and on the west by Turkey and Iraq. Until the world-shaking events of 1978–9 the West knew relatively little about my country. Oil was known to be its major product: it had intensified the Anglo-Russian rivalry which had started in the age of expansion and colonialism in the nineteenth century, and had been the cause of a crisis in the 1950s when the British were forced to withdraw. Churchill, Roosevelt and Stalin had attended an important conference in Tehran during World War II. But otherwise Persia had always been characterized as a romantic place, a land of nightingales and roses, of richly woven carpets and of great caravanserais on the Silk Route from China. Abroad, Omar Khayyam was the most famous of its many poets – though not its best – because of Edward Fitzgerald's translation. Travellers had brought back tales of Persia's ancient cities, such as Shiraz and Esfahan, and the wonders of their magnificent Islamic architecture.

At the end of the eighteenth century the capital was moved from Esfahan to Tehran, and it was here in December 1946 that I was born. My father, Sadegh Samimi, was a historian who had studied history of art and archaeology and was an expert in the cultures of the West as well as those of the East. For many years he was Director General of the Archaeological Museum of Iran and an adviser to the Iranian Minister of Culture. Though my mother had never gone to university she was a cultured woman who placed great value upon the education of her children. She taught me to read and write at a very early age, and by the age of four I could read the headlines in a newspaper. At five I had taken the examination to enter primary school, even though Iranian children do not normally begin their schooling until they are seven. From the age of three I also had ballet lessons.

My ballet teacher, Miss Corneli, was a Russian who had escaped to neighbouring Iran after the 1917 Revolution. She had subsequently founded an excellent ballet school in Tehran. The majority of her pupils were from the Armenian Christian minority; others included the daughters of diplomats or children from mixed Persian and European marriages. It was significant that there were no girls from strictly Islamic families.

Miss Corneli was a tall, slim, red-haired lady, then about fifty. She wore spectacles and always carried a stick with which she pointed out our every mistake. She was strict, impatient, and hated having to repeat anything. I did not enjoy going to her dance classes, although she was happy with my progress. But today I know that Miss Corneli, who died in Tehran in the 1970s in poverty and loneliness, bullied me and trained me into a mobility and sense of physical co-ordination which I could otherwise never have possessed. Above all, it is thanks to her that I developed a strict sense of self-discipline. I often still think of those days when the melodic sounds of her piano would echo across the street, punctuated by her instructions.

From the age of eight I was taught the piano. I learnt to play Mozart, Beethoven and Chopin with an Armenian lady who lived in our neighbourhood. I remember her flat well, permeated with the scent of fresh croissants and Turkish coffee. What a contrast to my ballet teacher! She was friendly, chubby and collected dolls from every corner of the world – which, of course, delighted me. Even today I can conjure up her living room in every detail. Behind the piano hung a framed picture of Leopold Mozart proudly playing the violin, with his young son Wolfgang Amadeus seated at the cembalo and his elder daughter singing. An ancient bookcase filled one entire wall; it was filled in jolly disarray with her many books and those wonderful dolls. The massive sofa, piled high with cushions on which her black cat seemed always to be sleeping, gave the whole room a sense of comfort and warmth which made the tuition seem less formal. The room's single, small window looked out across a little back garden, and all you could see were the dark green branches of an ancient pine tree. We always had to place a lighted lamp on the piano. How I looked forward to those Wednesday afternoons sitting at the piano with my teacher beside me.

My primary school was called Hefdah Dey, and its name commemorated 8 January 1935, the day the use of the veil was abolished by Reza Shah. For the same reason that day was known in Iran as Women's Liberation Day. After six years there I moved to Nemouneh, the most up-to-date girls' secondary school in Tehran. Even our uniforms, unlike those of other schools which were made of drab grey linen, were fashionably designed. Here, as always, my mother supported and encouraged me and helped me when I had problems with my school work. She also tried to complement my formal education by introducing me to Persian literature. On many an evening – and these were the loveliest moments of my childhood – my mother would read me the works of Persian poets, for example poems from Saadi's *Rose Garden*. Saadi, a twelfth-century poet from Shiraz, wrote in a simple, natural style, and often in the form of parables meant for ordinary people. His intention was moral and didactic, and his poems were easily comprehensible even to a child.

> Torment not the ant who is bearing food on her back
> She too is alive and filled with the joy of living.

My father did not interfere with our upbringing, as he firmly believed in my mother's views on the physical and intellectual education of children. He had given her a free hand in governing his and our lives; a freedom which ran against the Islamic traditions that the father and husband governed the household as well as the family relationships with the outside world. We all loved, respected and obeyed my mother. I remember that my father often discussed his professional problems with her and received moral support and advice. Later he admitted to me that without her he would never have received such rapid advancement in his career. My mother was indisputably our focal point, a formidable source of inspiration, encouragement and joy.

Despite their different temperaments – my father restless, vivacious, talkative and witty, my mother quiet, cool and reserved – they had a harmonious relationship, complementing each other. I never heard them arguing. If my father became angry about anything, his ire would soon be cooled by my mother's subtlety. Although I think she was an exceptional woman, her position in the family was paralleled in many other educated Iranian families. Not all women in Iran were subjected to patriarchy and male domination. Through their own assertive efforts educated Iranian women acquired status and self-respect and sometimes even the upper hand in running the family's entire affairs.

My close relationship to my mother was in no way affected when my two brothers Mehrdad and Mehran were born – on the contrary, as her only daughter I was still very much loved by her. This attitude towards a daughter is not typical of all Iranian families. In the old patriarchal social system which governed family relationships sons have always been more welcome than daughters, and were treated accordingly. But in my family things were quite different. My parents did not share the conventional Iranian view, which had its roots in Islam; they both came from unorthodox educated middle-class backgrounds and our lifestyle did not really fit into any clearly defined social category.

As an archaeologist, my father had devoted his life to the restoration and preservation of the Persian historical legacy, and it was from him that I learnt about my country's ancient past. My father characterized Iran as a land of invasions, a land of mixtures: mixtures of peoples and cultures without parallel in world history. Here, in the heart of central Asia, the riches of Persia had enticed invaders from all points of the compass.

The two names for the country – Persia and Iran – refer to ancient geographical boundaries, though for centuries the terms were used interchangeably. About one thousand years BC people known as Aryans spread southwards and westwards from southern Russia and Turkestan. That, my father told us, was where the name 'Iran' came from. 'Persia', which derives from the word 'Fars', strictly speaking encompassed the high mountain area around Shiraz with its nucleus at Persepolis, the cradle of Iranian civilization. Iran, on the other hand, was a vast territory bounded by what are now the southern republics of the Soviet Union, northern Greece and Turkey, Libya, Egypt and Ethiopia, the Arab Emirates, and Pakistan and Afghanistan – all forming the ancient Persian Empire. I also learnt that my mother tongue, Farsi, is an Indo-European language, even though it is written in Arabic script and includes many Arabic words assimilated since the country's conversion to Islam in the seventh century AD.

During the 1950s my parents took us on an educational tour to Esfahan, Shiraz and Persepolis in the southern part of the country, west of the Zagros mountains. Many of the monuments were erected more than two thousand years ago when the famous Achaemenian kings, Cyrus, Darius and Xerxes, were founding their empire and bringing its culture to a pinnacle of achievement. In Persepolis we looked in fascination at the ruins of their palaces, and in Pasargadae and Naghsh-e-Rostam at their tombs. My father told us of the rise and fall of this dynasty and of the defeat of their last king, Darius III, at the hands of the Greek conqueror, Alexander the Great, in 323 BC. Here and there he deciphered for us an inscription in the ancient Persian language etched into the cave walls, or explained to us the reliefs that are a testimony to the magnificent achievements of these kings.

After this period, he told us, Seleucus, one of Alexander's generals, founded a new Hellenistic-Persian civilization, but it was destroyed a century later by an invasion of Parthian nomads from the north-east. Their rule lasted for five and a half centuries, but they retained the existing culture and made themselves masters of Mesopotamia as well. In their time Persia was strong enough to repulse the forces of the Roman general Mark Anthony, who invaded the country in 36 BC. After an uprising the nationalist Sassanians ousted the Parthians, and established a dynasty which ruled for four hundred years, enlivening and preserving the Persian national spirit. Their decline took place simultaneously with the spread of Islam throughout the neighbouring countries, and in AD 646 the Sassanians were defeated and an Islamic state was inaugurated. By this time the Persian population contained elements of

Greek, Turk and Arab origin, as well as some from the borders of China and India.

Despite the cultural importance of Genghis Khan's invasion in AD 1220, and the subsequent Mongol rule which lasted for three hundred years, my father believed that the decisive turning point in Persian history was the earlier Arab invasion and the country's conversion to Islam in the seventh century. In his view Persian cultural history consisted of two major epochs: a pre-Islamic Aryan one, and a post-Islamic Arab one. The adoption of Islam brought about a fundamental metamorphosis in the social order and mentality of the Persian people – something that had not occurred at the time of any of the other cultural invasions that had affected Persia. For Islam survived even the Mongols, and has remained the social and moral nucleus of the country to the present day.

My father also explained that since Cyrus the Great, who proclaimed himself King of Persia in 546 BC, our state system had continued to be a monarchy and our history marked by the rise and fall of successive dynasties. I learnt that there had been many despotic monarchs and a very few enlightened ones, such as Shah Abbas in the sixteenth century. It was the king's performance as a warrior and conqueror that guaranteed his power – or lack of it. Nader Shah Afshar, for example, who ruled from 1736 to 1747, had apparently been a weak ruler, yet he is greatly revered as a brilliant warior who conducted a glorious campaign in India and captured the legendary Peacock Throne.

In Esfahan we visited many mosques and palaces belonging to the post-Islamic period. Those fascinating mosaics and blue cupolas transported my childish imagination into the land of the Thousand and One Nights. What could be more emotionally overwhelming than the call to prayer resounding from the minarets? We looked too at the Tshehel-Sotun, the dreamlike palace of the Safavid kings, who ruled in the sixteenth century when the Mongols had been toppled from power. These kings changed the form of the Islamic religion of Persia from Sunnism to Shiism and made Esfahan their capital. We strolled along beneath the ancient plane trees and the poplars in that magical palace garden, intoxicated by the scent of the roses and the jasmine and spellbound by the stories of the past that my father told. Many years later and thousands of miles from Persia, I came upon the following poem in the turn-of-the-century Prague-born poet Rainer Maria Rilke's *Sonnets to Orpheus*, which never fails to arouse in me a longing for those Persian rose gardens:

> Sing those gardens, my heart, poured as into a glass,
> Gardens you have not known, transparent, untrampled.
> Waters and roses of Isphahan or Shiraz,
> Blissfully sing them, praise them, the unexampled.

My mother too had told me much about Islam and read me some of the simpler verses of the Koran. On many occasions she read to me from a history book describing the life and deeds of Shia saints. So far as I can judge from the impressions of my childhood, my mother was not religious in any orthodox sense. I would rather call her a moralist possessing her own ethical code of values and wishing to acquaint me through reading with what was good and evil in the human world – an admirable philosophy of education, especially since she was a mother teaching her daughter in the Iran of the 1950s, when many other women still thought in far more rigid, old-fashioned ways. She never ignored any question I asked.

Today I also realize why she frequently took me to the slum districts in the south of Tehran. We would take clothes, blankets, toys and food with us and give them to families in need. Even then I was beginning to reflect about my mother's charitable activities, which seemed to me like so many drops of water on a hot stone. It was shattering to watch little children run after us and beg in the vain hope of getting something, when we had already given away everything we had with us. 'Poverty is so widespread that we can't help everybody even if we sell all our possessions,' my mother replied when I accused her of not having taken enough.

As far as Islam was concerned, what my mother told me conveyed a sense of melancholy rather than joy and liveliness. Even today this religion arouses in me associations of death and sorrow. They stem both from the religious stories of suffering that my mother told me, and from my first physical contact with Islam.

I was barely ten when my mother took me for the first time to a religious procession to mark the martyrdom of a particularly highly regarded Shia saint, Imam Hossein. It was early evening and my mother was wearing a black veil. I had only ever seen her twice before in such clothes, and that was at funerals. I was made to wear thick stockings beneath my dress and to cover my head with a scarf.

'Why can't we go along in our ordinary clothes? Why do we have to hide ourselves like this?' I asked my mother.

'It's an Islamic day of mourning,' she replied. 'The people who are in this procession all share a deep faith. If they see any woman unveiled in the street they may well come and beat her.'

I could not understand why we had to watch this procession at all, but my mother thought it right that I should experience such an occasion.

I shall never forget that hot summer evening. My mother seemed much paler than usual beneath her black veil; perhaps she too was rather afraid. On the way we fetched my aunt, who was also veiled in black yet insisted on telling us jokes and stories to lighten the atmosphere. In physique and personality she was totally different from her sister: while my mother was slim, reflective and introverted, my aunt was large, jolly and loquacious. I liked her very much because she was so unaffected, warm-hearted and full of life. When we reached our vantage point we found that hundreds of people draped in black were already gathered at the side of the street to see the procession go by. 'Don't they look like black ravens?' whispered my aunt, holding my hand firmly in hers. For a moment my fears vanished, only to return as the procession approached. A group of black-clad men of unnerving appearance, carrying black placards and holding fluttering flags high above their heads, bore down on us with rhythmic steps. With monotonous insistence and intensity they kept chanting the name of Imam Hossein. Behind them came another group of men, naked to the waist, who were flagellating themselves with iron chains to the rhythm of the chorus. Though their skin was criss-crossed with great red weals they continued lashing themselves while the onlookers shrieked and cried hysterically. Faced with this sight of indescribable and total ecstasy I crept beneath my mother's veil, peeping out from my place of safety at the spectacle before me.

Even my jolly aunt seemed to be affected by the atmosphere and fell silent.

In the meantime night had fallen and the street lamps shone across the path of the mourners. My mother comforted me, saying that the procession was now over and a play would begin. I had often been to the theatre with my parents, but always to see a comedy, so for me a play meant something that made you laugh. This performance was totally different. It was called a passion play and presented episodes from the lives of holy martyrs. Suddenly we were left in total darkness and a dreadful silence descended all around. I clung to my mother's legs, shaking all over. Then burning torches pierced the darkness and there appeared the figure of Imam Hossein dressed as a warrior and riding a white horse, followed by two mounted disciples. From the other side the Imam's opponent, Yazid, dressed in startling red and on a black horse, suddenly rode into the light. They engaged in a fierce sword fight to the clatter of their horses' hooves. Reeling from a sword-stroke to the stomach the Imam fell to the ground, gushing with blood that covered the pavement. The torches were extinguished for a moment, till, in the light of innumerable candles held aloft in many-branched candlesticks, I saw giant, ghostlike figures coming towards us in long white garments, singing a lament for the death of their Imam.

The Imam, my mother told me, had fallen 1300 years before in a battle near Karbela, today in Iraq, and re-enacted annually in this play. She went on to explain that the white garments represented Islamic shrouds, and that Moslems always wrap their dead in thick white winding sheets before they are buried.

It was late when we returned home and I went straight to bed, but I was so upset that I could not sleep. When I did I was gripped by nightmares and woke my parents with my screams. I had a high temperature. I heard my father tell my mother that she should never have taken me to watch the procession, which was unsuitable for children. But hadn't I seen many other children there? Did that mean that they too felt as I did? Today I know that my reaction was simply the result of my own modern, relatively secular upbringing.

It was my father who told me about the religions of Persia

before the Arab conquest. For 1500 years, he said, during their pre-Islamic period the Persians had been followers of Zoroaster, the first prophet in history to encompass the idea of a divinity and a scripture. Through Zoroaster's doctrines the Persians came to worship a single god, Ahuramazda, the embodiment of good, while they abhorred his rival, Ahriman, the symbol of evil. An unceasing battle raged between these two forces; yet good usually conquered evil. The same moral principle is at work in the human soul. The thinking person should allow good to triumph over evil in the inner battle of his mind and so create a balance between himself and the world. For Zoroastrians earth, water, fire and air were holy elements of human existence which must not be polluted. Sacrifices were forbidden, and so animals were spared. All in all, my father concluded, it was a gentle and progressive religion.

At the beginning of the seventh century, when Islam was beginning to establish itself in the neighbouring Arab countries, there were already signs in Persia of the decline of Sassanian rule. According to ancient tradition the kings of Persia were the direct representatives on earth of Ahuramazda; but the Sassanians had taken advantage of their spiritual and earthly monopoly, to create from the doctrines of Zoroaster an elitist religion. They had scant regard for the ordinary people, who suffered social injustice and inequality and had long felt alienated from this aristocratic religion. The Arab rulers, on the other hand, thanks to their tribal democracy, led a relatively modest nomadic life, though this did not prevent them from envying the extravagance of the Persian nobility and their cultural superiority. The emergence of Islam gave the Arabs an identity from which came a powerful sense of political unity and the stimulus to use their attractive new faith as a weapon to be turned against the decadent Zoroastrianism. But the conquest of a country so superior in culture, together with the pomp of the Sassanian court, corrupted the simple, democratically minded Arabs, and soon their liberal tribal system was replaced by a feudal pattern along Persian lines.

Despite their physical victory the Arabs never succeeded, my father insisted, on turning our country into an Arab one since the spiritual resistance continued. Although this resistance was not capable of blocking Arab influence on religion, language and literature in Persia, it nevertheless made a major contribution to preserving Persian identity in the centuries that followed.

Later I learnt the details of the history of the Shia religion, Iran's branch of Islam. After Mohammed's death in AD 632, a dynastic quarrel concerning the succession broke out between two Arab families within the Qureish tribe, of which the prophet had been a member. Through elections the Bani-Omayieh family had acquired Mohammed's power, while his true descendants led a simple, modest life. While the Arabs adhered to the Omayiehs and remained traditionalists or Sunnis, the Persians demonstrated solidarity with the latter faction and branched off, calling themselves Shias. They rebelled against their new Sunni rulers, declaring themselves to be followers of the prophet's son-in-law, Ali, and making him their first Imam. The definitive split took place when the elected Sunni Caliph Omar was murdered by a Persian slave in AD 644. The feud grew stronger. Ali was murdered in retaliation while at prayer in the mosque. His elder son and successor, Imam Hassan, was poisoned, while his brother, the next Imam, Hossein, whose commemorative procession I had watched in such fear, was killed in a battle against the Bani-Omayiehs in AD 680. Thus it was that the cult of martyrdom came to characterize Shiism, according to which twelve Imams followed the prophet. The twelfth, so legend has it, disappeared in AD 873 and will one day reveal himself to the world again, save mankind and re-establish justice on earth. And thus the problem of a successor both to the prophet Mohammed and to the twelfth Imam was solved.

In 1978 and 1979, in the wake of the Revolution which ended the rule of the Shah, I was to witness how the Shia spirit of suffering and martyr-worship was still able to inspire millions of believers in my country. With a sense of shock I realized that all the Shah's efforts to transform Iran into a modern, Western-style, industrialized state had not influenced in any way the archaic religious convictions of the majority of his people. And Ayatollah Khomeini, returning from exile, was surely greeted as the incarnation of the long-hidden twelfth Imam, who was supposed to end all injustice on earth.

But meanwhile the Shia religion still needed a source of continuity, and so was born the idea that representatives for the hidden Imam should be sought on earth. Called *Mujtahed*, they are, above all, interpreters of the Koran. They live from the donations of their followers and are therefore independent of any earthly regime. But as time passed a hierarchy also evolved among these clergy, or mullahs as they are known. Those who distinguished themselves through profound studies of the humanities gained in prestige and fame and so increased the numbers of their followers. Such mullahs are known as ayatollahs – literally, 'signs of God'. Gradually, they developed a sphere of power independent of and outside the state.

I was afraid of the bearded mullahs with their long robes and turbans because I had only seen them as a child when at a funeral. By the age of eight I had experienced two deaths in our own family, and my parents took me to each of these burials. After the funerals the mullah sang verses in Arabic from the Koran, of which I understood not a word, and then narrated a story of martyrdom, presumably to lighten our pain. According to the mystic philosophy of the Sufis, a sect that emerged in the twelfth century, death should not be represented as something fearful, for according to Islamic mysticism man emerges from the earth only to return to it. This philosophy occupies a special place in the mind of every Persian. But the sight of a Persian cemetery does not inspire a sense of peace and harmony, for they are bleak and ugly places.

As we went in through the main entrance of the cemetery where my paternal grandmother was to be buried I set eyes upon two huge men erecting a tombstone and who looked at me, as I thought, with a sinister expression. At their feet lay many engraved but otherwise incomplete tombstones. These masons, it seemed to me as I hurried past, were maliciously waiting for yet more people to die. Hardly had I recovered from this frightening sight when a great crowd of sick-looking beggars came down on us, demanding alms. When you pressed a coin into their hands they suddenly began to pray loudly and hypocritically for the soul of our departed relative, but the next instant they cast evil looks upon us as if they wished us to be dead too. In front of my eyes my grandmother's corpse, wrapped in a long white winding sheet, was cast into its grave. Today the symbolism of this type of burial is clearer to me – it is intended to display humility, modesty and equality before God; but as a child it aroused in me only fear. At home, Iranian mourning continues for a further forty days, and on the third, seventh and fortieth day after the death it achieves a peak of intensity. At these times a mullah comes to the house and stays for several hours, declaiming a divine service of mourning and singing funereal songs. Mourning and suffering are the very basis of the Moslem Shia religion.

My grandmother had lived with us and, although towards the end she could no longer walk and was mostly confined to her room, her departure left a great gap in our lives. I missed her most because she particularly liked me and was upset if my parents were angry with me. And then there were those delightful old Persian fairy stories, known to no one else, which she would recount to me. At this time we lived in an old house which had been built in the traditional Persian manner with pillars and a verandah, and stood in a large garden. The best part of the garden was the stream which ran through it and helped to make the heat of a Tehran summer more bearable. On one side of the stream beside an ancient wall stood two weeping willows, beneath which my brother Mehrdad and I would play to our hearts' content during the summer.

The district we lived in was called Absardar, from *ab* meaning 'water' and *sardar* meaning 'commandant'. At the turn of the century one Agha Bala Khan Sardar had a well on his estate here and, as was the custom in those times, had irrigation channels constructed to help the local inhabitants. Irrigation is an ancient tradition in Persia. For thousands of years a shortage of water had been the most pressing problem in the country, since it lies in a rain-starved band that stretches from the Sahara to the deserts of China. As early as the seventh century BC the Persians had developed sophisticated techniques for constructing irrigation channels and subterranean reservoirs for their agriculture, which are still in use today. It was the Persians' skill in irrigation that also enabled the gardens for which the country is famous to flourish. Thanks to the charitable commandant, the sound of rushing water gave our garden in Tehran a sense of greenness and peace, which returns to me whenever I think nostalgically of those days.

After my grandmother's death Naneh, my mother's old nurse, tried to fill the gap by spending far more time with me than she had previously done, and taking me with her now and then to the colourful Tehran bazaar. There we bought cloth, sweets, fruit and vegetables and Naneh would visit her brother, who had a little spice shop. Frequently he gave me a present of a tiny bottle of rosewater. When we got back home we would tell the house-keeper, Fatemeh, what we had seen and done. She was a tall, robust woman who had grown up in a Kordish tribe in the north-west and was better at riding horses than at washing crockery and dusting the house. She was constantly breaking things and my mother was often cross with her. Naneh and Fatemeh didn't get on, and quarrelled incessantly about trivialities.

Naneh, who in earlier years had received tuition in the Koran and was able to write and read a little, regarded the wretched Fatemeh as stupid and uneducated as she had never gone to school, and tried to put her down at every opportunity. But Fatemeh was a proud nomad woman, inflexible and unwilling to take orders from Naneh. In any case, she was almost twice the size of Naneh and whenever they had a row I was always afraid that she would pick up fragile old Naneh and throw her to the ground! Only when one of my uncles, Mehdi Ehterami, an army officer, came to visit us did the two women reduce their mutual hostility to a mere exchange of angry looks.

In the impressive uniform which he nearly always wore, with his stiff military bearing and moustache, my uncle seemed a strict and dictatorial figure, but beneath the façade he was very kind and gentle. His life revolved around order and discipline. Profound respect for the Shah and complete devotion to the fatherland were evident in his every word. As a young officer he had been decorated by the Shah, and after rapid promotion he eventually became one of the most influential generals in the Shah's army. My uncle wanted us children to be influenced by the Shah's sense of nationalist pride, and so at every New Year festival he would give us a portrait of the Shah and often took us to the celebratory military parades.

My father, on the other hand, was a liberal man of the world, a cosmopolitan. As a historian he distanced himself from the events of the present just as much as he distanced himself from the processes of history; he was an observer and analyst. Repeatedly he would quote to us a poem by Saadi, which was intended to arouse in us a more broadly based view of our position in the world.

> To no one man nor land should you tie your heart,
> For far flung are the realms of earth and sea
> And many are the men that live thereon.

As a young man my father had been sent to the military academy but, although he had done well and had been encouraged by his superiors to think of an army career, once his studies were over he left the army. Yet my father had interesting memories from those years. At that time Reza Shah, the father of the last Shah, was the ruler of our country. Although my father regarded him as an absolute monarch he still greatly admired him for his openness and for the persistence with which he carried out his plans for the modernization of Iran. He did not rely simply on the reports of his ministers, but would appear in person, unannounced, at a hospital or a road-building scheme or a barracks to see for himself how things were going. One morning Reza Shah appeared in the kitchens of the infantry division with which my father was serving and looked at the porridge cooking on the stove. My father told us that Reza Shah had discovered the sole of a shoe cooking in the pot. This had so enraged him that he not only slapped the cook and sacked him on the spot, but dismissed the commander of the division as well.

Reza Shah founded the Pahlavi dynasty when he was elected Shah in 1925. Coming from a modest military background, he was anxious to imbue his family with the dignity of the pre-Islamic monarchic dynasties. In 1926 he adopted for his dynasty the name Pahlavi – the language spoken by the ancient Parthians, on which modern Farsi is based. Possessed of a very powerful personality, Reza Shah had a tough manner and imposing looks: he was tall and robust, with piercing eyes, and wore simple military uniforms similar to those he had worn as a soldier in the Russian-commanded Persian Cossack army before rising to power. Full of admiration, my father told me how much he frightened his ministers by demanding absolute honesty in the fulfilment of their duties. Later, when I came to work in Reza Shah's son's administration, ministers and high officials still regarded the Shah with fear. But the son, who had succeeded him in 1941, had not inherited his father's integrity. What I saw among the Shah's ministers was not a fear of corruption and incompetence being uncovered, but simply a fear of being replaced by a new favourite.

My father seldom spoke of our Shah. Just occasionally I heard him say that in comparison to the old Shah he was far too weak and could not administer the country properly, but his disapproval was limited to these brief remarks. He never joined a political party, for instance, nor did he try to enter Parliament or to associate himself with the political opposition to the Shah.

His younger brother, Mansour, however, responded to the situation in a different way. Once my father came across anti-Shah writings in his room, and a loud and serious argument ensued. My father warned him of the consequences of keeping this kind of material in the house and told him to burn it immediately. I was still too young to have a clear understanding of what was going on. This uncle, then a student at the University of Tehran, was temporarily lodging with us; I rarely saw him because he left the house very early and did not return until late at night. Occasionally he came home earlier, with a group of friends, who would lock themselves in his room, smoking and talking for hours. Old Naneh told me once in a whisper, when my parents had gone out, that my uncle was a supporter of Mossadegh and held these sessions to discuss politics and to organize anti-Shah rallies.

Naneh said that the Shah did not like Mossadegh, but had been forced to make him his Prime Minister in 1951. Mohammed Mossadegh had opposed the Shah and his family for many years and could not forgive them for having accumulated so much personal wealth in less than a generation, through the expropriation of landowners. He also accused the Shah of being a mere puppet of Britain and of allowing the British to exploit Iran's vital oil resources. Mossadegh had become a national hero by fomenting Iranian hatred of foreign domination, symbolized by the Anglo-Iranian Oil Company. He succeeded in nationalizing oil, forcing the British to leave Iran and thus reducing the Shah's power as a monarch. I can vividly remember the time when, in August 1953, Mossadegh exiled the Shah. He had already expelled the Shah's twin sister Princess Ashraf, whom he believed wielded an evil influence on her brother. I was seven and witnessed the culmination of this crisis.

All the statues of the Shah in Tehran were pulled down, the schools had to close and we remained at home. But from inside the house I could hear the demonstrators shouting: 'Death to the Shah and the Pahlavis, servants of the aliens!' But only a few days later, to my confusion, the slogans changed; this time I heard them chanting: 'Death to Mossadegh, the traitor!' I just did not understand what was going on. Mossadegh was arrested and the Shah returned with his then wife, Queen Soraya, from exile in Rome.

Three times in those unsettled years my uncle was arrested for taking part in demonstrations against the regime, but thanks to declarations made by my father on his behalf he was always released. On one occasion he was so brutally beaten after being arrested that he lost all his teeth and had to spend a long time in hospital.

All this was extremely puzzling for me as a schoolchild. I had two uncles, each representing a diametrically opposed political view. One was a convinced royalist, the other a militant socialist who opposed the monarchy. In my first year at primary school I had been taught the language of patriotism and of reverence for the Shah. Our teacher would tell us of the good deeds of the benevolent Shah who loved his people and his country above everything else: therefore, she said, we too should love him. But my mother never spoke to me of the Shah and his family. Thanks to her, by the age of twelve I had acquired a keen social conscience and a strong sense of compassion. And at that point my childhood ended. That happy life together, in a liberal, unprejudiced family circle was torn abruptly apart, for quite unexpectedly my beloved mother died.

One day I came home from school to find her lying in bed in great pain, her old nanny standing helplessly by her side. My mother looked deathly pale and her forehead was damp with cold sweat. I did not know what to do. My father had gone on an archaeological excavation in a remote province and could not be contacted. I called my officer uncle and we took my mother to hospital in his car. The diagnosis was appendicitis, and she had to be operated on instantly. A week later she developed an internal infection, and her condition deteriorated with great speed. By this time my father had come back and wanted to send her to Europe for treatment, but the surgeon said it was too late. My mother was only thirty-five and had always enjoyed perfect health – it seemed ridiculous that she should suddenly die like this. For the first time fate had decided to show me its dark side. Today I blame the incompetent and irresponsible medical staff of the Iranian hospital for her death.

My mother had been an extraordinary woman: intelligent, graceful and exceptionally beautiful. As she lay on her deathbed I gripped her hand in mine as it grew colder. At that moment she looked to me, with her marble skin and luxuriant black hair, like a Greek goddess. Her last smile, which became petrified on her pale lips, remains indelibly printed upon my memory. When she parted from me I saw a white cloud drifting past the window.

It still intrigues me to consider how conscious my mother always was of death. For her, death was part of life – something that should be confronted. She taught me not to be tied to material things but to enrich my inner self. On many occasions when we were alone together she would say to me: 'Minou, you must know that life is not eternal. We are all mere visitors on this earth. One day I have to depart, another day your father.' And I remember her saying repeatedly: 'The only thing that remains of us is good deeds; it can be in the form of helping a needy person, writing a verse that can delight the heart, or planting a tree from whose beauty and shade people may benefit.'

The idea of transience is central to my country's philosophy of mysticism and it occupies a special place in Persian literature. It is a philosophy which regards everything in the material world as temporary, and so looks beyond it. The inner, invisible world becomes a source of mystic longing. Omar Khayyam's concept of death is a pessimistic one. He captured his thoughts on man's vulnerability in the image of a potter's workshop:

There in the potter's room I saw
Two thousand pots of clay, silent but eloquent:
Suddenly one raised its voice and cried,
'Where is our potter, who will sell us, who will buy?'

It is the same distress at the transience of human existence that leads Hafez to his epicurean hedonism. The mystical unity with God is reached through the intense experience of earthly pleasures. But for Molavi, the Islamic mystic whom my mother loved so much, it is in death that we reach the highest point of human knowledge.

The death of my mother marked the end of a decisive chapter in my life – a chapter in which I derived my first knowledge and which laid the foundation for the further development of my personality and attitudes. From that moment I felt like a fruit, consisting only of kernel and flesh and lacking a skin, open and vulnerable to all the vicissitudes of life. Good parents are like protective walls standing between their children and the world; if you lose one or both while still a child, all your security disappears and you become like a feather blown by the winds. That, indeed, was to be my fate.

How could my poor father possibly raise three children, aged twelve, nine and one, on his own? And at that time there were no good boarding schools in Iran to which he could send us. So he decided that we should go abroad. Our household was dispersed. Deeply saddened, old Naneh looked for comfort from her brother, the spice merchant in the bazaar, and settled down with him and his family. Fatemeh returned to Kordistan, hoping that she would still be able to fit into the life of the nomads. The Savak, the newly formed security police, possessed damning evidence against my militant socialist uncle, who moved to live with a friend of similar persuasion. Both remained under permanent police surveillance. My brothers and I were sent to Switzerland to grow up, each to a different boarding school in a different part of that distant land. In order not to lose all influence on our education my father settled in Paris, having arranged early retirement from his post as Director General of the Archaeological Museum.

I have never fully recovered from the consequences of my mother's tragic death. Throughout the years that followed I was constantly searching for some substance, some identity which could forge a tie between the culture of my birth and my subsequent experiences in the Western world. My links with Iran were restricted to the books which my father sent me from Paris and the occasional letter from my relatives, but these gradually dwindled to New Year cards. Only my uncle in the army was determined that my love of the fatherland should not be diminished by living abroad, and he continued to write regularly and to send me newspapers from home. Every Persian New Year he would send me, as before, a portrait of the Shah. One of my drawers at boarding school was filled with these portraits, which I instinctively never wanted to hang on the wall. But in my spare time I read Persian stories and poems which carried me back to my dreamlike past in Persia, to the warmth of our lovely house, to the hubbub of the Tehran bazaar and to the scented gardens of Esfahan. But now that all seemed as distant and unattainable as my mother.

3

The View from Switzerland

My boarding school in Dolder lay in the middle of a dense oak and pine forest on a steep mountainside above Zurich. From down below on the Römerhofplatz you could travel up to Dolder by cable car, above an idyllic mountain landscape. From there a narrow path led to the school, which was run by a middle-aged Swiss couple from Appenzell. In this solid old redbrick building lived children from all over the world. They came predominantly from diplomatic families or broken marriages, but there were also others whose parents simply believed in Swiss education and could afford to send their children to school there. It was a small establishment with only twenty boarders and ten day pupils. My father had decided to leave Mehrdad and me there, and to find a nursery for little Mehran. He thought that in a small school we were much more likely to receive personal care and attention than in a large one. He was right, because the headmaster and his wife, conscious of the fact that we had lost our mother, did their best to make us feel happy and secure.

The first task facing us was to learn German and to adapt to the Swiss system of education so that we could follow the lessons. Sadly, after a couple of months Mehrdad and I were separated, because we spoke too much Persian together. Mehrdad was sent to school near Teufen, but I continued to live at Dolder until I took my school leaving certificate. For two years I attended school there, and then I was transferred to a girls' secondary school in the middle of Zurich, while continuing to live at Dolder as a lodger.

My room was in the garret. Through its tiny windows I could look down over the trees to the old cable railway – a view which made me feel that I wasn't completely isolated. Pride and self-control were qualities that my mother had cultivated in me, so I never showed my feelings to anybody. But at times I would run up to my room and cry for hours in secret. Yet my liberal upbringing, together with the facility for languages which I soon discovered, helped me to adjust to my new life quickly, to do well academically, and to remain lively and friendly. But it was not possible for me to cope with my grief without some external symptoms. It was at this time that I developed the stomach pains which heralded the severe ulcer that was to strike me down at the age of twenty-one. The problem stayed with me, even after major surgery, for several years.

School life was characterized by discipline, order and a sense of duty, but that does not mean that we were brought up in an authoritarian manner. Our relationship with the teachers was generally based on understanding and common sense. Even the headmaster, who taught us mathematics and history and was regarded as strict, combined firmness with logic, so that we accepted our duties and the restrictions imposed on us. We were constantly reminded that we had to prove ourselves useful as members of the community, but we were also encouraged to develop our own opinions and to express them.

The headmaster's wife was a small, round, affectionate woman, full of fun. I never saw her in a bad mood. For many of us she became a second mother; when we had problems we could always go to her for advice and comfort. She was the only person in the school who hugged and kissed the children, and she would occasionally spoil us with delicious cakes and chocolates from a famous patisserie in town. But these were special treats for homesick children. Normally, the school's discipline extended to the dining table too. Both before and after meals we would pray and thank God for his gifts, and it was plain that we had to eat everything on our plate to the very last crumb. Frugality was one of the chief virtues instilled into us.

The deputy headmistress was bony, long-nosed and wore glasses. She was not very popular, but she was an excellent teacher. It was thanks to her that I made such rapid progress in learning German, because she gave me extra lessons three times a week and asked me to write long essays which she would correct in front of me, explaining everything with great patience. I always enjoyed language lessons, and learning grammar and syntax was never a problem; I soon became fluent in French and English as well as in German. But mathematics was real torture; I simply had no head for figures. When I went to secondary school it was confirmed that my strengths lay in arts subjects, and I had to make an enormous effort to pass my mathematics, chemistry and physics examinations.

My ensuing classical education led me into the fascinating world of the ancient European civilizations. The origins of Western cultural history lay revealed as I became absorbed in the classical myths and heroic legends of Greek and Roman antiquity. Of course, at that time I could not realize the central importance of the figure of Prometheus, who rebelled against Zeus, stole fire from the gods and brought it to man. It was not until later, when I began to reflect about the contrast between the Persian way of looking at the world and the ethics and philosophy of the West, that the decisive symbolic role played by Prometheus's revolt in the development of Western thought became apparent to me. After the fall of the Roman Empire a Christian culture emerged which was dominated by a monotheistic subservience to God, but Prometheus's maxims re-emerged in the Renaissance, the beginning of the modern age. It was not that man became irreligious, but that man himself became the centre of worldly events while his faith was secularized.

The Persian way of thinking, however, moved in a different direction. Man remained powerless, subject to a fatalistic view of the world, seeking salvation in mystical unity with his creator and descending into a melancholy *Weltschmerz*. The Works of Hafez, Omar Khayyam and Molavi are predominantly characterized by their determinism. Even the various religions of Persian antiquity, for the most part deriving their doctrines from the teachings of Zoroaster, rest ultimately on fatalism. In Islam, human will is of only minor significance. In Islamic culture it is Allah who is at the centre, and not man. The Islamic religion and its mysticism have continued to provide the fundamental concepts in the philosophic thought of Iran, and for this reason my country's philosophy never separated itself from idealism. And so it was that humanism and the materialism of the scientific eighteenth century could grow no roots in Persia. The nineteenth-century German sociologist Max Weber was certainly right to say that capitalism was the product of the Protestant ethic and a materialistic view of the world which could only emerge in the West.

But my school preoccupations were punctuated by visits to the very different world of modern Paris. Mehran, now aged four, lived there with our father and a French nanny. Our house in Tehran was let, and my father augmented the rent from it, and his retirement pension, by working as a consultant to several museums and antique dealers in Paris and by writing articles for French and Persian cultural magazines. He also finished a book about his experiences restoring historical monuments in Iran. Mehrdad and I visited him during the school holidays, which enabled us to practise our French and to get to know Paris. These reunions were always wonderful. My father was kind, understanding and affectionate; he had not lost his sense of humour, and made us laugh all the time. My two brothers were perhaps too young to realize what a sacrifice he had made in giving up his career in order to devote himself totally to us. But I knew well, as he talked to me frequently about those days back in Tehran, that he was not a happy man.

In 1963 my father visited us in Switzerland and announced that he was considering remarriage to his former secretary at the Archaeological Museum in Tehran. I remembered that on one of our visits to Paris she had come to my father's flat and we had had lunch with her. She seemed kind and friendly, and I had the feeling that she had remained in touch with my father during his years of absence from Tehran.

My father wanted to know what I felt about his marrying Safieh. He was worried that I would not be happy about another woman in effect supplanting my mother. But at seventeen I was now mature enough to understand that he could not live a solitary life for ever. Apart from that, I had the feeling that Safieh was a woman who could give him support and emotional security. She was not beautiful, like my mother, but came from a distinguished family. Her first marriage had failed after only a year, and since then she had lived alone, which was quite unusual for an Iranian woman.

And so my father and young Mehran returned to Tehran, and soon afterwards he and Safieh were married. I realized that my father's financial situation was not as comfortable as it had been when we first came to Europe. He had begged us to be careful with money, to study diligently and not to waste time, since his resources were now diminishing rapidly. As a result, after a year Mehrdad had to join them in Tehran as well, because my father could no longer afford to keep us both in Switzerland. I was now quite alone. By this time I had got my school leaving certificate and longed to go to university, but on account of the shortage of funds I had to go to a language and business school instead. I was bitterly disappointed.

In 1965, while I was at this college, I also attended lectures on literature at the University of Zurich. There I first came into contact with the publications of the Confederation of Iranian Students Abroad, whose activities were directed against the Shah and his regime. It was through these writings that I became familiar with the political history of my country. I came to realize that political events in Iran after World War II had led directly to the oil crisis of the 1950s, which had of course precipitated a series of economic and political crises later.

The events of the early fifties, marked by the crisis that Mossadegh had sparked off to nationalize Iranian oil, interested me particularly. I had certain memories of those days – of the street demonstrations, and of my socialist uncle and his conspiratorial friends – but I had really been too young to understand. Now I learnt what it had all been about.

The account that the Shah's opponents abroad gave of Mossadegh, the nationalization of Iranian oil, the British involvement in Iran and the nature of the Shah's regime appealed to me enormously. It awakened in me a sense of nationalism as it revealed the extent of the foreign domination to which my country had been subjected because of its oil resources and its strategic geographical location.

My father had warned me repeatedly against the Confederation, which was politically active in many European countries. Becoming a member would destroy all my chances of returning to Iran and having a career, he told me. I had myself heard of students who had flown back home to see their parents and who had been instantly arrested at Tehran airport because of their political connections. So I always kept well away from the Confederation's supporters and only read their publications in secret. I learnt among other things why Mossadegh, a true nationalist who essentially wanted an independent Iran – an Iran capable of deciding its own fate, and not one dictated to by a foreign power – was disposed of by the USA and Britain.

As far back as 1901, during the Qajar dynasty, a sixty-year concession for exploration, production and oil refining rights had been given to an Englishman named William D'Arcy. He had agreed to pay Iran a royalty of only 16 per cent of his annual profits. Oil was first found in Ahvaz, in the south-western province of Khuzestan, in May 1908. The formation of the Anglo-Persian (after 1933 Anglo-Iranian) Oil Company followed in 1909, and production started in 1912. I discovered how cheap oil began to be shipped in generous quantities to Britain, becoming a major factor in the development of British industry and transport during World War I. Meanwhile the Iranian economy and infrastructure remained backward. I did not blame Britain, so much as the Iranian government: it was the ignorance and weakness of the government, which was easily swayed by the short-term allure of ready cash, which made it possible for the British to impose such terms on a poor country such as Iran at the beginning of this century. Between 1911 and 1919 Iran received a total of £335,000.

In 1925, when Reza Shah seized power and founded a new dynasty, the Iranian annual oil revenue had reached £1 million. The old D'Arcy Agreement was revised in 1933, and a new contract was signed in which the Iranian share of the profits from the sale of the oil was altered to a fixed sum of four shillings per ton. It looked as if the new terms were more profitable for Iran, but in reality the government had been fooled again.

It was distressing for me to discover, as a young student, how an uncompromising, incorruptible man such as Mossadegh had been humiliated and destroyed by foreign powers because of his efforts to nationalize Iranian oil and to restore Iranian dignity. I learnt now that he had been totally misunderstood by the Shah, by the USA and by Britain. His view of Iran was not a Communist one, as they presumed. He was merely postulating and defending a parliamentary system and a constitutional monarchy, the foundations of which had been laid in the Iranian constitution in 1906. What amazed me was that the USA and Britain, both great symbols of Western democracy, did not want a parliamentary system in Iran.

The 1906 constitution for the first time separated the power of the Shah from the executive and judiciary powers, and defined the roles and duties of each social institution. This constitution was called to life as a response to a popular movement instigated at the turn of the century by the Shia religious leaders initially to protest against a tobacco concession granted to the British in 1891. The protest was soon transformed into a constitutional league directed against the absolutism of the Qajar dynasty. But it was only in 1906 that the basis of a constitutional monarchy was laid down in a formal document, which also guaranteed the preservation of the principles of the Shia Moslem faith through the creation of a council of five religious elders to be consulted by the government on political and social issues. A parliament was created, which in theory allowed the elected representatives of the Iranian people to assemble. But in practise the Shahs continued to maintain absolute power and to manipulate elections. Mossadegh wanted to introduce real elections and to allow Iranians to express their views through parliamentary representation. He wanted the judiciary system to become totally independent of the monarchy so that it could start fighting corruption. He was anxious to establish a democratic government of politicians not nominated by the Shah, but selected by Parliament. But all these progressive ideas, I discovered, were labelled 'Communist' and buried in the authoritarian rule of the Shah, brought back to life by the Western powers.

Mossadegh's liberalism gave rise to a new political consciousness in the country, but sadly it was to be short-lived. It appeared to me, reading about those days, as if the lid of a pressure cooker were being lifted: views were openly expressed in Parliament, and the freedom of the press had been restored. But Mossadegh's major achievement had been to nationalize oil, although after Britain's withdrawal the Iranian oil industry remained virtually shut down for three years. Obviously this development disenchanted Britain enormously, as her oil supplies from the Iranian oilfields had dried up. In addition Britain's ally, the Shah, had had his authority as an absolute ruler reduced to a purely ceremonial role, until he was forced in August 1953 to leave Iran.

But long before this, behind the scenes, Britain and the USA were sketching out a different Iran, in which their economic and political interests would be safeguarded. Britain was trying to persuade America of the dangers of Mossadegh's popular support and the gradual shift of his government in the direction of Communism. But Mossadegh had had to do whatever he could to combat the subversive efforts of the Western powers; for this reason he did not object to the support of Tudeh, Iran's Communist party, which had been declared illegal by the Shah after World War II. The British government hired an Iranian family, the brothers Rashidi, to supply her with up-to-date information about Iran's internal affairs and to engineer a plot to topple Mossadegh's government. The CIA joined the conspiracy and financed the subversion. Bribes were distributed by the Rashidi brothers and their associates among Iranian bodybuilders and weightlifters, who formed a kind of syndicate in Iran, with a huge popular following and contacts with the underworld. The syndicate was led and inspired by a massively built athlete known as Shaaban Bimokh, which means Brainless Shaaban. Backed by a high-ranking army officer, General Zahedi, and his son Ardeshir, Brainless Shaaban organized the riots in the capital which I had watched as a child – though without comprehending the sudden swing of public opinion in favour of the Shah; now I knew why. A Tehran mob smashed up the Prime Minister's office and arrested Mossadegh. Tanks were sent into the streets and martial law was declared.

With the assistance of the USA and Britain to stage-manage the *coup*, Mossadegh's democratic government was brought down and the Shah restored to his Peacock Throne. Brainless Shaaban vanished from the political scene but General Zahedi became Prime Minister and his son Ardeshir was appointed Ambassador to Washington and later Foreign Minister. Mossadegh was sentenced to three years' imprisonment, then remained under house arrest until he died in 1967.

What would Iran have looked like today, I wonder, if Mossadegh had been given the chance to lay the foundations of a parliamentary democracy in the fifties? In my view the Shah's abuse of power paved the way for the emergence of the religious extremism with which Iran is now confronted. I think that, unlike the Shah, Mossadegh would have achieved a compromise solution with the moderate religious leaders of the country and would never have attempted to turn Iran into a Western-style capitalist state.

After the *coup d'état* of 1953 the Shah became ever more determined to consolidate his power by suppressing all opposition. He banned all political parties with the exception of two state-controlled ones, Melliyoun (Nationalist) and Mardom (People's), and prevented free elections. In 1957, with American technical and financial assistance, the Shah established his notorious secret police, Savak, which became the key instrument of political repression in Iran. President Eisenhower granted the Shah initial financial aid of $500 million, with much more to follow. The setting-up of Savak was also assisted by security experts from the Israeli intelligence agency, Mossad. Both the USA and Israel helped the Shah in building up strong armed forces as well. In this way Iran, a Moslem country situated in the Arab Middle East, virtually separated itself from the Islamic world and Arab nationalism. News of the link with Israel was received with great dismay by most Arab states.

Why was the USA so keen on helping Iran? If Britain's interest in Iran had been more economic than political, America certainly was now planning to turn the country into an important strategic area to block Soviet influence. This of course led to the instrumental role that America gradually confided to the Shah as the Persian Gulf's policeman. Iran's geographical situation, sharing a border with the Soviet Union in the north and with the Arab states in the south, and with its access through the Persian Gulf to the Indian Ocean, has always served the West one way or another. Once Iran was a bridge connecting Europe with British possessions in the Far East. Since the discovery of oil the Gulf has become a crucial shipping area for the world's tankers. And in the two world wars Iran had been occupied by Russian forces.

In both occupations the Soviet government encouraged a Communist separatist movement in the north. As early as 1907 the British and the Russians had reached an agreement to divide up Iran into zones of influence; Britain took the southern part and Russia the northern area, while the Iranian government was left with the centre. But despite the Anglo-Russian treaty it was Britain's influence which remained uppermost. It was through British support that Reza Shah, then a jingoistic army officer, succeeded in overthrowing the Qajar dynasty.

During World War II Reza Shah's sympathies with Nazi Germany had made it impossible for the Allied forces to use Iran as a southern supply route to the Soviet Union during the German invasion of 1941. As a result the Allies entered Iran and forced Reza Shah to abdicate in favour of his son, Mohammed Reza. Reza Shah was then exiled to Johannesburg in South Africa, where he died in 1944. I remember my father telling me how humiliating it was for Iranians not to be able to move around in their own country without a passport, or to be refused permission to enter a foreign-dominated zone. When the war ended the Soviet troops refused to leave, although the British and American forces had withdrawn. This led to what was called the Azerbaijan crisis; with Anglo-American backing the young Shah freed Azerbaijan from Soviet domination.

After the return of the Shah in 1953 British interests in the Iranian oil industry, which had virtually closed down from 1951 to 1954, were also restored. The Anglo-Iranian Oil Company was replaced by a new consortium in which BP held the majority shareholding of 40 per cent. Soon the formation of an Iranian national oil company became necessary, since 50 per cent of the oil revenues were still going into foreign pockets. But despite all its efforts Iran only improved its position in relation to the consortium after it joined OPEC, the Organization of Petroleum Exporting Countries. It was Iran's militancy within OPEC that led to the oil crisis in the early seventies.

Now, as a young student and in command of all these facts, I could at last appreciate how crucial the *coup d'état* of 1953, which restored the power of the Western-oriented Shah, was to both the USA and Britain.

In 1963, while I was still in Switzerland, the Shah was to be confronted with another crisis. In June there was an uprising in Tehran organized by the radical mullahs and directed against his modernization programme. The uprising was suppressed by the army and many of the demonstrators were arrested. The most prominent of those interned – so my uncle, who was now a colonel in the Shah's infantry and had come to visit me in Switzerland, told me – was the Ayatollah Ruhollah Khomeini. He apparently remained under arrest with my uncle's division until the Shah decided to exile him to Iraq. Neither the Shah nor my uncle could possibly have foreseen that one day this modest mullah would be Iran's most important figure.

Khomeini was born in April 1900 at Kohmein near Esfahan in central Iran; his father, grandfather and elder brother were all religious leaders. He studied theology under his brother and then moved to the holy city of Qom, where he began to teach Islamic philosophy. Soon a keen group of seminary students surrounded him. He postulated a theocracy as the ideal government for Iran, opposed Reza Shah for abolishing the veil for women, and regarded our Shah as a Western puppet. Since Mossadegh's overthrow in 1953 he had become one of the leaders of the opposition to the Shah. His popularity grew as his views regarding the monarchy and Western civilization became more and more radical.

The Ayatollah's exile set off another uprising. The Shah responded by strengthening his secret police and extending its powers into all aspects of society. But the disturbances of that summer in Tehran produced no headlines in the Western press, and soon they were also extinguished from memory within Iran. The figure of the revolutionary Shia mullah remained hidden from public gaze until 1978, when he returned to the political stage and unleashed a maelstrom of events that were to rock the world. But my uncle, Mehdi Ehterami, later fell from the Shah's favour and was never to experience this historic era. Years before the triumphant return of Ayatollah Khomeini to Iran he had himself died of cancer in a London clinic.

In 1972, on his way to London, my uncle stopped off in Switzerland and spent a few days with me; I was at that time the Iranian Ambassador's secretary. Previously a man with a firm military bearing, he had shrunk to a thin, frail-looking creature. My uncle now told me for the first time that the straightforwardness and honesty which had initially impressed the Shah had made him unpopular in the higher echelons of the army. It was not only jealousy that caused antagonism, he explained, but hypocrisy. Financial corruption was rife in the army, and my uncle's rivals wanted to keep it from the Shah. My uncle had always fought against corruption and was himself utterly incorruptible. Despite his unpopularity he had risen to the rank of general; the fact that he and his wife were invited to private imperial receptions revealed his closeness to the monarch. But suddenly his good fortune was reversed.

The Shah liked to nominate his ministers and military and civil advisers personally, sometimes in a curious haste and under most unsuitable circumstances. In the winter of 1970 the Shah and Empress Farah were at Tehran airport waiting to fly to Switzerland for their annual skiing holiday. My uncle had been told two days before that the Shah was going to make him commander of the Royal Guard. His family had been greatly excited, and on the day his chauffeur drove my uncle, wearing all his military decorations, to the airport. Here, however, he was greeted by General Aryana, a close military adviser of the Shah, who told him with regret that His Imperial Majesty had decided against his promotion. Confused, humiliated and broken-hearted, my uncle returned home. He never saw the Shah again.

Exiling the Ayatollah Khomeini did not, however, remove all the opposition to the Shah, for he had many other opponents of different persuasions. First there were Mossadegh's followers in the National Front party who had either fled abroad or remained in Iran, keeping a low profile. Another major source of opposition abroad was the Confederation of Iranian Students, which I had first encountered in Zurich and which encompassed several ideologies. Some had links to the National Front, others belonged to Tudeh, and yet others were Marxist-Leninist, Trotskyite or Maoist. An extreme left-wing Islamic group known as Mujahidin was also developing underground, and beside them a non-religious Marxist guerilla movement, the Fedayin. Their armed confrontation with the regime was not, however, to begin until the 1970s.

All opposition factions apart from the National Front regarded the Shah's social reforms, which he had initiated in 1960 thanks to American aid, as no more than cosmetic. In their view, Iran's social problems could only be solved by a revolution from below.

Reading the Confederation of Iranian Students' reports and opinions I realized how powerful Savak had become. Opposition political views were ruthlessly suppressed. The prisons, I gathered, were full of the Shah's political enemies, ranging from students and teachers to clergy and ordinary people. If the Shah punished his opponents without mercy, so they said, he rewarded those who supported him very generously – though I was to learn from my uncle's story just how arbitrary and fickle he could be. After the Mossadegh experience the Shah did not trust anybody but his very close friends, an attitude that, I was later to discover personally, he was never to relinquish. Gradually all the key posts in Iran were occupied by members of the Imperial Family or their friends and allies. He surrounded himself with hypocritical, incompetent and subservient men from whom he demanded only loyalty and praise, and was satisfied with nothing less than absolute power.

When, in 1967, my studies in Switzerland were nearly over, I was already confused and sceptical. However, I had to think seriously about my future. A difficult decision faced me. Either I could remain in Switzerland, where I had spent the formative years of my youth, or I could return to Iran after nine years of absence. I had influential Swiss friends who could easily have obtained a work permit for me. My Swiss education had given my life its governing values and direction: I was industrious, duty-conscious, self-disciplined, and above all I did not accept everything uncritically; this was an idiosyncrasy that proved most disadvantageous for my career within the Shah's administration. Yet despite my Swiss upbringing I had remained faithful to my own culture. For several years I had had private tuition in Farsi, which enabled me to read Persian texts sent by my father. My feelings were torn between two quite different spheres: the emotional, romantic world of my childhood and the rational, disciplined world of my Swiss youth. At times I longed for the warmth and simplicity of the East, at others I admired the logical organization and systematic functioning of things in the West. Furthermore, as a twenty-year-old woman I enjoyed relative freedom in Switzerland and did not relish losing this within an Oriental society. I knew that in Iran social convention would make it very difficult for me to live on my own, yet I was too independent to imagine myself living with my father, his wife and my brothers. Nor did I like the prospect of living in a country where freedom of opinion was suppressed. Nevertheless I was intrigued by the landscape of my childhood memories, and this curiosity brought me to the decision to return to my homeland after all.

— 4 —

Return to Iran

My return in 1967 coincided with the coronation of the Shah. Although he had been on the throne for a quarter of a century, there were good reasons why his kingship had not been confirmed for so many years. In the forties, as a young monarch, he had found himself a mere puppet subject to the whims of the Great Powers. He had had a hard struggle to detach himself from them and to restore the territorial sovereignty of his country. In the fifties the trial of strength with Mossadegh had led to an erosion of his power. Even after his authority had been reinstated in 1953, the Shah still felt insecure without an heir. Now, at long last, the Iranian monarch was basking in the sunshine of divine favour. After all visible internal opposition had been suppressed by Savak, he had been able to instigate his US-financed programme of social reform to give his regime a *raison d'être*. And finally his third wife, Empress Farah, had fulfilled his long-treasured wish and given birth in 1960 to Crown Prince Reza.

The Swiss newspaper reports of the forthcoming celebrations were not uncritical. Magnificent cloaks encrusted with diamonds, sapphires and emeralds were being made for the sovereigns by Iranian and foreign designers, and this represented only a small fraction of what was going to be spent on the festivities. The journalists had accusingly recounted that the crown which made the Shah the ruler by divine right over a desperately poor nation was encrusted with 3380 diamonds, 388 pearls, five emeralds, and two sapphires. The Empress's diadem, which was made of gold and platinum, bore 1469 diamonds, 105 pearls, 36 emeralds and 36 rubies. At the same time informed sources in Switzerland were aware of the immense poverty in Iran. I had myself often watched films on Swiss television showing the deplorable living conditions of the majority of my compatriots – despite the unscrupulous censorship exercised by Savak, Western journalists occasionally managed to smuggle out of Iran films and photographs which testified to the grim reality behind the ostentatious façade. The poor, of whom there were many, lived in low, mud-brick houses with no sanitation or electricity, their filthy children running barefoot through alleys strewn with refuse. But these distressing circumstances did not inhibit the Shah from crowning himself King of Kings of Persia, identifying the Pahlavi dynasty with the glories of Persian antiquity.

The Shah's marriage to Farah Diba in 1959 had captured the imagination of the Western public, who saw it as a story from the Thousand and One Nights: a handsome prince looking everywhere for a beautiful princess to share his life in a dream palace in some remote and wonderful land. But the Shah had already shared his life with two other wives before Farah. His first marriage, to King Farouk of Egypt's sister, Princess Fawzia, in 1939, had been an arranged one; the Shah had not even set eyes on his bride before the wedding. To make up for his own modest military background, the Shah's father had wanted to marry his son into proper royalty, but the marriage failed soon after their daughter, Princess Shahnaz, was born. Fawzia returned to Egypt, leaving her daughter to grow up at the Iranian Imperial Court.

A few years later the Shah met the half-German Soraya Esfandiary. The Bakhtiari tribe, from which Soraya's wealthy father came, is one of the largest and most prosperous tribes in Iran, settled in the area between Esfahan and the southern oilfields. The Shah had long known of Soraya's legendary beauty – when he finally met her he fell instantly in love and married her soon afterwards. But sadly Soraya was unable to have children. As time passed and all medical treatment failed, the Shah felt compelled to divorce her in order to produce a male heir. According to the constitution only a male descendant could succeed to the throne, and so without an heir the Pahlavi dynasty would cease upon Mohammed Reza's death. Broken-hearted, Soraya left Iran for Europe. Both Fawzia and Soraya were granted generous alimony by the Shah's Court.

Now the Shah was searching again for a suitable wife who would be able to end his dynastic insecurity. Good fortune came the way of Farah Diba, a young Iranian girl studying architecture in Paris, who was introduced to the Shah when he visited that city. Farah was not as beautiful as Fawzia or Soraya, but she impressed the Shah with her simplicity and openness. He also appreciated her slim, athletic figure. It must have been quite overwhelming for a girl such as Farah, who led a very ordinary student's life in Paris, to be courted by the Shah. At their third meeting, back in Tehran, the Shah, a keen pilot, took Farah up in a private plane. There, high over his capital, he proposed to her. A year after their fairytale wedding Crown Prince Reza was born.

Farah soon made herself popular in Iran and abroad as a warm-hearted, socially conscious young Empress. Western women started to copy her hairstyle, and eagerly read glossy magazine articles about her new life at the Shah's Court. I myself found Farah far more sympathetic than the Shah's two former wives, who had shown no real interest in the people of Iran. Farah, unlike her predecessors, came from a middle-class background. Her father, an officer in Reza Shah's army, had died when she was a child, and she had been brought up by her mother. Life became more and more of a financial burden for the family, and it was Farah's uncle who paid for her education and sent her abroad to study on a modest allowance. These experiences made Farah seem to me far more human and natural than Fawzia or Soraya, whose only quality was their beauty.

But I did not return to my country merely to see the Shah's coronation, nor did the newly won stability of his regime serve as a motive. I wanted above all to see my family after such a long separation, and to relive the memories of my childhood.

I was only familiar with the social and political problems of my country through what I had heard and read, and I had little idea of the realities. My romantic memories of Tehran, where I had been born, were soon blown away. I found myself in a city of artifice and no character, submerged beneath monuments to a newly industralized society. To reach the city from Mehrabad airport meant driving along a broad, factory-lined freeway. New suburbs stretched out to the north, east and west. The permament traffic jams on the streets leading into the city were eloquent testimony to the massive increase in Tehran's population, and the skyline was dominated by grey office blocks and apartment buildings. What struck me most was the architecture – I wondered if the Iranian construction industry had worked to any plan at all.

I looked at this metamorphosis in bewilderment and found it impossible to identify myself with any of it. In vain I searched for some familiar sight from my childhood. It was not until I visited the old town and walked through the colourful bazaar, and drove with friends through the old villages north of Tehran, nestling beneath the brown slopes, and sat at midday beneath the cool shade of the walnut trees, admiring an azure sky and eating Persian yoghurt with fresh country bread, that I could say joyfully that my home city had not lost all its charm. And then there were the people. My relatives were so warm-hearted, so hospitable and so generous. I hadn't experienced such love, warmth and friendliness since my childhood.

My father and stepmother received me with affection and immediately made me feel at home. It was wonderful to see my father in such good form, enjoying a happy family life again. He was now working as a consultant to the Foundation for the Restoration of Archaeological Monuments, which had links with several Iranian universities. In addition he and Safieh had set up a private primary school, which she was now enthusiastically running. My brothers were doing well at school and my father was thinking of sending them both to England for their higher education.

Two days after my arrival I went to visit my mother's grave, in a cemetery named after a Moslem Shia saint, Imamzadeh Abdollah, whose shrine is kept there. I had forgotten that my father had bought up a family mausoleum cared for by an old verger. He asked whether I wanted to light candles in memory of my mother's soul, which is the custom in Iran. When he left to fetch the candles I knelt to touch her tombstone and began to pray. Tears rolled uncontrollably down my cheeks, and the same sense of grief that I had felt as a twelve-year-old child, holding her hand as she lay dying, swept over me again.

Every time my path took me to this cemetery I passed through the poor southern districts of Tehran, and every time I wondered why the Shah had done nothing to improve living conditions here. This area was still as decaying and primitive as it had been when I had visited it as a child, with my mother. People continued to live in miserable clay hovels. Poverty, however, was not restricted to south Tehran, and was an all too common sight in Iran. But hadn't the Shah promised social dignity for everyone? What was the purpose behind his enormous administration, the gigantic bureaucracy in all those ministeries which had amazed me after a few weeks of living in Tehran? Surely it was precisely to solve such problems? But then I would reflect that it was unreasonable to expect reforms initiated only in 1960 to have eliminated poverty and backwardness within such a short time.

Since there was as yet no significant help from the state to free them from the misery of everyday life, the poor and the uneducated sought refuge in their faith. Religion, I discovered, was a dominant force in the lower echelons of society: the presence of God was as powerful as ever in the life of the ordinary Iranian. In their prayers it was as if they shared a permanent personal relationship with God and as if there was no barrier of any kind between them and their creator. These true believers in Islam continued their religious rituals despite the Westernization process set in motion by the Shah. Pilgrimages to Shia shrines had remained an important source of consolation for them. Their wives still wore the veil, which had been officially abolished thirty years earlier, and I could not see how anyone could persuade them to abandon it. It was as if they occupied a totally different reality. Nobody at that time, not even Savak, took any notice of the circulation at this level of society of Ayatollah Khomeini's teachings, which his disciples were smuggling in from Iraq.

With the exception of holy cities such as Qom and Mashhad, where Islam permeated every aspect of public life, there was little sign of the influence of religion among other social groups. The women wore elegant, modern, Western-style clothes and used make-up. Whenever I came into contact with a mullah I could sense his outrage that I was not wearing the veil. But what annoyed them even more was the hedonistic Western habits that the privileged classes had adopted: the consumption of alcohol, the increasingly permissive relationships between young men and women, and the startling exposure of their bodies on beaches and at swimming pools. The clerics held the Shah and his father responsible for this change. I do not think they were against the rights that women had seemingly gained in society – rather it was the vulgarity displayed by those imitating Western manners. All they could see of Western life, as reflected by the distorting mirror of its Iranian imitators, was the quest for pleasure. The mullahs were, for instance, utterly outraged by a remarkable social event that took place in 1968 – the marriage between the sons of two of the Shah's top military advisers, General Khosravani and General Djahanbani. As well as her Western haute couture clothes, Empress Farah also had a traditional-style Persian wardrobe, of which General Khosravani's son, Keyvan, was the designer. This public wedding held at Tehran's Hotel Commodore, was celebrated in the capital of the Pahlavis at a time when homosexuality was still illegal in most of Europe. In any case it is prohibited by Islam.

It would be wrong, though, to think that the middle and upper classes had become totally irreligious. A firm belief in God as a supreme force governing all aspects of life, narrowing down the scope for human decision, remained the common cultural bond. Yet those who had access to Western ideas and had enjoyed the individual freedoms existing there could not accept the shackles of Islamic morality. And as the authorities sought to suppress the impact of Islam where it came into conflict with modernization, Westernized Iranians became more and more alienated from their religion. I discovered, for instance, that the Shia cult of paying homage to saints and martyrs had been banned; those overwhelming religious processions, such as the one which I remembered from my childhood, could no longer take place. I was told that the Shah was against the self-mutilation and flagellation practised in these processions because he thought them barbaric. To demonstrate that he had not lost all affinity to the country's religion, however, the Shah occasionally visited a Shia shrine, and his Court organized luncheons on religious feast days; and the Shia religion was certainly used as a pillar of national unity.

The substitute for religion was nationalism. Everywhere I

encountered huge, full-length posters of the Shah, standing like a god greeting his nation. Especially in schools the emphasis was laid far more on patriotism and on love of the Shah than on Islamic religious tuition. Once, to my amazement, I came across a poster which bore the legend 'God – Fatherland – Shah' in a triangle. It was the word 'Shah', not 'God', that occupied the most important position at the top of the triangle. Savak, in whose hands the whole propaganda machine lay, deliberately portrayed him as a supernatural figure.

It was this artificiality that disturbed me so much. People were afraid to talk freely and were in constant terror of the omnipresent Savak. Friends warned me in particular not to talk to taxi drivers, as they were largely hired by Savak for intelligence purposes. A totally apolitical person, who might in the course of a casual conversation have said something against the Shah or the state of affairs in the country, could easily be reported to the authorities and end up in prison. I could not understand the reason for this oppression. It made all the innovative aspects of the Shah's reforms, such as women's rights, seem purely cosmetic, because liberation could only make sense in a society that was itself free. For instance we now had the right to vote and be elected to Parliament. If free elections had been allowed, the rights granted to women by the new law would have had some meaning. But the elections were grossly manipulated and all the seats went to candidates selected by Savak.

Princess Ashraf, the Shah's twin sister who was notorious for her ruthlessness and immorality, was encouraged by her brother to set up an organization for women's liberation. This was a typical example of the appalling nepotism, waste and incompetence that were rife at this time. (The princess was also the Shah's envoy to the United Nations Commission on Human Rights; whenever she attended a conference in New York she would stop off in the south of France to meet a new lover and gamble away millions of pounds at a casino. On one dramatic occasion in the 1970s her enemies caught up with her while she was driving along the Corniche. Her car was riddled with bullets, a female companion killed and her twenty-five-year-old lover wounded. Miraculously, Princess Ashraf herself escaped unscathed.) A group of hypocritical, shallow and profit-seeking women joined her new organization. Inspired by Savak propaganda, they became the female demagogues of the regime's philosophy. Eventually the women's organization was turned into a complete ministry with its own budget, from which the Princess and her followers benefited. The minister, Mahnaz Afkhami, a close friend of Princess Ashraf's, spent astronomical sums on clothes from European couturiers. One particular photograph of her, wearing an Yves St Laurent outfit with large Dior sunglasses, and talking to a peasant woman in an Iranian village, became a standing joke in intellectual circles.

It was in the same social climate that Farokhrou Parsa, the wife of one of the Shah's generals, became Minister of Education. After a few years of shamelessly plundering the ministry's financial resources she was replaced. But her deeds were not forgiven by the Iranian people: she was the only female former minister to be executed by Khomeini's revolutionary Islamic government in 1979.

On several occasions I talked to women lecturers at Tehran University, or to women students, all with varied political convictions. They were truly horrified by the dimension of vulgarity that women's liberation had taken in Iranian society. But since dissenting political opinions were brutally suppressed by Savak, they never had a chance to make their views known to the public.

In this rather discouraging atmosphere there was still Empress Farah, who inspired many women with her sincere and unpretentious ideas. Her popularity among cultured, progressive Iranian women was a thorn in Princess Ashraf's side. She was jealous and resentful of Farah's active participation in social and cultural life, and of the originality of her ideas. Initially Farah wanted to stimulate women to acquaint themselves with the history and traditions of their country and thus save them from the threat posed by the wholesale importation of Western lifestyles. This intellectual approach to the country's most crucial dilemma naturally appealed to the majority of educated women or women with a modern inclination – those who did not reject the assimilation of Western technology and who believed in a moderate and sensible adoption of Western influences without losing their own cultural identity. Later, unfortunately, even Farah succumbed to the hypocrisy of her husband's regime, but at that stage I still admired her enormously and saw in her cultural plans a sense of purpose, a humane goal in which I could invest my energy.

As far as the Shah's position was concerned, the propaganda exercised by Savak in the mass media proved quite effective. At first the people of Iran felt the *coup d'état* of 1953 to have been imperialistic, alien and undemocratic, but as the Shah proceeded to institute his social reforms and to set about persuading his people of his good will, they gradually forgot that he had only returned to power with the assistance of the Americans.

Ironically enough, from the outset the Shah imbued his reforms with a pseudo-democratic quality by calling for a referendum and a public debate on the six main points of his programme. As far as I could make out from the facts and figures published by the regime itself, 100 per cent of the population had agreed with the Shah's intended reforms. The six points were, first, land reform: the landowners were to be expropriated and their estates redistributed to the peasants – in short the feudal social order was to be destroyed. Secondly, all private forests and natural resources were to be nationalized. Thirdly, the electoral system was to be reformed, above all to include the emancipation of women that I have just described. Fourthly, there was to be a sale of shares in state companies to enable expropriated landowners to reinvest in industry the monies that they had received as compensation. Fifthly, profit-sharing schemes were to be introduced for workers. Finally, an educational corps was to be established to fight illiteracy.

The few parliamentary voices raised in opposition were less critical about the reforms than about the position of the Shah himself within the state. They wanted to know whether the Shah intended to rule the country as an absolute or as a constitutional monarch. For since 1906 the Iranian state system had in theory consisted of a constitutional monarchy – in other words the Shah should act only as head of state and have no political involvement. But this concept had never been put into practice and Iran was doomed to be ruled by dictators. Even those faint sceptical voices in Parliament who had questioned the position of the Shah faded away with the overwhelming result of the referendum.

The Shah made frequent public speeches expressing increasingly doctrinaire preconceived ideas. I clearly identified the Shah's need for a rationale to support his political programme and to consolidate his power. He was assisted in this task by his Iranian advisers and theoreticians, who evolved the framework of a philosophy known as the Revolution of the Shah and His People. Ideologically his social revolution postulated nationalism and monarchism, and praised and emulated the pre-Islamic history of Persia which had produced mighty kings such as Cyrus the Great. In theory, a close bond was to be forged between the monarch and the people, who together would carry out the long-term programme of reforms. Today, looking back at those years, I think that this bond could have become reality if the Shah had remained honest to his people. He could have gained their confidence and increased his own credibility if he had been a modest, approachable ruler with a genuine understanding of their cultural make-up and aspirations. I am certain that he would not have needed a secret police nor a strong army to protect him against internal dangers. I would have liked to see the Shah, as I had seen the federal ministers in Switzerland, for instance, mingling with ordinary people and talking to them spontaneously and openly. But the Shah did not have the common touch.

I had the impression that, despite the absolute power he wielded, he still felt the need to assert himself. This need may have stemmed from a childhood complex. My father remembered that he had been a pale, weak, sickly-looking child, dominated by his powerful father and strong-minded twin sister. The Shah was of a much smaller physical build than his father, which also contributed to his inferiority complex. Another factor that seemed to annoy the Shah was the family's relatively humble origins. But the Shah himself had enjoyed a privileged, protected life as the Crown Prince, learning the principles of kingship.

He was born in 1919, and was therefore seven at the time of his father's coronation. Unlike his father, who could barely read and write, the Shah was given a proper education, first in Tehran with carefully selected sons of high-ranking officials, and subsequently at the Ecole Le Rosey in Switzerland alongside the sons of wealthy and famous Europeans. It was there that he developed the fascination with Western lifestyles and culture that later turned him into a fanatical, self-destructive imitator of Western progress. Industrialization and mechanization became his obsessive priority, and he ignored the grass-roots social problems of his country. I could see why he was regarded in the West as a modern-thinking enlightened monarch: it was because he was in himself a totally Westernized person. He spoke fluent English and French; he was charming, elegant and well-mannered. He appealed to a Western public accustomed to less fashionable, idiosyncratic figures as the heads of state of developing countries. But these are not issues of interest for a developing country. The West identified itself with the Shah, but the majority of Iranians felt alienated from him.

It was an exciting and instructive time for me to explore what lay beneath the surface of my own country. There was certainly no lack of financial means in oil-rich Iran to close the last gap between poor and rich, between knowledge and ignorance, and to achieve social equality. But in every field of social life the tension between the old and the new, between tradition and modernity, between Western and Eastern values, was only too palpable. Daily I would encounter this confrontation between the rationality of Western technology and the irrationality of the way people thought in the East. It wasn't simply that people lacked qualifications and experience; their whole attitude and ethical values simply didn't fit. The Persian philosophy of life, based as it was on fatalism and submission to God, was incapable of keeping pace with the rapid process of modernization. Rationalism, precision, the concept of the value of work and a sense of time and cost – all vital in dealing with Western technology – were missing at all levels of Iranian society, from the upper- and middle-class Westernized groups to the common man with his rigid religious persuasions. Expertise, systematic organization and long-term planning were replaced by incompetence, inefficiency and indifference.

The Tehran traffic presented a perfect example of another mental stumbling-block. In the West, people had long since learnt that their private interests were dependent on public control. Every ordinary citizen accepts the traffic regulations, for instance, not only to protect himself and his vehicle, but also because if he doesn't heed the interests of others and endangers the life of his fellow citizens, they will behave towards him in the same way. In other words, do as you would be done by – the alternative is anarchy. We had traffic regulations in Tehran too, of course, but nobody took any notice of them and the result was chaos.

Iranians are essentially a most friendly and hospitable people. What I could not understand, therefore, was how at the public level they could be so selfish. Europeans seemed to me to be less warm and hospitable in private, but they did possess an extraordinary sense of community. In trade, in industry, in agriculture, in banking, my people behaved as if they were behind the wheel of a car in a Tehran traffic jam. How could a solid private sector develop from the short-sightedness and irrationality of businessmen who only had their own egocentric, profit-seeking interests at heart, and from the lack of planning and co-ordination between the various elements of Iran's industrial and business sectors? A genuine middle class with a coherent awareness of its own identity, such as one encounters in the West, could never emerge in my country.

It was not only the clash between tradition and innovation that I found confusing but also the ethnic complexity of Iranian society. Iran is a vast country. Although, in comparison with its glorious past, it has diminished drastically in size, it still covers nearly seven times the area of the British Isles, or one-sixth that of the USA. It is difficult to imagine the problems of ruling such a country without knowing something about its sources of potential division.

Migrations and foreign invasions in the 2500 years of Persian history have left a profound mark. Towards the west rise broad mountains, home of the Lors and Kords, who have also settled over the border in Iraq and Turkey. South of Shiraz live the Qashqai tribe, formerly Turkish, and beyond that the Khamseh, an ethnic mixture of Turks and Arabs living south of Lorestan. The region south of Esfahan is inhabited by the wealthy Bakhtiari tribe. Oil-bearing Khuzestan, which embraces the southern areas around the Persian Gulf, is inhabited by Iranian Arabs. In the south-east, the most arid region of Iran, live the Baluchis; their villages extend also to the adjacent parts of Pakistan and Afghanistan. In Azerbaijan, in the north-west of the country near the Turkish and Russian borders, reside the Iranian Turks, while in the north-east are the Turkomans, a Mongolian tribe. Right in the north, on the shores of the Caspian Sea which Iran shares with the USSR, are the settlements of the Guilanis and the Mazandaranis.

All these diverse tribes and peoples have their own languages, customs and dress which, on my return to Iran after so many years abroad, utterly fascinated me. But I could see how hard it must have been for the Shah to integrate this cultural and geographical complexity and to attempt to forge it into a single homogeneous nation. One means adopted was to declare Farsi the official state language to be taught in all schools.

As far as religion was concerned, 90 per cent of the Iranian population are Shia Moslems, and again for reasons of national unity the Shah had confirmed the Shia faith as the official religion. But there are also Sunni Moslems in Iran – mostly among the Kords, Turkomans and Arab Khuzestanis – as well as other religious minorities such as Christian Armenians, Jews, Zoroastrians, Assyrians and Bahais. The Armenians, who stemmed from the area named after them straddling north-east Turkey and the southern USSR, fled from persecution by the Ottoman Turks to Iran in the sixteenth century. Shah Abbas Safavid, then ruler of Iran, welcomed them as a sworn enemy of the Ottoman Empire and allowed them to establish themselves close to Esfahan, even giving their new lands the same name, Julfa, as their former homeland and letting them continue to practise Christianity and build churches.

Iranian believers in the ancient Zoroastrian religion form a small group of only a few thousand who mainly live in Yazd and Kerman. Bahais are not very numerous either. Bahaism, the modern manifestation of the Shia branch of Islam, emerged in Iran at the beginning of the nineteenth century. It outpaces Shiism by attributing even more divinity to the Imams, whom it regards as the doors or *Bab* to the knowledge of God. Since the twelfth Imam disappeared, perfect men were to establish the continuity of communication with God. While the Shias worship their martyr saints and receive divine blessings from their spiritual leaders or ayatollahs, the Bahais are taught and inspired by *Bab*. It was the doctrine of divine representation on earth that gave the impetus to the teachings of Mirza Ali Mohammed Shirazi, who in 1844 declared himself to be the *Bab*. He quickly acquired a large and influential following. The Shias could not tolerate this new version of Islam and Mirza Shirazi was executed in 1850. Persecution of Bahais forced Shirazi's leading followers to leave Iran. It was in exile that one of these refugees, Baha'ullah, together with his son Abdul Baha, founded modern Bahaism. Unlike the Jews, the Christians and the Zoroastrians, however, Bahais were not granted any political rights in the otherwise remarkably democratic Iranian constitution of 1906.

Yet despite this ethnic and religious fragmentation, since the land reforms the Shah and Empress seemed to be more popular with the Iranian peasants. At least that was the impression given on Iranian television, which was of course controlled by Savak precisely to project the popularity of the sovereigns. When they made official visits to villages they were seen to be mobbed by enthusiastic crowds. Though at this time the land reform was only in its early phases, a substantial transformation in the social and economic systems of rural Iran was anticipated. Agriculture was gradually going to become mechanized, and those peasants who had been given land were hoping to cultivate fields belonging to them in their own right.

Until 1960 Iranian villages and land had been the private property of feudal rulers, members of the Court, tribal chiefs and wealthy merchants, though worked by the peasants. Now the land was allotted on fifteen-year mortgages to those peasants as members of a state co-operative. At the end of the fifteen-year period the co-operatives were required to have paid for the land. The dispossessed landowners were to be compensated by the state with long-term tax concessions, but they were disaffected and many of them were to become the Shah's political opponents. Some, however, invested in new industries and soon became powerful magnates. *Plus ça change* . . . A few years later I saw that corruption had penetrated rural life as well. Peasants were being driven from their holdings, co-operatives' funds were being embezzled, and the technical aid granted to the peasants by the state gradually declined. The result was a mass migration to the cities. The emphasis of the regime remained sharply on the promotion and expansion of industry; agriculture was gradually ignored and abandoned.

But when I returned in 1967, the situation seemed to be very positive and promising, particularly since both the USA and the Soviet Union approved the Shah's plans for the industrialization of Iran. The political aspirations of his opponents abroad seemed to me no more than pipe dreams, for the massive Western and Soviet investments in development projects demonstrated foreign confidence in his regime. The Russians had built steel mills and heavy engineering plant, and had agreed to purchase Iran's first gas exports. The idea was to diversify the economy of the country away from an over-emphasis on oil. The oil industry itself was beginning to expand into a petrochemical sector in which Western companies were keen to invest. Textiles and foodstuffs were the first areas of the economy to become industralized, followed by steel and other metals in the seventies. But a communications network, a national grid, a transport system and a skilled industrial workforce were all missing when the Shah began to industralize the country – there was simply no infrastructure. As a result the new industries were faced with inefficiency and high costs.

Though I had returned to Iran to renew old relationships, it had also been my intention to find myself a job. My father thought that my best chances lay with international firms or one of the many oil companies, who would be able to make use of my languages. But I envisaged a different future for myself, working in one of the national institutions in direct contact with the Iranian people, where my training and abilities could be of use to Iran itself.

It was my father, though, with his greater experience of the way things worked in Iran, who helped me to find my first job. One day he caught me eagerly leafing through the Tehran daily paper, *Keyhan*, looking for job advertisements. He burst out laughing and then looked at me with sympathy in his eyes.

'Everything here is done through connections,' he told me. 'If you want a good job I've no choice but to speak to one of my influential friends.'

'No, please don't do that,' I begged him. 'It's not necessary. I have excellent references and I'm quite sure that I can find work myself.'

Since Iran had adopted so many Western values I was sure that it must be a meritocracy where I could make my way on the basis of my own abilities. But that turned out to be an illusion. The top posts in both the private and public sectors, I discovered, were still occupied almost exclusively by the sons and daughters of the upper class. Education alone counted for nothing. My father told me that it was impossible even for a distinguished expert to be promoted beyond a certain level if he was not associated in some way with the Court. He himself had managed to break through this barrier, but he was undoubtedly a rare exception. After a year of unemployment I had no alternative but to go back to my father. He did not want to see my energy suppressed or my aspirations disappointed, so he knew that I would have to begin my career in a responsible and stimulating job. He thought that I should be launched with the help of an old school friend of his who now held a prominent position in the Foreign Ministry, and one evening my father told me that his friend was willing to interview me.

The Iranian Foreign Ministry lies in the heart of Tehran, halfway to the famous bazaar and close to the Archaeological Museum. To reach it you have to drive along the busy Ferdowsi Avenue, where most of the embassies, banks, airline offices, hotels, carpet shops and jewellers are situated. The old town, including the Golestan Palace, which is the oldest building in the city, the Shah Mosque and the Marble Palace, which was erected in the time of Reza Shah, lies just south of this thoroughfare. Although this district was not particularly old, for the capital had only been moved to Tehran some two hundred years earlier, I loved it because of its aura of history and culture. Going that October afternoon to my interview with my father's old friend, I found Ferdowsi Avenue packed with tourists, elegantly dressed Iranians, men and women in rainbow-hued costumes from every province, villagers wearing baggy black trousers and felt caps, veiled women, and mullahs in long brown capes and white or black turbans. It presented a colourful and heterogeneous picture – doubtless a testimony to the economic development of modern Iran, but to me it all seemed profoundly paradoxical.

It was the first time that I had been inside the Foreign Ministry with its great inner courtyards, high ceilings, broad staircases and long, dark, red-carpeted corridors. Large pictures of the Imperial Family hung on the walls. In contrast to the atmosphere in the other ministries I had visited, an almost unpleasant silence reigned throughout the building. A commissionaire took me to the Permanent Secretary's office on the first floor and announced me. The official's two fashionable secretaries sat nonchalantly drinking tea, chatting and filing their nails. They ignored me for a full ten minutes. Finally, one of them turned and asked me in an offhand manner just what I wanted.

'I have an appointment with His Excellency the Permanent Secretary at ten o'clock,' I replied, glancing automatically at my watch. It was already nearly twenty past ten.

'Oh, His Excellency is frightfully busy today, I'm afraid,' she replied. 'You really will have to wait a very long time before you can speak to him,' she warned me, graciously motioning me to a chair in a corner.

Two young men then came in and began to talk and joke with the secretaries. Though they were obviously anxious for me not to overhear them, I soon began to learn quite a lot about how things worked in the Foreign Ministry. The minister, Ardeshir Zahedi, was flown to his office every day in a private helicopter from his villa in Hessarak, north-east of Tehran. All his advisers and assistants had the dubious honour of being addressed by some derogatory nickname; if, for example, he wanted to speak to the 'Rascal' or the 'Bastard', everyone knew exactly whom he was referring to. It was also apparent that he had a particular weakness for beautiful women, something which created a good deal of gossip among his staff. My father had told me that he had once been a guest at the Iranian Embassy in Washington in the late fifties when Zahedi was Ambassador there, and had observed him at a reception flirting outrageously with a beautiful American girl sitting on his lap. He was at that time married to Princess Shahnaz, the Shah's daughter from his first marriage. Then, she had merely walked out in a fury; but she had since divorced him. On the whole, however, Zahedi could do as he wished, for he and his father had played a decisive role in the Shah's return to power in 1953.

While I was quietly taking in all this information several other people had been ushered into the Permanent Secretary's office, even though I was still kept waiting.

'You didn't tell me why you are here,' the self-satisfied secretary said to me.

'His Excellency is an old friend of my father's,' I told her. 'He wants to offer me a post here in Iran.'

'Who is your father?' she asked with great curiosity.

'My father is the former Director General of the Archaeological Museum,' I replied. 'He resigned many years ago.'

Suddenly it dawned on me that I shouldn't reveal any more about myself than was absolutely necessary. 'Savak has its agents everywhere,' my father had warned me. 'Think very carefully about your every word.' But the secretary continued to ask me this question and that, which I evaded with answers as brief as possible.

At last I was asked to go into the Permanent Secretary's office. As I did so, I began a new chapter in my life that was destined to reveal to me the true nature of the regime.

— 5 —

Diplomacy Iranian Style

The Permanent Secretary, Parviz Khonsari, was seated at an enormous walnut desk in a huge office. Behind him hung a majestic portrait of the Shah, the Empress and the Crown Prince in a gold frame. His numerous telephones never stopped ringing. He glanced briefly at me over his glasses and indicated with a quick, nervous movement of the hand that I should take a seat. I sank into a wide armchair covered in grey velvet. Mr Khonsari continued to deal with his papers and to answer his telephones.

Then I noticed that three men were also present. They were sitting on an old sofa in the darkest corner, chatting quietly among themselves. Now they began to direct penetrating, enquiring stares at me. I looked down at the large Persian carpet which covered most of the floor. 'It must be an old Esfahan,' I thought – one of the very finest.

A servant in dark blue uniform came in and served tea in traditional glasses with antique silver holders. A young diplomat in a grey pinstripe suit came bursting in behind him, approached the Secretary's desk hastily, bowed in respect, opened a folder and whispered something into his ear. The boss also gave his orders in a low voice and the diplomat left the room.

I began to wonder if the Permanent Secretary really wanted to speak to me at all, but I dared not utter a word. The three gentlemen in the corner did not appear to be in much of a hurry, for they carried on chatting cosily and waiting like good boys until their master deigned to speak to them. I almost wished I had brought a book with me to while away the time. This thought had hardly passed through my mind when a door opened and in walked a tall, slim, elegant man accompanied by four other important-looking people.

Mr Khonsari jumped from his chair like a coiled spring and approached the guest with arms extended. I heard one of the three men waiting in the corner say to the other two: 'Oh, that's Dr Loghman-Adham, the Grand Master of Ceremonies at the Imperial Court!' At that, they all rose respectfully.

From the conversation between the Permanent Secretary and the Court's Master of Ceremonies I gathered that the latter had come to the Foreign Ministry to select a dinner service for the Court banquets. It seemed that they had sent for various European manufacturers' catalogues, from which he was now to make his choice. I did not know whether to stand or remain seated. However I soon began to feel rather uncomfortable, since I was now the only person in the room still sitting, so I decided after all to stand up. At that moment Dr Loghman-Adham became aware of my presence and smiled at me.

Suddenly I remembered the poor taxi driver who was waiting for me in the car park. I did not know then that my father, being thoroughly versed in the Persian system of administration, had ordered the taxi for the whole day.

Khonsari, who had now noticed that I was standing about uneasily, quickly introduced me to Dr Loghman-Adham. 'She speaks four languages!' he exclaimed. 'Isn't that extraordinary?' Then he told him that I had been brought up in Switzerland and had only recently returned to Iran.

The courtier's eyes lit up with enthusiasm, and after he had looked me over from head to toe he said: 'What a lucky coincidence that you should be here at this particular moment!'

'We absolutely must find a job for her,' declared Khonsari, and whispered something into his guest's ear.

Then the Shah's Master of Ceremonies asked me various questions, some in French: how long I had lived in Switzerland, which schools I had been to, and whether I was now planning to remain in Iran. He also enquired about my age, and I told him I was twenty-one.

Finally they both shook hands with me and I was free to go. Before I left the room, the Permanent Secretary asked me to ring him in a few days. Confused by this rather mysterious meeting and the authoritarian atmosphere in the Foreign Ministry, I plunged through the connecting door into the administrative office. His formerly arrogant receptionist, who had come in frequently while we were talking, now treated me much more kindly.

As I left the ministry building and went to look for my taxi I still had no idea that this had been the first informal interview for my admission into the Shah's administration. I made myself comfortable in the back seat of the taxi and wondered what the Master of Ceremonies had meant when he had talked about a lucky coincidence. The cool reception, the unexpected appearance of a prominent personage, the questions about Switzerland, the change in the Permanent Secretary's attitude, and finally the fact that I had been requested to get in touch with him in a few days were all, for the moment, extremely puzzling.

The driver, who kept glancing back at me in the rear-view mirror, asked me if my visit had been a success.

'Oh, I really don't know,' I answered cautiously. It was always a possibility that taxi drivers could be Savak agents.

'*Inshallah*, I hope everything will turn out just the way you want it,' was his kind and comforting reply.

The very next day I received a telephone call from the Imperial Court. A pleasant female voice informed me that His Excellency the Grand Master of Ceremonies wished to speak to me. Immediately my heart began to beat faster and I could see that the hand holding the receiver was trembling.

'I should like to know if you will come to Switzerland with me,' he said, and continued: 'In the near future I shall be sent to Berne as the Ambassador of His Imperial Majesty Shahanshah Aryamehr. It would be in your interest to sit the entrance examination for service in the Foreign Ministry, which as luck would have it is taking place next week, and to regularize your position as an employee.' If I decided to go to the Iranian Embassy in Berne as his secretary, he added, it would be best to take up my post a few weeks before his own arrival, in order to familiarize myself with the work.

This was a breathtaking offer for a young girl such as myself, but

I still asked for a few days to consider his proposal. My father thought that I should seize this unique opportunity, but I hesitated, for my original intention had been to live in Iran and get to know it more deeply after my years of absence. That was why I had not considered working for international organizations, in spite of the attractive conditions of employment which they offered. I wanted to come into contact with real Iranians – but fate, my family situation and the nature of my knowledge and experience had now led me into the circles of the Iranian élite, so there was also the attraction of finding out about Iran on a higher level, and my curiosity led me to a momentous decision.

I sat and passed the entrance examination for the Foreign Ministry, which consisted of a language paper and some questions on the internal politics of Iran, the aims of the Shah's social reforms, and the achievements of the reform programme. The questions were doctrinal and were consciously aimed at a kind of opinion research, which made the answers that much more confined. It was not only the candidates' knowledge which was being tested, but the extent of their nationalism and their loyalty to the Shah. There was also a paper that concentrated on Iran's foreign policy, on its relations with the Gulf States and the leading role played by the Shah in the political stabilization of the Middle East, and lastly on Iran's relations with the Western states and with the Soviet Union.

Clearly this was no examination of the kind I had known at school and college. It was a form of written catechism designed by the Shah's state security organization. I was rapidly becoming more and more aware of the omnipresence of Savak. The job application which I had to fill out after the examination proved that detailed information about us and our families was already known. While the new Ambassador to Switzerland, Dr Hossein Ali Loghman-Adham, certainly wanted me to be his secretary, no posts could be filled without clearance from Savak – hence the investigation of my views in the examination and the enquiries into my family background. This didn't mean that you received a contract if you were not regarded as a security risk – contracts and contractual obligations on the part of the employer were unheard of in Iran. The job was effectively in the gift of Savak, and if you displeased them you could be suspended instantly and without appeal.

From that time onwards the shadow of Savak followed wherever I went. At the beginning I found it rather exciting and felt like a character in a spy novel, but as time went on the constant surveillance became unbearable. Why was it necessary? Was no one to be trusted in this regime? Was it possible to work at all under such conditions? Experience itself soon provided me with the answers to these and to many other increasingly sceptical questions. It also became clear to me that once you had worked in the higher echelons of the Shah's administration it was not easy to leave, and you remained at the mercy of Savak.

Shortly before I left for Switzerland I was given an intensive course in the security department of the Foreign Ministry on the dangers of espionage, disloyalty to the Shah and to Iran, the art of discretion, and the safe methods of storing documents. My private life had to be restricted from now on. I would not be allowed to associate with any Iranians who were not members of the Embassy staff, nor with persons of any other nationality, including the Swiss and all foreign diplomats. It was not until the plane actually took off and we were surrounded by thick clouds that I was suddenly stricken by fear of what lay ahead. I knew nothing about the Embassy beyond the number of diplomats who were already in Berne or who were to be sent by the Foreign Ministry at the request of the new Ambassador – it appeared that I was the only female member of staff. The Ambassador himself had given me this sole piece of information briefly on the telephone, and asked me to treat it confidentially. Everything in this system seemed to be labelled 'Confidential'.

In order to overcome my apprehension I took out of my bag a book which I had brought to read on the flight. It was Dürrenmatt's comedy *Romulus the Great*, an ironical choice, as it later turned out, because Dürrenmatt is a Swiss writer and his play concerns the last Emperor of Rome. In the play, Romulus is a tragi-comic figure who runs a large chicken farm. The full irony became apparent to me several years later: I had been flying to Switzerland to take up my first post in an administration which, twelve years later, was to collapse and to take with it an ancient monarchical system and its last emperor, Mohammed Reza Pahlavi.

Dürrenmatt's note on the play shows the affinity, but also the decisive differences, between these two rulers, one invented, the other real. Romulus was:

> . . . witty, relaxed, humane, certainly, but in the final analysis a person who is extremely hard and ruthless in his actions, and who does not shrink from also demanding the absolute from others, a dangerous fellow who has made death his aim; that is the terrible thing about this imperial hen breeder, this man who passes judgement on the world but is disguised as a fool, whose tragedy lies in the very comedy of his end, in his retirement, which he then – and only this makes him great – has the insight and the wisdom to accept!

Unlike Romulus, the Shah never wanted to accept his retirement.

Suddenly a man in a dark suit who was sitting next to me, and had not so far uttered one word, asked what I was reading so avidly. I told him the story with some pleasure but – as I could see from his reaction – he did not find it funny at all. At the time I thought he simply lacked a sense of humour. Later, however, when I discovered with some dismay who he was, I understood why he had not shared my joke and what a bad mistake I had made at the very beginning of my career.

When we arrived at Zurich airport I said goodbye to my humourless travelling companion. My journey was not over yet: I still had to catch the train to Berne, where a hotel room had been reserved for me. It was evening in Zurich and it was snowing. The magnificently lit, elegant Bahnhofstrasse looked like a shimmering piece of jewellery behind the lightly falling snowflakes. In spite of the cold and of having no one with me I felt safe, for I knew the city well. I bought a copy of the *Neue Zürcher Zeitung* at the station bookstall and followed an elderly porter to the platform. The train to Berne had not yet arrived, so I sat down, wrapped myself up snugly in my coat, pulled the brim of my hat down over my ears, and began to read my paper.

Suddenly a man's voice made me jump – it was asking me

something in Persian. At first I thought I must be dreaming. But then I recognised the man who had been sitting next to me in the plane.

'Are you going to Berne, too?' he repeated.

'Yes, I am,' I answered with hesitation.

'Have you got somewhere to stay tonight?' he wanted to know.

I told him that I had a hotel room, but that I would soon have to look for an apartment.

'I see. So you are staying in Berne for some time,' he said.

He helped me with my cases, as our train was now approaching the platform, and soon we were sitting opposite each other in an empty first-class compartment. I stretched out my legs and closed my eyes, which were burning with sheer exhaustion, and abandoned myself to the monotonous sound of the express.

'So you're an envoy of the Foreign Ministry?' I heard him asking loudly.

'What gives you that idea?' I asked in amazement.

He laughed and explained that it was not difficult to guess. 'A small town like Berne, with nothing but embassies,' he continued, 'could otherwise have few attractions for a young lady like you.'

I enquired jokingly if he was also from the Foreign Ministry.

'No,' he replied hesitantly, 'but I shall have quite a lot to do with the Embassy.'

I saw that he did not want to talk about himself any more, so I said nothing else until we arrived in Berne.

The second secretary from the Embassy came to meet me at the station. He also shook hands with my companion and addressed him as 'Colonel'. Then he drove us in his silver-grey Mercedes to my hotel in the old town. Who was this colonel who had followed me like a shadow from Tehran to Berne and was now, it seemed, lurking in the same hotel and on the same floor? Was it merely coincidence? The ancient town clock struck one, and I knew I had to report to the Embassy at eight. I snuggled deep down under the covers and closed my eyes, but my heart was pounding and I knew I would sleep only fitfully.

Morning brought an end to this discomfort. It was a sparkling day – the sun shone gloriously over the snow-covered city, and I felt it was a good omen for the beginning of my working life. I took a taxi through the city centre to the Luisenstrasse where the Iranian Embassy was situated. After telling me briefly what my work would entail, the chargé d'affaires asked if I knew why I had been sent with such urgency. 'Their Imperial Majesties, the Shahanshah and the Shahbanou, are to spend their winter holidays in Switzerland,' he said quietly. 'We must do our best to see that their stay passes off as smoothly as possible. The head of security of the Imperial Guard is already here too,' he added. 'In fact I think you've met him. Colonel Vaziri is staying at the same hotel as you.' Only now, as if in passing, was I told the identity of my mysterious travelling companion. All this time he had been checking on me as a newcomer to the Embassy, to ascertain if I had links with the Shah's opponents abroad. The preparations for the visit were to be put in hand immediately, the chargé d'affaires continued, and were to be top secret. Then he took me up to the first floor and introduced me to the rest of the staff.

The consul kept himself very much to himself, and never had any contact with people requesting visas to visit Iran. This was all dealt with by a Swiss-educated Iranian assistant who, unlike the consul, could actually speak German. The cultural attaché's main task seemed to be to keep an eye on Iranian students in Switzerland, especially those who opposed the Shah and on whom he regularly sent coded reports to Tehran. Financial matters were handled by the first secretary, whose only other function was to accompany the Ambassador on his walks. There were also two second secretaries who were supposed to prepare political reports for transmission to Tehran, but they were convinced that no one ever read them, they told me later, and they spent most of their time picking up women in the back streets of Berne. That was the sum total of Iran's diplomatic efforts in Switzerland. In the months to come my fellow diplomats' animosity was to be aroused as the Ambassador came to rely on me, the sole woman in the Embassy, more and more, and to give me the kind of responsibility and independence that my more senior colleagues did not themselves enjoy.

My ground-floor office was connected to the Ambassador's office by a small waiting room. It had large windows opening on to a back courtyard, so that it was full of light. I sat down at my desk and looked around. An informal picture of the Shah and the Empress smiled down at me from one wall. Behind me stood four old, locked filing cabinets. I opened my desk drawers and searched in vain for some keys to the cabinets, from which I hoped to glean some information about the imperial visit. I had not the vaguest idea what steps should be taken for the preparation of an important visit of this sort – it was, after all, my first post. But I had understood one thing from the start: no one was able to tell me how to do my job. I had to get down to work myself and perform as best I could the responsible and diplomatic task which had been set me, using all my self-reliance and intuition.

The door opened and Colonel Vaziri walked in. As he sat down and took off his hat, I noticed that he had very thick, coal-black hair – so he was not as old as I had thought. When tea had been brought I said to him jokingly: 'What an odd coincidence that we came on the same flight to Switzerland and even sat next to each other on the plane!'

The merest flicker of a smile greeted my remark. Colonel Vaziri sipped his tea, still holding the black briefcase on his lap tightly with his left hand. His strange behaviour and his silence irritated me. Minutes slipped by and still the colonel said nothing.

'What can I do for you, Colonel?' I asked cautiously.

'The chargé d'affaires must surely have told you why I am here,' he answered in a somewhat offended manner.

'Yes, of course!' I assured him. 'Shouldn't we discuss the matter – for instance, could you let me have Their Imperial Majesties' travel plans so that I can start work?'

He stuttered, speechless, in amazement.

'It's impossible for me to make any arrangements without the travel plans,' I went on. 'I need to know exactly when and where they are arriving, where they intend to go after that, and how long they are going to stay in Switzerland.'

But he seemed not to trust me. My openness made him uneasy, I suspected, and I realized that from now on I should have to appear much more reserved in order to win his confidence.

'Make an appointment for me with the federal police,' he said, 'and tell them that the matter is extremely urgent.' He also gave me to understand that he did not wish the nature of his involvement to be divulged. While I was looking up the telephone number the colonel made sure that all the doors were closed and that no one had overheard our conversation. I asked for the department responsible for security measures during visits by prominent persons from abroad. When I had finished I told the colonel, who was pacing up and down, that I had arranged an appointment with the head of the department for the next day. Immediately he put on his hat and began to leave.

'Wait a moment, Colonel!' I said, 'I'll write down the details for you.' And I quickly noted down the name of the person concerned and the address of the office.

'You can keep the address,' he told me, and then explained in a friendlier tone, 'You are coming with me tomorrow, you see. We are going there together.'

As he left I sank down in my chair with relief, although I still had not extracted any real information about the visit from him. But at least I had passed my first practical test, and I now believed that the mentality of the Shah's administration would be easier for me to comprehend.

The next morning we met again at the Embassy. After a more restful night I felt more self-confident. I had had dinner in a little Italian restaurant near my hotel and then gone for a stroll in the quaint, narrow streets of the old town. Berne really was a tiny place, and the large numbers of diplomatic limousines with their green CD plates were the first thing to catch one's eye on its streets.

The Ambassador's young Italian Swiss chauffeur drove the colonel and me in a Mercedes to the Swiss police headquarters. Throughout the journey the colonel remained silent and glanced suspiciously first at me, then at the driver, because we were talking in French. The chauffeur was curious to know what sort of man his new boss was, and I in turn found out a few things about the situation at the Ambassador's residence in the fashionable suburb of Muri.

I soon realized that the colonel could speak only Persian, and was therefore completely dependent on me. As soon as we had sat down with the representatives of the Swiss security police the colonel opened his black briefcase, from which he was never

Tehran before the revolution. The poet Ferdowsi confronts double decker buses from his plinth (Camera Press).

Above left: Sadegh Samimi, the author's father, receiving Konrad Adenauer at the Archaeological Museum in Tehran, 1955. Above right: The author's mother in 1950. Below left: Minou Reeves in 1952. Below right: At the Embassy in Berne, 1970.

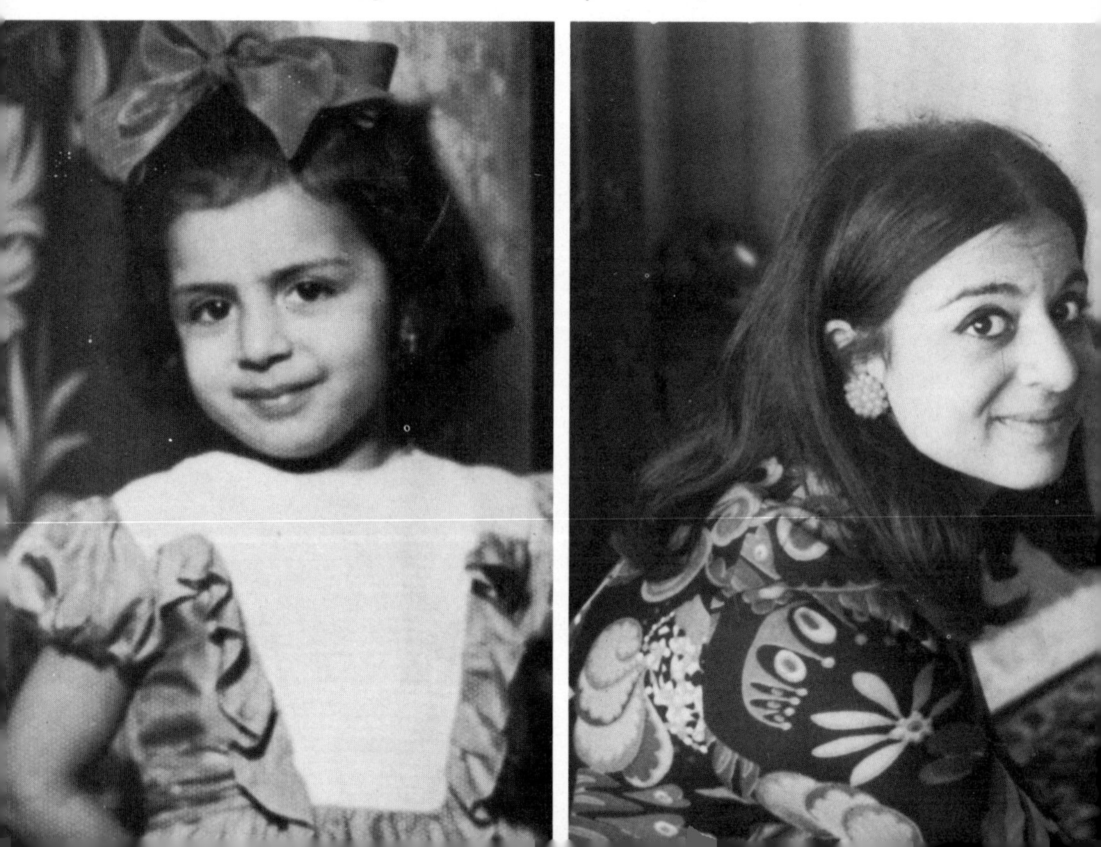

Above: The Abadan oil refinery, run by Anglo-Iranian Oil Company in 1951 (Camera Press).

Below: Modern Esfahan (Camera Press).

Above: The Shah and the Empress at a reception in the Golestan Palace (Camera Press).

Below: The Empress kneels before the Shah and the Peacock Throne at her coronation (Associated Press).

separated, took out various documents and spread them carefully on the table. Then he turned to me and muttered in Persian: 'Tell the gentlemen that His Imperial Majesty, the illustrious King of Kings, the Light of the Aryans, wishes to spend his winter holidays in Switzerland at the beginning of the coming month. The necessary security measures must be taken in good time.'

Using my own discretion and experience of the Swiss, I tried to reproduce the colonel's words in German, and in a more digestible form, for the gentlemen of the police – I always omitted, for instance, the Shah's pompous titles and simply translated 'His Majesty the Shah of Iran'.

It took quite a long time to find out what the plans were. The Shah and the Empress were to land at Zurich in a private plane. We were to reserve two floors in the Grand Hotel Dolder, where they would be staying for a week, for them and their entourage of forty. After that they wanted to spend a further two weeks skiing at St Moritz. Of the forty people accompanying the imperial couple twenty-five were security officers and bodyguards. During the visit about forty large cars with reliable drivers would be required, as well as ten taxiplanes. The more of the secret plan that was revealed, the greater became the colonel's agitation. After lengthy and pained consideration, the Swiss finally agreed that they would provide a further twenty-five security police to ensure that there would be no trouble.

The colonel now replaced all his documents in his briefcase and locked them away, except for one carefully folded sheet which he pushed towards me. 'That's the list of the political enemies of His Imperial Majesty, the illustrious King of Kings, the Light of the Aryans, who live abroad,' he said. 'Tell the gentlemen,' he again demanded, 'that every person on this list must be refused an entry visa to Switzerland for the duration of the imperial visit!' He then pointed out that it would of course be most preferable 'if all applications by Iranian nationals to enter the country during that time could be rejected or delayed'. What a grotesque demand, I thought, and I was sure that the Swiss would be amused at it. The colonel still thought he was in Iran, where he did have the power to issue orders for all sorts of ridiculous measures.

Tact was essential, for both sides were looking at me in

anticipation and the Swiss police were already eyeing the list which I had unfolded. In embarrassment I explained to them what the colonel was talking about and what he was demanding. All three immediately burst out laughing. The colonel gave me a black look, as if I had committed a terrible crime.

'I'm afraid there can be no question of that!' asserted one of them. 'Switzerland is a free, democratic country, and yet you want our consulates abroad to refuse visas to Iranian citizens who wish to come to Switzerland as tourists!' While I now attempted to explain their view of his ludicrous demand to my blinkered colleague, they continued to deliberate.

The colonel was clearly displeased. He pointed to one name on the list which was underlined in red, and insisted that I should at least convince the police of the danger posed by that particular person. 'Tell them that he is at present living in Iraq,' he said, 'but his family has been living in Geneva for some considerable time.' The name was that of General Bakhtiar, the first head of Savak. After building it up into a strong organization he fell out of favour and the Shah dismissed him, I was later told by the Ambassador. He was said to have harboured ambitions to become Shah himself. A year later he was sent into exile, and he was now working with the government in Baghdad, who opposed the Shah and his regime. He was also backed by the Iranian Communist party, Tudeh.

The Swiss officials noted this special case and copied the list of personae non gratae, with the proviso that they were unable to prevent their possible entry into Switzerland. I thanked them for their assistance, especially since this was only a private visit. 'You know,' said one of them to me as we were leaving, 'the problem is not confined to the Iranian side. We too have student organizations who are opposed to totalitarian political systems. And the Shah's recent coronation led to harsh criticism in the Swiss media. The danger of a demonstration', he warned, 'cannot be ruled out.' However, he assured me that they would do everything reasonable to prevent such an eventuality.

In the car I told Colonel Vaziri what had just been said to me. I too was of the opinion that the Shah's visit could be just as much subject to protest from his critics in Switzerland as from the Iranian opposition. Though the security chief did not take this argument seriously, he was convinced soon enough. A big, forty-eight-hour anti-Shah demonstration, mainly organized by Swiss students, took place in front of the Grand Hotel Dolder while the Emperor and Empress were staying there. Ironically, it was the colonel who had to receive the students' resolution, in which they criticized the Shah's monopolization of power and demanded the democratization of Iranian institutions and the release of political prisoners.

I am sure it was not a pleasant initiation for my Ambassador, who had presented his credentials only two weeks before the arrival of the Imperial Family. Coming from the Court itself he was close to the Emperor and Empress and was more familiar with their personal habits and private problems than with the vicissitudes of Iran's domestic or foreign policy. Presumably that was why they had posted him to Switzerland, so that they could spend peaceful holidays there.

At Zurich airport there were about fifty people awaiting the arrival of the imperial plane. I could not believe my eyes, for I had expected everything to go according to plan, and the plan did not include crowds. The Ambassador seemed particularly nervous, I thought. I tried to calm him down and asked him who all these people were, standing in a row like schoolchildren.

'They are His Imperial Majesty's Ambassadors to various other European countries,' he answered. 'It's all obsequious fawning, you know. Why do they have to bother His Majesty on a private visit to Switzerland, when he wants to get away from official duties?'

Yet shortly afterwards the Ambassador introduced me to the Chef de Protocol of the Swiss Foreign Ministry, who had now arrived to greet the visitors. What a grotesque contradiction, I thought – a moment ago he was calling all his colleagues hypocrites, and now I found that he had secretly persuaded the Swiss Chef de Protocol to receive the Shah and the Empress in person, as if this were a state visit!

At last the plane landed on the runway and taxied up to the VIP platform where we were waiting. The day before, their luggage had arrived in two other private planes. The Shah and the Empress emerged, smartly dressed – the Shah in a navy blue camel-hair overcoat and the Empress wrapped in furs – and were greeted by the Chef de Protocol. The Ambassador bowed and kissed their hands. Then we saw their entourage getting out of the plane. The Ambassador's wife, who was standing next to me, whispered who they were. A small and dainty lady-in-waiting was apparently the Empress's aunt. The four gentlemen who had now also joined the imperial couple were the Court Minister, Assadollah Alam, the Shah's personal doctor, General Dr Ayadi, a close friend, Prince Davalou, and the clown, Gholi Nasseri.

'The clown?' I asked in amazement. 'Do you mean to say that the Shah has a court jester? It's like the Middle Ages!'

'His Majesty has a tendency to fits of depression,' she told me. 'The clown tells him jokes – political jokes and blue jokes. He cheers him up.'

There were many other people with them whom she did not know. Colonel Vaziri and the very obvious-looking bodyguards lined up behind the Emperor and Empress. The Ambassador whispered something to the Shah, at which he and the Empress came over and hurriedly shook hands with us. However, the Shah ignored the Ambassadors who had come to Zurich from all over Europe, despite the fact that they all bowed low as a sign of veneration. He climbed straight into a Ferrari, accompanied by his Court Minister, and drove off, leaving the Empress behind. No one had any idea where they were going, but it was certainly not to the Grand Hotel Dolder, where they were all supposed to be staying. He did not turn up again until the early evening. I was told later by the amused Ambassador that the Shah had spent the entire afternoon in the company of a well-known film actress. The Empress and her ladies-in-waiting, meanwhile, were driven to the hotel in a Rolls-Royce.

The Swiss Confederation had thus officially welcomed the Shah and his Empress, but that did not mean that their visit was welcomed by all the Swiss. The large demonstration next day, which I have already mentioned, took us by surprise. This inconvenient event was not taken seriously by either my colleagues at the Embassy or the Iranian security officers, who were relying heavily on the support of the Swiss authorities. But I had dark forebodings.

As we drove back to Berne it had already begun to snow. My colleagues were all hoping for an enjoyable skiing holiday for the royal visitors, and had not seemed particularly surprised by events at the airport; they appeared quite cheerful and carefree. But I had my own opinions. On the one hand I had heard the Shah's speeches in Iran about the country's progress towards a better future and, like my compatriots, had imagined that the Shah was a shining example at the head of his people, the principal servant of the reform programme. But how was I supposed to reconcile these commendable intentions with the demonstration of pomp, irresponsible escapades such as that with the actress, and the obvious incompetence and sycophancy of his high state officials? But from then on I was so busy with my work that I hardly had time for such reflections.

I was originally supposed to be the Ambassador's secretary; however, I soon found myself overloaded with a mountain of other work and did not know if it was going to be physically possible for me to manage it all. As I had grown up in Switzerland, could speak the languages of the country and had rapidly gained some insight into the functioning of the Swiss administration, I became, after a time, a kind of omniscient figure upon whom the entire Embassy depended. One of my most difficult jobs – ridiculous as it may sound – was to see to the immediate fulfilment of any odd little requests made by Their Imperial Majesties during their stay. The Ambassador became panic-stricken every time we received a telephone call or a note from the Court Minister or the Shah's personal doctor, informing us of his wishes; the Empress usually rang in person if she wanted something, or wrote us a little note. The Ambassador had warned me right at the beginning that no mistakes were to be made in carrying out these requests from Their Majesties, nor those from their entourage. He was so afraid of these people that I often felt really sorry for him. But he was not alone – everyone seemed to go in fear of the Shah and his retinue. They treated him like Almighty God.

The events of one winter afternoon were typical. I was sitting in my office looking out at the snow-covered fir trees and wishing that I were free of all the responsibilities that were pressing down on my shoulders. I was translating a newspaper article about Iran.

It was entitled *Opium, the daily bread of the Persians*, and I could imagine what kind of effect it would have on our authorities. I wondered if the Ambassador would allow this, along with all the other reports about Iran, to be sent to the Shah in St Moritz. From my own observation, however, I had concluded that only articles full of praise were presented for his perusal, while the critical ones were held back.

This thought had hardly passed through my mind when the Ambassador stood before me, saying in a trembling voice: 'Just leave everything. We have terribly urgent business to attend to. You see,' he said, 'His Imperial Majesty, the King of Kings, the Light of the Aryans, is suffering from a chronic skin allergy – itching eczema on the hands. A cream containing cortisone, which is supposed to be very effective, is apparently available in Switzerland.' It seemed that someone from the entourage had recommended this magic potion to him, and His Majesty wanted it right now.

My first thought was to go to the nearest chemist's shop and enquire whether this product was obtainable at all. The Ambassador's chauffeur drove me there; he was always very sympathetic, since he knew that my entire time was taken up on errands like this and that I had no private life at all.

After checking in his thick pharmacopoeia the chemist told me, as I feared, that the product we were looking for was not manufactured in Switzerland. He offered me two or three alternative products.

'No,' I said. 'It must be this cream.'

Back at the Embassy, the Ambassador raised hell. 'That's impossible! How can you simply take the word of some stupid idiot at the corner chemist's?' he screamed at me.

I did not take offence at the Ambassador's strident tones: I knew he was sick with fear and worry. So I spent the whole day going from one chemist to the next, flanked by the Ambassador's chauffeur, all in vain. We even drove over the border into Germany and tried there. The longer I spent driving around the more furious I became. Just because some person at Court had carelessly dropped a name – possibly in a garbled form – I had to run around like a puppet on strings being pulled by a madman. I was convinced that I would get the same answer everywhere: I knew how efficient the Swiss were. If that product had indeed been available, a Swiss chemist could have helped me.

It was getting on for six when we finally returned, empty-handed, and my boss turned chalk-white when I told him. I was sure that the Court Minister, who had accompanied the Imperial Family to St Moritz, had been pressing him all day.

'Ring up the head of the customs office,' the Ambassador said in desperation. 'Perhaps they've got the cream on their list.'

'It's already past their closing time,' I protested. 'There won't be anybody there.' We did manage to get through to the switchboard, though, but the person on duty could not give us any information.

'Ask for the director's private number,' hissed my boss.

'That's quite out of the question,' was the emphatic reply at the other end when I made this request.

My boss was close to a breakdown, so I begged and pleaded: 'It's an emergency. It really is. It's a matter of life and death.' I was disgusted with myself. The woman finally agreed to inform her boss, who would then be able to ring us back if he wished. He did ring back, and I explained the situation to him. He was annoyed. Iranian diplomats were always causing him trouble.

'Wait until tomorrow. When I'm at the office I'll look it up.'

I translated this to my boss, who then snatched the receiver from my hand and spouted into it a torrent of broken French. His tone became more and more anguished. In the end he achieved his aim: on condition that we sent a chauffeur-driven car for him, the customs director agreed to go back to his office and look up the product that evening.

He rang us again at about nine. The cream in question was not a Swiss product, he confirmed. 'It could be manufactured in England or in America,' he suggested. Accordingly, that night my boss telephoned the Iranian embassies in Washington and London. I was sure that the same absurd panic would now reign there, too.

At last, next morning, came the news that the skin cream could be obtained in chemists' shops in England. However, it was possible to buy eczema ointments containing cortisone in Switzerland, too – but under a different name. This might have provided a solution, but my boss did not dare send the Shah a cream with a different name. There could be no quibbling with the words of the Emperor.

So a private plane was sent to London and a courier brought twenty tubes of the stuff to Zurich, where a car was waiting to take it straight to St Moritz. Another small nightmare was over.

I was often forced to question my position at the Embassy. Performing the tasks for which I was responsible became more and more of a burden to me, because I was inwardly opposed to them and somehow dissatisfied. The duties and functions of our Embassy contradicted my ideas of the purpose of the representatives abroad of a dynamic, developing country such as Iran, especially since there was so much talk of the virtues of its ruler in every newspaper and magazine at home. Under the 'wise' leadership of its Emperor, Iran would supposedly be able, at the very latest by the end of the century, to compete with highly developed countries such as France and Sweden. The Iranian newspapers were full of the rhetorical speeches of the Shah and his advisers on the sacred principles of his social revolution: conscientiousness, dynamism, thrift, self-sacrifice and loyalty to Shah and fatherland. The Shah and his Empress were constantly opening new factories, motorways, dams and bridges, ultra-modern hospitals and many other magnificent buildings in various parts of Iran. All these reports bore witness to a country undergoing rapid economic and social development, and to an enlightened monarch. But should not we, as his representatives abroad, also be concerning ourselves with more meaningful and more constructive activities than, for example, wasting time and human energy and money searching for a specific skin cream to combat His Majesty's itches?

The Swiss knew very little about the recent progress of our country. The Embassy was in a good position to enlighten them, without giving the impression of being propaganda merchants. We could have set up photographic exhibitions and film evenings, or organized lectures about various aspects of the new Iran. The Swiss public would probably have been more tolerant of the Imperial Family's regular visits to their country if they had also been made aware of what they had achieved for the Iranian people.

Unfortunately, however, our main function was to arrange the costly and ostentatious trips made by the Shah and his vast entourage to Switzerland, and to fill the various private orders that came throughout the year from the Imperial Court in Tehran. These orders ranged from Mercedes, Ferrari and Maserati cars to the most intimate medicines, from Danish furniture to Swiss watches and jewellery. One of the strangest requirements resulted from a recommendation by the imperial horse breeder. He had heard of the wonderful abilities of ginseng to increase potency and achieve general regeneration, and commissioned us to supply him with this expensive substance. It must be assumed that these were not just empty claims, for the orders increased so greatly that it soon became impossible to send them in the diplomatic bag, and they were instead delivered regularly by air freight to the male members of the Imperial Court.

The gentlemen at Court believed that we were magic dispensing machines, whose buttons they could press at any time. I had already grown quite accustomed to being woken by the telephone in the middle of the night and informed of their ridiculous orders by the Ambassador. I had taken a flat near the Embassy so that I could drive quickly to the office in the event of emergency. A list of important telephone numbers and addresses stood next to my telephone at home. One Sunday evening, when the Shah was back in Tehran, the Ambassador rang me at home to announce a catastrophe. Before the receiver was even halfway to my ear I heard his anxious voice asking me to take pen and paper immediately and make careful notes.

'His Imperial Majesty, the King of Kings, has toothache,' he informed me. 'The Swiss dentist must be informed immediately. Ring him straightaway and organize his trip. I shall stay here by the telephone to hear from you. Don't forget, the Court Minister will want to know tonight what we have been able to achieve.'

I put the telephone down and wondered if I could possibly disturb someone at home at this hour in Switzerland. In any case, since it was Sunday there would be no chance of booking a flight. It annoyed me very much that the Ambassador, who had presumably spent time as a diplomat in European countries, had not even thought that far. He should have told the Court Minister that we could do nothing until the Monday. How could we know that the Swiss dentist was even prepared to fly to Tehran at such short notice? And anyway, weren't there any good dentists in Iran who could have treated their Emperor's aching tooth? Of course there were, but the Iranian Imperial Court made every normal situation complicated. On the other hand, I wondered why well-educated grown men such as the Ambassador were scared to death of the Shah. Was he really so dreadful, or did the people around him just make him seem to have the effect of a latter-day Ivan the Terrible? My subsequent encounters with the Shah and his close entourage opened my eyes on this score, too. The Shah revelled in having his every whim satisfied and thrived on the subservience of those surrounding him. Since they were utterly dependent on his good will for their future, they were only too willing to pamper him.

There was no alternative for me but to find the dentist. It was 11 p.m. as I dialled his home number. Quite a long time passed before I heard a soft female voice.

'Hello, who is it?' she asked reproachfully.

'I am very sorry to disturb you. This is the Iranian Embassy. I have an urgent message for the dentist,' I said, and asked, feeling rather awkward, if I could speak to him.

'Which embassy did you say?'

'The Iranian Embassy,' I replied, and hoped that she would call the dentist to the telephone.

'My son-in-law is on holiday at present. Can I give him a message? But I won't be able to reach him until tomorrow.'

'It's vital that I speak to him this evening,' I explained, and asked if she could give me his holiday number – she refused, of course. The poor woman had no idea how I was feeling or what was at stake. I was certain that the Ambassador had been trying to ring me and that my engaged line was sending him mad.

After a long conversation I managed to persuade her to give me the dentist's telephone number in Tessin. Although his mother-in-law had asked me to wait until the next day I dialled the number at once. When he answered I politely explained the situation and tried, as diplomatically as possible, to prepare him for his urgent mission.

It was all in vain. Overcome by rage, he shouted down the telephone at me. 'It's quite out of the question! I've just about had enough,' he stormed. 'Even when I'm on holiday they can't leave me in peace! Listen carefully, young lady. You can tell your boss that not even God himself can get me away from my holidays, and that's that. Have I made myself quite clear?'

'But doctor, I beg you, please don't be angry. I'm sorry to have upset you so much,' I said. 'I do appreciate how you feel. Let me assure you that the Imperial Court will pay a handsome fee for your expertise. Please let me book you a flight to Tehran tomorrow. I'm sure that you won't have to stay there for more than a couple of days.'

'No, that's impossible,' he said, but now in a milder tone of voice. 'You have to understand that the Shah of Iran is not my only patient. I have a considerable number of other commitments during the year, and at the moment I'm trying to take a rest from them, if you don't mind. In any case, I can't just leave my wife alone here.'

'It can quite easily be arranged for your wife to go with you to Tehran,' I said. There was an embarrassing silence, and then I asked, 'Are you still there, doctor? What do you think? Ask your wife if she agrees.'

'Just a moment, please,' was the reply, and I heard footsteps receding into the distance. While I was waiting I thought how ludicrous the whole situation was and asked myself just how long I would survive in this senseless job. But my tactics must have worked, for the dentist returned with the good news that his wife would like to accompany him.

The Ambassador was absolutely delighted when he heard, and wanted to tell Tehran immediately, even though the flight was not yet booked. It was quite clear to me that he was worried less about the tooth of his illustrious Emperor than about his own plans. He had spent ten years as Master of Ceremonies at the Shah's Court before being appointed Ambassador to Switzerland in 1968. Whenever he talked about those splendid years at the Iranian Court I could not help noticing how disappointed and upset he sounded no longer to have direct access to the Shah. I felt that he regarded his present diplomatic appointment as a kind of enforced retirement, although, unlike the Shah's other Ambassadors, he still enjoyed what he called the great honour of serving the Emperor's family during their holidays in Switzerland.

I gathered from his remarks that, in view of his long service as Master of Ceremonies, he had hoped that the Shah would in the end appoint him Court Minister. Unfortunately, this post was currently filled by Assadollah Alam who, aware of the ambitions of his rival, had persuaded the Shah to send him far away to Europe. The Ambassador's chief concern in life was to make his unswerving devotion clear to the Shah at every opportunity, thus smoothing the way for his return to the Imperial Court. And what opportunity could be more suitable than helping to cure his master's aching tooth as speedily as possible? Scarcely eighteen hours after the imperial order had been issued the dentist was on board a Swissair jumbo jet, first class. His reward was much greater than he had ever imagined: in addition to a huge fee and a two-week tour of the historic cities of Shiraz, Esfahan and Persepolis with his wife, as guests of the Imperial Palace, the dentist was also presented with a valuable silk carpet. But the Ambassador never got his long-desired post from the Shah.

The imperial entourage obviously now assumed that the excesses which they were able to indulge in at home, as a result of their unlimited power, could be perpetuated in Switzerland. It was not just an endless supply of expensive consumer goods that they craved. They smuggled opium and heroin, and made a lot of money in various other illegal ways. When they got their knuckles rapped by the Swiss authorities, I had to negotiate until the authorities were again prepared to turn a blind eye.

At first I was quite convinced that the Shah knew nothing of these machinations, but then I began to have doubts. The Emperor's own demands were no less grotesque and absurd than those of his courtiers. I pinned all my hopes on the Empress, whom I admired so greatly. My work at the Embassy, with its many disagreeable aspects, was made bearable for me because I told myself I was working for her.

Every time the imperial couple visited Switzerland we could expect to have to deal with exasperating incidents. One day, for example, I received a call from the Omega watch company who told me that two diplomats from our Embassy, who had been allowed to purchase their products at half price under an agreement between the Embassy and the company, had offered to sell ten valuable watches to a shop in Zurich at a higher price. We found out that those involved were not our diplomats, but two of the Shah's bodyguards.

In January 1971, another embarrassing incident occurred. I was sitting in my office, checking through a long list to see if I had omitted anything in the preparations for the imminent imperial visit, when I was interrupted by a telephone call.

'This is the Federal Swiss Office of Aviation,' a man's voice said. 'Two weeks ago you informed me that two jumbo jets loaded with holiday luggage for the Shah and Empress would arrive at Zurich airport.'

'Yes, of course!' I answered. 'Is there something wrong?'

'The first of these planes arrived today,' he then said, 'and not in Zurich but in Berne!'

A horrible feeling crept up on me and took my breath away. I asked him, appalled, how such a thing could have happened when I had long since informed our authorities in Tehran of the flight plan approved by the Swiss aviation office.

'This sort of thing just shouldn't happen,' he told me gravely.

We both knew that unannounced aircraft flying in Swiss air space could easily be taken for an enemy and were in danger of being shot down by the Swiss air force.

'I am afraid this plane must fly back to Tehran with all its contents,' he continued.

I begged him not to do anything until I had discussed the matter with my Ambassador.

'You had better tell your Ambassador also that customs at Berne airport have discovered that the cargo does not consist merely of the royal luggage. It includes a quantity of revolvers and ammunition, said to belong to the Shah's bodyguards, for which a licence should have been obtained in advance.'

I knew that the Swiss found this kind of behaviour outrageous and would not be prepared to turn a blind eye again. I remembered that a year before I had had to deal with the complaints of the Swiss customs about two Arab horses that had unexpectedly been found on board a plane supposed to be bringing the Shah's luggage.

The moment I informed the Ambassador he sprang into action,

as such diplomatic mistakes could have cost him his job. He rang up his good old contact, the Chef de Protocol at the Swiss Foreign Ministry, who arranged for the suspect plane to be allowed to fly to Zurich, where the canton authorities issued a licence for the imported weapons. The sheer quantity of the royal couple's luggage was in itself incomprehensible to me. Was all this extravagance really necessary? But to me these were not the most distressing aspects of the regime, as I had become more and more concerned by the political situation at home.

The Shah, so we heard from the Swiss press, had built up Savak into one of the largest security services in the world; 50,000 employees were now spying on every Iranian citizen. The prisons were bursting at the seams with political detainees. Gruesome methods of torture, such as electric shocks, foot crushing, and unspeakable atrocities performed on the genitals and anus, were commonplace. The Shah had not used his oil billions to alleviate the poverty of his people; instead he had made his empire the most repressive system and the greatest military power in the Middle East.

I had been suffering a recurrence of my old stomach trouble in recent weeks, and now I began to understand why. It was not my work that had brought it back, but my scruples, my doubts, and the realization that I was serving a rotten cause. One morning I collapsed at the Embassy in terrible pain. They called a doctor, who sent me straight to hospital where I was found to be suffering from severe internal haemorrhages. For two weeks it was not certain whether I would live or die. Then the doctors decided to operate, and after that I spent another six weeks in hospital.

No sooner had I been discharged than I was confronted with the problem of paying the bill. The surgeon's fees and the cost of my stay in hospital were astronomical, and I told my boss that I could not pay. He hesitated, then said he thought that the Foreign Ministry would probably be open to reason. After long discussions the ministry agreed to bear half the cost; my father paid the other half. My boss told me that I ought to be very grateful for the obliging attitude of the Court.

I was not grateful. I was disappointed, frustrated, embittered – not only because of the refusal of the Court to pay for my entire treatment, but, above all, because I no longer believed that my service to the Court was also a service to my country. In this frame of mind I decided to give up my post in the diplomatic service. But on the very morning on which I arrived at the Embassy in Berne with my letter of resignation in my pocket, my boss met me with a beaming smile.

'Minou, I have a surprise for you. The Empress would like to meet you!'

— 6 —

St Moritz: the Winter Capital of Iran

The lively winter season in Switzerland begins in January when snow covers the high Alpine chains and their famous coniferous forests with a dense white veil, and when the innumerable ski slopes, ski and chair lifts and cable cars are opened to wealthy winter sports enthusiasts from all over the world. The Shah and his entourage would arrive in Switzerland every winter between 15 and 20 January and return to Iran around 20 March, in order to celebrate the Persian New Year on 21 March in the palace in Tehran, and so as not to miss their annual spring holidays in the Noshahr Palace on the Caspian Sea.

St Moritz is one of the most exclusive and also one of the most inaccessible resorts, lying between four high mountain passes in the Upper Engadine in south-eastern Switzerland. These passes are only crossed with difficulty and in severe winters they can remain blocked for several weeks. It is quite likely that the Shah's security advisers had chosen this remote jet-set ski resort on purpose, to protect the Shah from the dangers posed by his political opponents abroad. The Imperial Family skied on public slopes with their bodyguards skiing close behind them.

Zurich was the first stopover on the imperial itinerary. Two entire floors were always reserved at the Grand Hotel Dolder for the two-month period, but normally the Shah and the Empress did not stay in Zurich for more than a week. After that they flew in embassy-hired taxiplanes to the small airport at Samedan, where their drivers were waiting to take them to St Moritz. A provisional administration then moved into the hotel in Zurich. It comprised functionaries from the Foreign Ministry, the Court Ministry and the security organization, and its purpose was to carry out the Emperor's orders during this period. A liaison office at the posh Hotel Suvretta in St Moritz passed on the imperial instructions to the central office in Zurich. Both offices had several telephone and telex systems, and the lines to Tehran were kept open for them. But the busiest link was the air traffic between Zurich and Tehran – the private planes in which the Emperor's couriers, their fur coats, gourmet foods, consumer goods and alcohol were flown backwards and forwards daily.

Were all these operations, while the Shah was spending most of the time on skis, really necessary, I wondered? On the one hand it was right that the Shah should be kept informed of events in his country, since, as an absolute monarch, he determined the politics of Iran, but did it have to be achieved at such great expense? It frequently happened, for instance, that his ministers, who had flown over to inform the 'Arbab', or the Big Boss – as the diplomats referred to him amongst themselves – about something important, had to wait several days at the Hotel Suvretta before being granted an audience.

It was in the winter of 1968, after the big anti-Shah demonstration outside the Grand Hotel Dolder in Zurich, that the Embassy had been ordered to look for a property for His Majesty in St Moritz. We came up with the Villa Suvretta, the most attractive property in the place. It was a very imposing, massive old granite building with large rooms, not far from the Hotel Suvretta, where other imperial guests could stay. In spite of its central position the villa itself stood apart from all the other houses in the village, and was secluded. The details, including photographs, were sent to the Imperial Court in Tehran, and soon afterwards the Embassy received authorization to buy the property and have various alterations and extensions carried out before the winter of 1969–70. Including interior decoration, which was entrusted to well-known French and Danish designers, the villa ended up costing about £3 million. In the face of strong Swiss criticism at the extravagance involved in this project, the Shah and the Empress spent their 1970 winter holiday in their new villa, and it was in the following winter that I was to meet the Empress there in person for the first time. It was also to be my only direct encounter with the Iranian 'winter court'.

It was a day in February, and I was very nervous. The Ambassador had told me hardly anything about Farah's personality; she seemed to me to be overshadowed by her husband and his male entourage. This first meeting turned out to be full of surprises and contradictions.

As I sat in the Shah's own Rolls-Royce on my way to St Moritz I remembered a story that the Ambassador had told me. When he was taking Their Imperial Majesties around the Villa Suvretta for the first time and showing them their elegant bedroom, which was full of magnificent roses chosen to match the room's decorative scheme, the Big Boss uttered an embarrassing remark and one that had apparently made the Empress extremely ill at ease. 'Whatever are you thinking of? Do you think I sleep in the same bed as the Empress?' the Shah had said, half-jokingly. His personal doctor, a prominent general, and his Court Minister, who dogged his footsteps and exerted a great influence on him, had bowed their heads in hypocritical bashfulness. How could the Ambassador, who had served His Majesty for ten years as the Court's Master of Ceremonies, possibly have committed such a grave error, these eminent gentlemen reproached him. The Ambassador told me that in the Imperial Palace in Tehran, too, the arrangement was that the Shah spent the night in his private apartments.

'Where does his personal doctor sleep, then?' I had asked, for I had heard that he was never allowed to leave the Shah alone.

'In the rooms set aside for him, which are connected with the Shah's bedroom suite,' was the answer.

So, under the supervision of the personal doctor and the Court Minister, the Ambassador had the interior of the Villa Suvretta remodelled to provide separate bedrooms. What conclusions could be drawn from the Shah's remark? What went on in his private apartments? I wondered at the time how an attractive, intelligent, modern woman such as the Empress – who had, after all, studied architecture in Paris before her marriage – could resign herself to this kind of existence, whose most intimate spheres were apparently controlled by a group of male chauvinists. In those days the prevailing view of Empress Farah was that she was cultured and sophisticated.

Now I glanced into the mirrors flanking the spacious back seat in the Rolls, which was majestically covering the section of motorway between Berne and Zurich, and tried to suppress my agitation. The Shah kept a number of expensive cars in Switzerland, all of which were maintained for him by the Embassy. The dashboard instruments and handles on this particular vehicle, which he had had specially made, were fashioned in real gold: I thought them vulgar.

It was a drive of several hours, and we had therefore left Berne early in the morning. I began to flick through the pages of the Empress's correspondence and of the diplomatic messages I was taking with me to St Moritz for the Ambassador, who was there already. Although it had snowed a great deal that winter, the weather was lovely that day, and we arrived much earlier than I had expected. Outside the famous Hotel Suvretta I asked the chauffeur to drive to the imperial villa and wait there. The hotel receptionist told me that the Ambassador was in the bar, so I cautiously opened the door and stood for a moment in the entrance, clutching my briefcase.

The bar was small and the Ambassador was sitting at a table near the window, talking to three other men and a very beautiful blonde woman. I recognized the Shah's personal doctor, Dr Ayadi, the Court Minister, Assadollah Alam, and the Foreign Minister, Ardeshir Zahedi. The Foreign Minister was avidly trying to attract the woman with his Oriental charm. He joked, made her laugh and laid his hand on her shoulder. The conversation alternated between English and French. The breathtaking beauty turned her head in my direction and smiled; her brown, almond-shaped eyes were radiant and she wore her luxuriant blonde hair pinned up. Her smile was very familiar to me and I could have sworn that I had seen her somewhere before. She continued speaking French in a cooing voice, and the Ambassador translated into Persian. The Foreign Minister then answered in English. The other two men were also laughing in obvious enchantment. Then I knew where I had seen her and why at the same time she seemed a stranger to me – I had only seen her in films. It was Brigitte Bardot!

At last the Ambassador noticed me. He jumped up, came towards me with open arms and quickly led me away to the large and splendid foyer. He confirmed that our audience was at four o'clock and that we still had some time to discuss a few matters. We sat down by a window with a magnificent view on to the Silvaplana lake and the Ambassador ordered tea. I handed him the briefcase, and he began to read the diplomatic messages. As he drank his tea I asked him who the blonde woman was. The Ambassador chose to ignore my question and began to discuss the papers with me, but I knew, as his confidante, that he would eventually tell me all about her.

The massive square granite structure of the Villa Suvretta, with its dark slate roof and barred windows, had a sinister look even on this sunny winter day. The entrance, especially, which was at the back in the courtyard, and overshadowed by the mountainside and by ancient trees, was very sombre. At the iron gates some heavy Iranian guards in civilian clothes came towards us, and the Ambassador told them we had an audience with the Empress. On the wide entrance steps we were greeted by the formerly mysterious, now familiar, Colonel Vaziri, who in 1968 had sat next to me in the plane to Switzerland and had later revealed himself as the security chief for the Emperor's foreign visits. Since then I had had to accompany him every year to the headquarters of the Swiss security police, with whom he was still unable to exchange one word, to discuss security arrangements for the next imperial visit. In spite of our three years of working together, I still felt that he distrusted me. Today, however, he was surprisingly friendly and led us into the room where we were to wait for our audience. This room, which always had to be artificially lit since it only had one small window opening on to the rear courtyard, was dominated by an enormous antique walnut bureau on which stood pictures of the Imperial Family. The Ambassador, who had noticed that I was feeling uneasy, smiled at me with a confident look as if to say: 'You see, your three years of effort in the Embassy have been worthwhile after all!' My reward was to have the great honour of being introduced to the Empress, by which means the Ambassador was hoping to raise my sunken work morale.

Empress Farah, who had spent the whole day skiing, received us smilingly in a spacious, light salon with a magnificent view over the snow-covered Silvaplana valley. Her informal appearance – she was wearing very elegant tweed trousers and a yellow angora pullover – and her warmth and kindness totally dispelled the grim impression that the villa had made on me from the outside.

'May I present to Your Imperial Majesty my assistant, who has indefatigably stood by me since I took over the post of Ambassador of His Imperial Majesty, in relation to the preparations for the illustrious royal visits?'

The Empress shook my hand, and when I bowed to her she expressed her gratitude with a movement of the head. I had rather hoped for a few words of appreciation. After we had sat down, she asked me a number of questions about my education, and when she heard that I had grown up in Switzerland and could speak several languages she said that my abilities ought perhaps to be used in Iran itself. While a servant in a white jacket and gloves served tea, the Ambassador asked the Empress if he might discuss the letters that we had received from all over Europe in connection with her visit. Her utter dedication and her interest even in the petitions lodged by quite simple people fascinated me as a young girl. She listened with sympathy, for example, to a petition from an invalided Italian worker in Switzerland describing his financial plight, and requesting help from the charitable Iranian Empress. The Empress was, however, of the opinion that she had a commitment to the Iranian people, some of whom also lived in great poverty, and therefore unfortunately she could not grant his request. She answered the questions put to her with a sense of reality and with a logic which I appreciated. She seemed to understand the simple outside world with its human problems, which set her apart in my eyes from those prominent Iranians whom I had so far encountered.

Her views and her goals in life became much clearer to me than they had previously been when we passed on to questions put to her in German by a Swiss women's organization. She noted that the organization wanted to know about her ideas and activities as the Empress of a developing country, and explained that she presided over about thirty-five institutions in Iran which were mainly concerned with social welfare, education, cultural history, and Persian art and literature. Her greatest ideals, she declared, were to combat poverty and illiteracy, to stimulate interest in the ancient culture of Iran and to promote contemporary art. The country, as we knew, was passing through a decisive transitional stage from a traditional feudal agricultural system to a modern industrial state. On no account should the spirit of Iran and its centuries-old traditions and cultural values be cast aside as a result of this Western-style modernization. She said how very pleased she was that many intellectual forces were supporting her in such a difficult and responsible undertaking. She was convinced, she assured us, that she had already achieved a great deal, and she was looking forward to the results of the new projects which had been initiated.

'If you will permit me, Your Majesty,' I broke in as politely as I knew how, 'I should like to draw your attention to a further question which this women's organization seems to find most interesting. What difficulties does Your Majesty, as the wife of a powerful Oriental monarch, find standing in the way of the realization of your social ideas?'

The Empress had listened to me most attentively, and after a moment's consideration she replied, 'The privileges and rights granted to us by His Imperial Majesty, my husband, in his progressive reform programme, give me, and every other Iranian woman, the opportunity of making a creative contribution to the development of our country. As for difficulties,' she went on, 'there are enough. But we don't want to fight with our men – we want to work together to save the country from stagnation. If I am not mistaken,' she added, 'only a few of the Swiss cantons have female suffrage. Most cantons voted against it in a referendum, didn't they? It seems to me that we Iranian women have acquired far more rights than the Swiss women. We can vote and be elected.'

Even then, young as I was, I was surprised by the ingenuousness displayed in the Empress's remarks in regard to women's liberation in Iran. Though I was, and for a long time remained, devoted to her, I caught my first glimpse of her unquestioning trust in her husband's view of things. Could she really believe that Iranian women enjoyed any freedom under the repressive political system which the Shah had evolved?

The audience was closed. The Ambassador, who had expressed his opinion on all the other letters addressed to the Empress and had answered her questions, was silent as this last case was dealt with. Finally he told the Empress that the Embassy had completed all the formalities for the visit of Soeur Claire, the former headmistress of the Ecole Jeanne d'Arc, the French school in Tehran where the Empress had been educated. Every year she visited the Empress in St Moritz from her home in Paris, and the two had become good friends. I thought it remarkable that Farah Diba, now the Empress of Iran and wife of the powerful Shahanshah, had not forgotten her old acquaintances and was still so fond of them. Later, however, when I discovered in Iran what a negative effect her former friends and school fellows had on her and how they monopolized the privilege of access to the Empress for themselves, my enthusiasm was somewhat dampened.

The Ambassador kissed the Empress's hand and I expressed my respect, and we left the villa. The chauffeur was waiting for us outside, this time in the Ambassador's Mercedes. The Ambassador got out at the Hotel Suvretta and went back to his colleagues, giving the chauffeur instructions to drive me to Samedan, from where I could fly back to Zurich and then catch the train to Berne.

It was only five o'clock in the afternoon, but the excitement of the day was swirling round in my head. I sank down in the comfortable back seat of the Mercedes and closed my eyes. Where were the royal children, I wondered. Empress Farah had not only given the Shah a successor to the throne, Crown Prince Reza, who was ten at that time, but also a second son, Ali-Reza, and two daughters, Farahnaz and Leila. I remembered that they were still in Tehran and would come to St Moritz later. Four European governesses were taking care of them under the supervision of the Empress's mother. The youngest child, Princess Leila, at that time barely a year old, had a Swiss nanny, the daughter of a prominent politician. Her employment at the Iranian Court, so despised in Switzerland for its profligacy and opulence, had caused a furore in her own country's press, and when her father, Monsieur Roger Bonvin, attempted to give a lecture at the University of Zurich about the economic situation in Switzerland the students pelted him with tomatoes and drowned him with shouts of: 'Get your salary from the Pahlavis!'

Governesses and nannies were, of course, essential since Farah was too busy as an Empress to remain at the Palace all the time. The Shah, however, was not by nature a family man, and was rarely seen with his children, even on holiday. He preferred to spend most of his time with his close male associates. On the rare occasions when the family did come together it was for photographic sessions or when they were visited at the villa by friends such as King Hussein of Jordan or King Juan Carlos of Spain.

Empress Farah had undoubtedly consolidated her position as the Shah's wife by becoming the mother of the heir to the throne and of her three other children, and had been appointed Regent by the Shah at his coronation. If the Shah died before the Crown Prince was twenty-one, the Empress would rule the country until he was of age. She had thus been granted a clear political status. What woman would have had the courage to forego such a privilege and such immeasurable wealth, especially since she loved her children? Nevertheless it seemed to me that for this reason the Empress was obliged to put up with a great deal in her marriage to the Shah, and frequently had to turn a blind eye to his behaviour. I remembered, for example, the incident at Zurich airport when the Shah had left her and disappeared with his Court Minister Alam in a Ferrari to spend the afternoon with a film actress.

While I waited for the train to Zurich, I felt as if all eyes were upon me and knew about my experiences that day. It was only three years before, newly arrived from Tehran, that I had been standing on the same platform with my luggage, waiting to travel to Berne and take up my position at the Embassy. My feelings at that time had been very different from those of today. How was I supposed to explain all these contradictions of which I had become aware during my years of service and, above all, on this February day in St Moritz? Reality fell far short of all the noble aims.

The Shah, too, had bound himself to the old privileges of the ruler and of men, which his reforms should have overthrown. I could not imagine, anyway, how such a playboy could be a serious political figure and leader of the nation. It was a few days later, in the foyer of the Hotel Schweizerhof in Berne, where we were awaiting the Iranian Ambassador to Vienna who was to spend a few days in Berne, that my Ambassador confirmed my suspicions about the blonde in the bar of the Hotel Suvretta. She was indeed Brigitte Bardot, and she had come to St Moritz to meet the Shah. How her visit had been kept secret from gossip-seeking journalists I could not imagine – presumably through some subterfuge on the part of the Shah's male entourage. The articles that appeared in European magazines concerning the Shah's many love affairs reaffirmed to me his attitude to women. Once I knew that this sort of thing went on I realized why the Shah was so emphatic about separate bedrooms. In Gstaad, another elegant Swiss ski resort, it was alleged that every year he met his former wife, the beautiful Empress Soraya, to renew his old love for her. A later affair with the Swedish American film actress, Ann Margret, with whom the Shah was said to have fallen in love, also made big headlines. At that time the papparazzi wrote: 'The beautiful, radiant smile has vanished from the lips of Empress Farah.' The photographs of her in the European press at that time were intended to show how embittered she had become.

Back in Tehran, the Shah's affairs were common knowledge among society women, who loved to gossip about them in the privacy of beauty salons and fashionable hairdressers.

Of course the Shah, as the ruler of an Islamic country, was perfectly entitled to have up to four wives and as many concubines as he wanted, so his behaviour was relatively restrained. But as a Westernized monarch he preferred the European practice, and possibly also the excitement, of monogamy combined with furtive affairs.

Apart from such affairs, major decisions on internal political measures in Iran were also on the agenda in St Moritz. The Shah's cunning ministers liked coming there to see the Big Boss, who was obviously on top form, to convince him about new, and for them very lucrative, projects for the country and to gain his approval to carry them through. Even important appointments in the Iranian armed forces and civil service were made in St Moritz. Most ironical of all was the nomination of Princess Shahnaz, the Shah's daughter from his first marriage to the Egyptian Princess Fawzieh, as governor of an Iranian province.

For some time Princess Shahnaz had been living with her fiancé, an avant-garde artist from the Iranian aristocracy, in a fashionable but, for her, somewhat modest apartment on Lake Geneva and drawing her large living allowance from her father's Embassy in Berne. The Shah was not at all pleased with this alliance, especially since the artist had long hair and, according to rumour, smoked hashish. Everyone knew that the princess had become sick of the pomp and hypocrisy at her father's Court, and that she wanted to lead a normal, independent life. The Shah could not tolerate this attitude and banned his daughter from the Court, which he regarded as a punishment. Not so his daughter; she was only too glad to lead an informal, quiet life. It was not the first time that the beautiful young princess had rebelled against her father; as I mentioned earlier, she had obtained a divorce from Ardeshir Zahedi, the son of the general who had saved the Shah's throne in 1953. Unlike her stepmother, Empress Farah, Princess Shahnaz was not prepared to endure her husband's dissipated behaviour. Empress Farah, who enjoyed a friendly relationship with the Princess, secretly admired her courage and wanted her back in Tehran; now she was attempting to make peace between father and daughter. But the Shah insisted on one condition, without which there could be no question of reconciliation; the fiancé was to have his hair cut short before he came to St Moritz with the Princess to regain her father's favour.

The Ambassador went to Geneva in person to bring the fiancé news of the Emperor's desires. 'Either His Majesty accepts me as I am, or I will do without seeing him,' was the response. When all attempts at persuasion had failed, the Ambassador engaged a top-class hairdresser from Geneva who finally succeeded in cutting off the disputed hair. The next day the Shah granted the young couple an audience, and nominated his daughter for the governor's post.

The Shah's double standards in questions of propriety amazed me. While he was able to justify his own multifarious relationships and those of his sister, Princess Ashraf, when his daughter became friendly with a social outsider he was suddenly concerned with the 'good reputation' of his Court. This inconsistency, however, was undoubtedly the result of sheer hypocrisy; he had also excluded from the Court one of his brothers, after he was reported to have behaved in a scandalous manner when drunk.

So as to protect them from their father's unsuitable influence the children of the disgraced Prince – a twelve-year-old boy and a fourteen-year-old girl – were sent to Switzerland on the orders of the Shah, who paid their fees at an exclusive international boarding school at Montreux on Lake Geneva. Since then they had been under the supervision of the Iranian Embassy in Berne. In 1969 the Ambassador told the student counsellor and me to visit the Shah's niece and nephew regularly and to write detailed, confidential reports on their progress for the Shah.

On our first visit the headmaster told us that their academic efforts were unsatisfactory, and that they were continually breaking the rules. The young prince had several times been caught smoking hashish, and often broke bounds to meet delinquent local riff-raff and to gamble away his pocket money. We talked to the children themselves and told them what the consequences of their behaviour would be, but their school reports grew worse every year, and eventually it was impossible for the Embassy to answer for them.

On one of my visits I had a very long private conversation with the children in an attempt to uncover their psychological problems and to work out how best we could help them. The young Princess had clearly suffered as a result of their broken home.

'Our father,' she said, 'left our mother, whose beauty was the talk of Tehran, because she was unfaithful, and married her sister, our aunt. After a while our father realized that his second wife, too, was deceiving him with other men.' The trouble had finally driven him to drink.

At this point her brother interrupted: 'It's unfair that His Majesty has banned our poor father from the Imperial Family – he isn't exactly the most holy person himself.'

The children were quite convinced that their father had been the victim of a vile injustice, and they begged me to arrange for them to speak to their uncle, the Shah, during his next visit to St Moritz. The Shah, however, declined their request and gave orders that they should be sent back to Tehran. The Ambassador told me to accompany the children on their flight, and it took me a long time to forget what happened in the VIP lounge of Tehran airport when I arrived with my charges. Two men from the Court Ministry were standing right at the exit to receive them, and before I could say goodbye to the children they all disappeared through the door. The reception party did not even ask me if I had somewhere to stay for the night in Tehran, and if they could drive me there in their car. I heard afterwards that the Shah's twin sister, Princess Ashraf, had taken custody of the children and that they were brought up by governesses in a separate palace in Tehran. But after that I heard no more of them.

At that time we were at the start of the glorious seventies, the Golden Age of the Pahlavi Empire, during which the Imperial Family multiplied their wealth many times over. In January 1972 a new building went up in the rear courtyard of the Villa Suvretta in St Moritz, equipped with all the most up-to-date gymnasium equipment. The Embassy bought an additional property in the exclusive Thunstrasse in Berne. But the Shah's visits to Switzerland became more and more unwelcome. In Tehran there was strict censorship of the press. Here in Switzerland it was different, for the newspapers carried detailed reports of the appalling extravagance of the Pahlavis. The criticism of the lavish festivities at Persepolis in October 1971 on the occasion of the 2500th anniversary celebrations of the Persian Empire was especially severe.

The Shah had had sixty-two tents pitched in the desert; their curtains were of purple velvet, and they were illuminated by gold-plated bronze chandeliers and equipped with pink marble tables. For a whole year, convoys of lorries drove through the desert; 165 chefs, butlers and waiters were flown in from Maxim's in Paris; 25,000 bottles of wine were laid down, each one costing $100. All the world's heads of state were invited.

The Swiss only sent a retired federal councillor, and there was a heated debate in the Swiss Parliament even about him. Why should they send a representative to this ridiculous spectacle at all? What did they have to lose if they did not take part? The Persian people live in poverty, they said, and we are supposed to go and watch the Shah and his wealthy guests served with caviar. In conclusion the main speaker told a short parable which I have never forgotten. A hungry Bedouin is searching in the desert for a bite of bread to eat. Just as he is about to give up hope, he catches sight of a fat purse lying under the bushes. Eagerly he grabs it and opens it. And what does he find inside? Some valuable pearls. 'What use are pearls to a hungry stomach in the desert?' demanded the speaker.

The Iranian Foreign Ministry was, of course, aware of the Imperial Family's poor reputation in Switzerland, since one of my duties was to translate into Farsi all newspaper articles about Iran and the royal visits, which were sent to Tehran. In an attempt to suppress these undesirable reports, just before Christmas every year the Foreign Ministry supplied us with expensive presents which I was supposed to pass on to Swiss journalists. Among these gifts were vast quantities of caviar, silk carpets, and gold and silver cigarette cases embossed with the imperial coat of arms. But in spite of these bribes the criticism became ever louder. The reputation of the Shah and his country abroad did not, however, affect the Shah's position at home. On the contrary, he was growing more powerful – so much so that he imagined that he could continue to ski in Switzerland just as before, and failed to notice the beginnings of a change in his fortunes.

The Empress still enjoyed some popularity in Switzerland, however. When she came on a visit we received many letters of support from various sections of the population. However, anti-Shah feelings reached a climax when there was an opium scandal in St Moritz.

While the imperial couple were skiing there, Prince Davalou, a relative and close friend of the Emperor's to whom he had transferred Iran's caviar export monopoly until it was nationalized, was caught at a drugs orgy by the Swiss police. His villa was searched and large quantities of opium were found. The Prince had been the only one of the Shah's advisers who received him after his flight to Rome in 1953 and offered him his funds; the Shah's own Ambassador had refused to do so.

At the Embassy we were appalled. This time it was useless to plead or to negotiate; the Prince was arrested. But not for long. The Master of Ceremonies from the Swiss Foreign Ministry intervened once again, and after some nerve-wracking to-ing and fro-ing Prince Davalou was released on bail of several million francs.

The incident was not without consequences, however. The Swiss press was up in arms. Some of the articles were choked with anger, others full of irony. One daily paper published a caricature of the Master of Ceremonies wearing a loose coat and with both arms outstretched; one arm was covering the Shah, and the other Prince Davalou. Under this mantle of protection he was escorting the two men to a plane. The contents of the newspaper article I mentioned earlier, *Opium, the daily bread of the Persians*, to which the Embassy had recently objected in a letter to the editor, suddenly seemed to have some justification after all.

The Swiss authorities took the logical step and transferred the Master of Ceremonies to Tehran as Ambassador. As for the Imperial Court, instead of blaming Prince Davalou for the scandal it blamed my boss. He was charged with the terrible crime of not having known how to sweep the dirt under the carpet. For just two or three months he was transferred to Bonn, and then debarred from all government posts.

My new boss, Mahmoud Esfandiary, was related to the Shah's second wife, Soraya. He was a cold, formidable character, a favourite of the Shah. In a country where freedom of the press existed, his biggest mistake was to prosecute the editor of a Swiss satirical journal which had portrayed the Shah as a tyrant. The court's decision was even more ridiculous: the editor was found guilty – in accordance with a law which protected foreign heads of state from press libel – but was merely fined 150 francs.

I, too, soon felt the effects of the new Ambassador's personality. When I came into my office one morning I was shocked to find that the keys to the filing cabinets had disappeared from my drawer. I ran into the Ambassador's office, where he told me that he had personally taken charge of the keys because I was a security risk. 'Savak has informed me that you mix in Marxist student circles,' he said. It was true that in my minimal free time in recent weeks I had been out a few times with a post graduate student of economics. I was twenty-five at that time, and we did not talk about politics.

'That's ridiculous!' I burst out.

The Ambassador shrugged his shoulders. 'Well, I have received instructions to reduce your responsibilities to a minimum.'

'In that case,' I said, 'I would prefer to give up my responsibilities altogether.'

Without saying goodbye, and slamming the door behind me, I left the Embassy. I had stomach ache. I felt sick. Why had I let myself get tangled up in this web of suspicion, corruption and intrigue? Money? There was no question of that. My salary was 1300 francs a month (about £400 in today's money), just enough for me to rent a small room. If my father had not sent me the occasional cheque I would not even have been able to buy the clothes which my official duties demanded. I paced up and down in my room and kept on saying to myself: 'I've had enough, that's it . . . I'm finished . . . I'm not going to go along with it any more.' I resolved to stay at home. But after only a few days I received a telephone call from the Ambassador. I was to come to the Embassy to speak to a representative of Savak. I had no choice but to go – I had no permit to stay in Switzerland except in a diplomatic post, and my family was in Tehran, where they were vulnerable to any reprisals that Savak might dream up.

The Savaki, who turned out to be a man with a protruding lower lip, slit eyes and obtrusively shiny patent leather shoes, tried to persuade me to resume my duties. He made one repeated condition: 'Drop this student.' He said it threateningly in a sinister voice. He said it with a smile, showing his yellow dentures. He said it in a fatherly manner and added, 'It's in your own interest.' Gradually I realized that I did not really care all that much about the student, but what did matter to me was my self-respect. So I refused.

In the end the matter resolved itself. The gentlemen with the yellow teeth and the patent leather shoes was accused of spying, made persona non grata and expelled from Switzerland, while 'my' student was given an influential post in the Shah's administration. Savak was not merely in the business of torture and repression; sometimes it bribed or bought political opponents if they could be useful. I had thus not, as had been threatened, ruined my 'brilliant career'. The keys to the filing cabinets were returned to me. Work could be resumed. But no one could have failed to notice that I had changed: when people came to me with absurd requests I resisted. I no longer said yes and so be it to everything. I spoke my opinion quite openly.

Left: The Messenger of Allah, Ayatollah Khomeini (Camera Press).

Below: Iran at prayer (Camera Press).

After the revolution women returned to wearing the chador or at least covering heads and legs (Camera Press)

Above: The Shah and the Empress inaugurate a centre for retarded children in 1975. Minou Reeves is second on the right.

Below left: Minou Reeves with the Queen Mother in 1974.

Below right: With Senator Edward Kennedy in 1975. the Empress's mother, Madame Farideh Diba, stands behind.

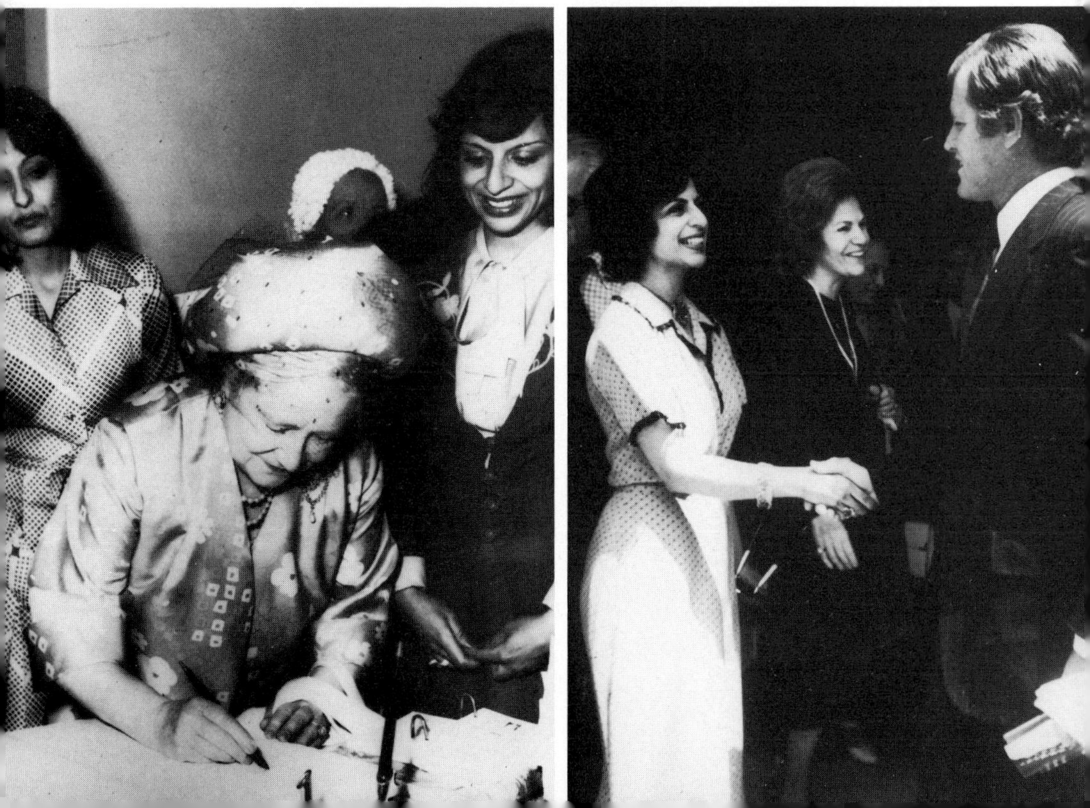

Above: The Shah in Switzerland with members of his entourage (Camera Press).

Below left: Crown Prince Reza, heir to the Peacock Throne (Camera Press).

Below right: Some peasant children benefited from the Shah's fight against illiteracy (Camera Press).

7

The Empress's Charity

People were running in every direction. Up and down the corridors of this bright new centre for mentally handicapped children you could see excitement on every face. Last-minute preparations were under way for a visit by Their Imperial Majesties. The cleaners were polishing the floor yet again; the shine hurt one's eyes and the tiles were now so slippery that they were almost dangerous. Other staff were inspecting every bedroom to ensure that each was absolutely perfect and that the bedclothes showed not the tiniest crease. The nurses carefully cleaned the wretched children's noses for the umpteenth time. Section heads issued urgent instructions about things that had suddenly occurred to them, and then hurried away to check the flowers once again. And everywhere, at every corner, on the roof, down in the basement, in the park, there were security police checking. The walls were decorated with pictures of Empress Farah visiting similar centres in other parts of Iran, for she was president of the National Organization for the Protection of Children, for which, since leaving the diplomatic service in 1973, I had worked as head of public relations. I had been recommended for this post by my first boss, Dr Hossein Ali Loghman-Adham, who had been posted back to Tehran and knew of my affection for the Empress and respect for her work. His brother, Dr Aligholi Loghman-Adham, was the head of the organization, and it was to him that I reported.

This charitable foundation, with its headquarters in the Evin Hills north of Tehran, had many different objectives: one of them was to concern itself with the welfare of mentally handicapped children. Our new occupational training centre for the mentally handicapped was at Vardavard, near Karaj, north-west of the capital, and had been built on a vast piece of land donated by a rich benefactor.

A month before the official opening Savak summoned me to a meeting at which the security arrangements would be discussed. As at the Embassy in Switzerland, an essential part of my job consisted of arranging visits to the organization's various centres by the Imperial Family, overseas dignitaries and high-ranking Iranian officials. This particular occasion was of special importance. I had been surprised that the Shah had decided to accompany the Empress, as for some years his interests had been directed almost exclusively towards industrial projects and military displays.

I had already submitted to Savak a list of names of everyone who would be present on the opening day, and three prominent officials now received me at their headquarters in order to go through this list. It was a very tricky operation, for the slightest mistake could have been misinterpreted as treason. In matters of this kind Savak was merciless. If anything went wrong they automatically laid the blame on those involved in the preparations: the mildest penalty was to be debarred from public office; a real breakdown in security could mean imprisonment. On many previous occasions forthcoming visits by VIPs had brought me into contact with the gentlemen of the secret police, but it was a long time before they were prepared to accept me as a woman in this post and to trust me. As a result I felt strained and apprehensive whenever a new visit had to be arranged, which meant once or twice a month.

The Savakis now told me that two weeks before the opening day they would create a safety zone around the Centre which could only be entered by people holding an identity card issued by them. When I heard the size of the area to be closed off I suddenly remembered what the Mayor of Tehran had told me just a few days before. For nearly a year I had been repeatedly requesting the Traffic Ministry to have the road leading from the Tehran-to-Karaj motorway to the Centre asphalted and properly signposted. All my efforts had been in vain until the Mayor had surprised me with a telephone call. He told me that he had met my boss that morning in the Parliament building – Dr Loghman-Adham was also a member of Parliament – and they had discussed the problem. The Mayor would speak to the Traffic Minister straightaway, he said, and make sure that the road would be asphalted. Then he asked when the opening day was. I replied that we were still awaiting confirmation from the Court, but so that he wouldn't forget his promise I made it quite plain that the opening was to take place in the very near future. I knew, of course, perfectly well when the Centre was to be opened, but had learnt from experience that such dates could not be revealed to outsiders.

Now, speaking to Savak, I realized that this road would fall within their safety zone. The work still had not begun, even though the Mayor had said that he would see to the matter personally. But soon workmen would appear and, having no identity cards, would be refused entry to the zone to do the asphalting for which we had waited so long. I told the Savakis how important this road improvement scheme was, especially in the context of the official opening. 'The only other way to get to the Centre is by a slow, winding lane off the old Tehran-to-Karaj road,' I explained. 'I'm sure it would be far more pleasant for Their Majesties and their retinue to drive along the motorway.'

'You are absolutely right,' they said. 'Can you give us a list of all the workmen?'

'I'll do my best,' I replied, but I knew that it would be exceedingly difficult. The ministry would have had to be unusually efficient and well-organized to prepare a list of that kind in advance. Unfortunately, I was only too aware of the ineptitude of the Traffic Ministry – and as for co-operation between one Iranian institution and another, that was practically non-existent. Anyway, I failed to understand why Savak, which had so much power in the country and was able to make the impossible possible, couldn't obtain this list themselves. Finally, after superhuman efforts, I managed to get them what they wanted, but it was at the cost of my stomach which started to cause me trouble again.

I was overloaded with work. Not only did I have to supervise the internal decoration of the new Centre in time for the official opening, but I was also responsible for publicity material and brochures, which, since my arrival, were now available in several languages. These now all needed to be updated and reprinted. And there was still the daily routine work. On top of that, the rivalry and hostility between the various heads of our organization had a negative effect on the staff, resulting in a lack of solidarity and co-operation between the various departments. Sabotage and intrigue were part of daily life here, a state of affairs which was widespread throughout public and private institutions. I later discovered, for instance, just why our request for the road to be asphalted had been ignored for so long – there was a long-standing feud between the Traffic Minister and the director of our organization. In Iran, it seemed, tasks of national importance were subject to purely personal squabbles!

Once the Traffic Minister discovered that Their Imperial Majesties were due to open our new Centre he immediately sent a gang of labourers to set about the work, only for them to be – as was, I suppose, inevitable – held up by security men. Every workman was taken back to Savak headquarters and individually vetted, a lengthy procedure which meant that the work, already seriously delayed, still couldn't begin. Yet suddenly the traffic minister began to show an extraordinary understanding of the needs of local people! Not only was the motorway link asphalted right through to the village where our Centre was, but expensive repairs were carried out along the whole stretch of motorway from Tehran to our turn-off – simply to impress the royal couple. And a week before the opening another gang of men appeared. The entire imperial route was to be swept. This made me really sad, and I wondered whether the Shah and his Empress were aware of such cosmetic deceptions. Surprisingly, I was to receive my answer from none other than the Shah himself.

When the opening ceremony was over and all the departments had been visited, the Shah turned to us and said, 'I'm sure your lovely new Centre will look just as perfect tomorrow as it does today.' Dr Loghman-Adham accepted this remark from His Majesty's lips at face value, and couldn't stop talking about his use of the word 'perfect'. But it was clear to me that the Shah was being sarcastic, and I was convinced that this Centre would also soon suffer neglect and become the victim of self-interest and corruption. Indeed, the more I observed the Shah in the coming years the more apparent it became to me that he did not really mind if his ministers and advisers were corrupt, provided that he thought they were loyal to him and displayed complete obedience. The ministers in their turn had no choice but to behave in a superficially loyal and sycophantic manner if they wanted to retain their posts.

It was a warm, sunny afternoon in early summer as my colleagues, children from the Centre and I awaited the arrival of Their Majesties. Dr Loghman-Adham had asked me to have a hundred invitation cards sent to various high-ranking state officials. I could understand that the Minister of Health, the Minister of Education and the benefactor of the institution should be present; I could also appreciate that protocol required the Court Minister, the chamberlain and ladies-in-waiting to accompany the imperial couple on such visits. But what seemed to me absurd was the enormous number of other guests, all from the top ranks of the army and the civil service, people who had nothing whatever to do with the Centre. It goes without saying that the Traffic Minister and the Mayor of Tehran also attended. It was this unnecessary pomp and ceremony that I disliked so much.

Despite the heat, the Shah and Empress seemed to be in good form. It was amazing to see the Shah so relaxed and cheerful. Over the last year we had grown used to seeing him nervous and irritable, a sign, as we were later to discover, of his incipient illness. With her tall, willowy figure and long, slim legs the Empress always wore her exclusive French and Italian haute couture clothes with the panache of a model; today she was wearing an elegant dress in crepe de chine patterned in pink and grey. The imperial couple were greeted by our director, and a twelve-year-old mentally handicapped child handed the Empress a bouquet. She kissed the child and talked to her.

While the honoured guests took cold refreshments in the reception hall, my staff of fifteen men and women and I distributed brochures and answered questions. Then Their Majesties were taken to a private reception room. While I was speaking to the guests in the hall a security officer came and told me that the director wanted to see me straightaway in the private reception room. My heart practically stopped from fear. Had something gone wrong? Had I made a mistake? Why did he want to talk to me so urgently? Filled with anxiety, I rushed to the royal couple's room and gingerly tapped on the door.

But nothing frightful awaited me – quite the contrary. For the first time since I had entered the service of the state my work had found recognition. I was introduced to the Shah and Empress, who were sitting on a sofa. The director, who was standing opposite the imperial couple together with the Prime Minister, the Court Minister and two senators, said: 'It gives me the greatest pleasure to be able to inform Your Majesties that with the help of this colleague we have, in the course of the past year, succeeded in doubling the number of our publications, which provide extensive information about the activities of our organization, and have been able to translate them into several European languages. It is our goal to inform the world about the charitable and progressive ideas of our beloved Empress, and to show people everywhere the high level of education, training, and physical and mental care that we offer handicapped children in Iran.'

The Shah, who was turning the pages of one of our French brochures, looked up at me in a friendly way and asked, jokingly, whether I could also write Persian, whereupon all those present obediently laughed.

'Of course, Your Majesty,' I said, and picking up a copy of the organization's weekly journal, which lay on the table, I showed the royal couple an article which I had written on the causes of mental disturbance among children. Upon being appointed, I had made it my business to read extensively on the topic in French, English and German specialist periodicals.

At this, the Shah became rather more serious, frowned and remarked: 'Has the number of applications to be accepted in your institutions grown larger through this publicity programme?'

But before I could answer my boss broke in and explained in a curiously nervous and hasty way that, thanks to the newly opened centres in several parts of the country, it was possible to help an increasing number of children.

The Shah and Empress would not have guessed the real motives behind this carefully worded reply. One morning my boss had called me to his office; I could tell that he wanted to say something important or confidential, because in such situations he always looked down at his desk. Churning through a mass of papers he whispered, without so much as glancing up at me: 'I must draw something of the greatest importance to your attention. You're making far too much publicity for us. That's perfectly in order as far as foreign countries are concerned, but if you continue with this here at home it can only cause a lot of trouble.'

'What do you mean – "trouble"?' I asked in amazement.

Lowering his voice still more, with a worried look spreading across his face, he continued, 'Since we started making our services known to the public, more and more people want to send their handicapped children to us. Now we mustn't let these lovely centres of ours become too full.'

'But I thought that it made sense to utilize our capacity to the full,' I said, annoyed. 'After all, we are the only institution in the country which cares for children of this kind at all!'

'Many of these children can perfectly well stay with their parents and simply receive advice from our specialists on how to bring them up and keep them healthy,' retorted my boss – and then added, in the greatest confidence, that it was the image of our organization that mattered. Publicity in Iran itself would increase the demand, and our model centres would become unattractive through overcrowding.

And now here he was twisting the truth when speaking to the Shah himself. In the meantime the Empress was listening to this conversation with great enthusiasm, and I could see how proud and happy she was that her husband had agreed to accompany her to this Centre. She smiled at me, and I wondered if she recognized me from our meeting in Switzerland.

We then followed the Shah and Empress into the main hall where, to general applause, they unveiled a plaque commemorating the opening. What a scene followed! About a hundred and fifty people, many of them journalists and security men, pushed and shoved to get closer to the imperial couple in the hope of being introduced and being able to convey their homage and devotion. But it was quite clearly impossible – there simply wasn't enough room for so many visitors at once. Consequently, most of the guests had to stay behind and simply listen to the information from me – no doubt they felt short-changed. I had known all along that we would be storing up trouble for ourselves if we invited so many people to the Centre at any one time, and before the invitations were sent out I had said as much to my boss. But he was adamant that not a single VIP should be left out. Embarrassing though it was, I had no choice but to try to cope with the situation. It's all absurd ostentation, I thought to myself. The Centre would have been much better served with a reception of modest proportions.

Only one touching little incident deflated my anger. As we were entering one room a small, physically handicapped boy tried to get up from the floor but promptly fell down again. As a nurse rushed forward to try and help him, he began to clap and sing: 'Look! Look! The Shah has come!' The Empress was so moved by the spontaneity of this child's sheer joy that she could not hold back her tears. She was a very soft-hearted woman and her emotions were easily affected. It was moving to see her heartfelt sympathy for people in need, and it was precisely this humanity, which manifested itself over and over again and was quite unlike anything I had encountered from any other member of the Court, that had determined me to continue to work in an organization under her patronage.

When we reached the park another little boy again surprised us with a display of spontaneous affection for the imperial couple. Suddenly he leaped out of the swimming pool, tore towards us and, before we could stop him, embraced the Empress, soaking her splendid silk dress. Then he begged to be photographed beside her. Without so much as a frown the Empress patted his head and allowed the photographers to take several pictures of them, which turned out very well. Not even the Shah was spared – the imperial trousers, too, were splashed all over. But no one minded.

One of the purposes of the Centre, which was fitted with the most advanced equipment, was to rehabilitate young invalids and encourage them to work for a living. During the visit the Shah showed particular interest in the modern workshops where these young people were trained in various crafts. He spent a long time in each one and asked questions of both the instructors and the patients. He was particularly interested to hear the views of the instructors, who had mostly been trained in the West.

But these expensive projects were almost too perfect to be

practical – they certainly enabled some invalids through training to live a fairly normal life, but these people were only the tip of the iceberg. Whilst the size of the administration grew relentlessly, the actual number of children benefiting steadily declined. It was not long after I had been employed in the Organization for the Protection of Children that I discovered to my horror that the principal function of these fine buildings and lavish facilities was indeed purely to impress overseas visitors.

I remember clearly, for example, the admiration shown by England's Queen Mother when she visited our Centre in 1974. She had been a guest of the imperial couple for a whole week, and Empress Farah's private office had arranged her visit to us. She was wearing a striking silk dress and looked remarkably sprightly and cheerful – I remember her friendly smile as she greeted us. I had arranged for orchids to be presented to her as she arrived, and as the British Embassy Rolls Royce drew up a little handicapped girl walked across to this massive car and handed them to the Queen Mother. By a happy coincidence the colour of the orchids exactly matched that of her dress, which was particularly pleasing for the journalists and photographers.

But to me something struck a discordant note – it was surely strange that the Empress had not accompanied the royal visitor? It seemed to me highly discourteous for the mother of the Queen of England to be accompanied only by an Iranian lady-in-waiting. But then irrevocable ceremonial errors of this kind occurred only too frequently in the Ministry of Court, which was staffed by people who had neither the sense nor the time for etiquette. They were busy with very different matters; pleasure-seeking and business interests took precedence. But it still seemed a mystery to me that Empress Farah, who appeared to be such a sensible, caring person, had not herself thought of this blunder. Had she, too, given way to the hypocrisy of the establishment? Did she now regard herself as some lofty goddess, not to be concerned with day-to-day practicalities?

Together with other directors of the organization, I accompanied the Queen Mother as she moved from one section to another in the Evin Centre, explaining the activities of each department as we went.

'I really did not know that you had such modern institutions in your country. And these methods for helping mentally handicapped children are quite remarkable,' she exclaimed. 'I must congratulate you!'

She was also deeply impressed by the park, which contained a number of swimming pools and sports facilities. Coming from a country where it rains so much, she asked in astonishment how we could keep the lawn so green during the heat of the Tehran summer. I explained to her that pipes had been laid beneath the grass, and that every evening the lawns were watered for several hours on end.

'Keeping the park in such good condition must be a very expensive matter for an arid country like Iran,' she suggested, quite fairly.

'You are absolutely correct, Your Majesty,' I answered, 'and it isn't only the park, but the whole operation which is extremely costly.'

'But then it must be worth it,' she said in conclusion, 'when you think of what excellent results you have achieved.'

What she meant by 'excellent results' was the maximum rehabilitation of people who would otherwise have been incapable of working and quite unproductive. Before she left she wished us success in our 'extremely exciting activity'.

Extremely exciting! That's just what I had thought, too, when I first came to work for one of the Empress's social welfare organizations. But the more I witnessed the sheer irrationality with which the Empress's modern ideas were being put into practice, the more apparent it became to me that my own efforts were absurd.

Surely, I thought, it would be possible to set up more modest centres for mentally handicapped children at far lower cost. Such centres could allow the parents to feel more comfortable and trusting, and they would have identified more easily. Above all, more children could be taken into care. But the greater a project, the more profitable it could be for those commissioned to undertake it, and that was precisely what was happening everywhere in Iran. In my country charity was all for show, a sort of public relations exercise for the West. Each charity was patronized by a member of the Imperial Family. It seemed particularly monstrous in the case of an operation which by law was designed to be humanitarian and non-profitmaking. We administered numerous other small centres throughout the country. In the provinces the demand was greater and the facilities far fewer, so we were nowhere near a position in which we could accept all those children who required help. While the intentions of the institutions of which the Empress was patron were more than praiseworthy, and from the outside the way they worked looked impressive, in practice they were defective and ineffectual.

Among the many prominent foreign personalities who were shown the activities of our organization was Senator Edward Kennedy, who on one occasion in the mid-1970s, accompanied by his sister and her daughters, came to the Evin Centre as guests of the Imperial Court. In contrast to the Queen Mother, who had been accompanied by an Iranian lady-in-waiting, they were escorted by the Empress Farah's mother. This time the orchids which a child presented seemed rather out of place: Edward Kennedy's young nieces were just wearing jeans, and his sister a simple cotton dress. But when you consider that our American guests were, after all, visiting a welfare organization, their appearance seemed entirely appropriate. They, too, were impressed by our work. As we visited the Centre's guidance clinic and a psychologist carried out an intelligence test on a child, the Senator said to me, 'You really must come and visit our Kennedy Centre for Mentally Handicapped Children. I am sure you would find it extremely interesting to see how we treat children with these problems in the States.' Unfortunately I was never able to accept his invitation, for at this point my career entered a serious crisis.

The staff in the Organization for the Protection of Children consisted of a team of specialists from various scientific fields – doctors and psychologists, educationalists, sociologists, nutritionists, social workers, physiotherapists and so on. Most of them had been trained abroad, but some had been educated at Iranian universities and it was extremely pleasing to see that by now Iran had so many home-grown experts. However, the majority were very dissatisfied with the low salaries they were paid in comparison with the incredibly high sums which the administrative élite received, together with many other privileges such as interest-free bank loans, duty-free importation of cars and invitations to imperial receptions. Thus morale was low and the staff did not work with any particular devotion. Every now and then they would hear of the money which found its way into the pockets of the upper levels of the organization's hierarchy, and these rumours did nothing to increase their enthusiasm.

But my own morale was still not totally destroyed, and I continued to try to carry out my duties in accordance with the Empress's high ideals. I firmly believed that if everyone went about his or her work in all honesty this could contribute to a gradual improvement of conditions and a reduction of corruption in the system. Indeed, I regarded the lethargy of my disillusioned colleagues, who were filled with doubts about the system, as a kind of corruption in itself. The country desperately needed educated people if it was to be liberated from backwardness. It wasn't easy to pursue this idea with full conviction without frequent disappointment, and one such disappointment was to turn, for me, into total disillusionment.

I was busy with preparations for the festivities to celebrate the United Nations International Year of the Child. Our efforts had been rewarded with generous donations in the form of cash and consumer goods, and we now intended to organize a series of festivals throughout the country to entertain Iranian children from all levels of society. There would be sports competitions, at which the presents we had received would be given away as prizes, and many well-known showbusiness personalities had said that they would help us. After endless meetings and strenuous efforts I also persuaded several ministries to participate in the festivities. Everything was systematically planned, and we hoped to give as many children as possible a whole week of fun and pleasure.

The problems started when I brought my detailed report on the planned festivities to my boss, who was rarely in the office as he had so many other profitable state posts and industrial directorships. I now needed his permission to set the plan into motion. The festivities were to begin with a speech by the Empress, which I had written for her and which was attached to the report. The speech looked at the future prospects of the country from the

Empress's point of view and summarized her views on the education of children and their physical and mental welfare. My boss had no objection to the text of the speech, but when it came to the events we had planned for the children he was far from happy. He certainly did not want all the money which had been donated to be disbursed as I had planned; his director of finances would take the matter in hand, he said, and together the two of them would decide what should be done with the money.

Despite all the work and energy which I had put into the organization of the festival I would not have been in total disagreement if some of the money had been, say, distributed to needy families in the slums of southern Tehran. The one thing I did not want was for the finance director and the head of the organization simply to pocket the cash, but sad to say much of it went astray, to the detriment of the children. I had already heard many rumours about embezzlement, and now I saw it happening before my very eyes. Right from the start I had had the impression that my ideas, my way of working and my sense of duty were a thorn in the flesh to my boss and the rest of the directors. They felt threatened and attempted to sabotage my plans and efforts, treating me like an outsider who didn't belong in their group.

The situation became more tense when we invited tenders for the purchase of milk powder. We received quotations from various European firms which I translated into Persian, sorted according to price and quality, and summarized in a list. The powder was intended for consumption by mentally handicapped children at all our centres. I knew that we had enough money to afford one of the higher-quality products, but when the board met to make a final decision our boss recommended that we should buy the poorest quality. The tender came from a Swedish firm which had expressly stated that in Sweden this milk was used only for feeding cattle, a clause which was suppressed in the report my boss had prepared.

I found it quite unacceptable that these particularly disadvantaged children should be fed with such a nutritionally inferior product. When we were all asked to sign our agreement I refused to do so, which created a very hostile atmosphere; I was attacked from all sides and accused of failing to fulfil my duties. Angrily, I asked my colleagues if it wasn't the height of irresponsibility to sign a falsified document and condemn children to the consumption of cattle food. In the end, when they were still unable to convince me that I should sign, my boss got up, came over to me and, placing his hands on my shoulders, said jokingly, 'I expect it's the imperial inspectors that you are afraid of, now that they have started to visit places like ours to check the books. Don't worry about them. We're all going to stick together, and if it comes to it then we can all have some fun together in prison!'

I now knew that my work for this organization, in which I had invested so much enthusiasm, had come to an end. I left the meeting, locked myself in my office and composed a letter of resignation. As the objectives of the organization directly contradicted the humanitarian maxims of the Empress Farah, I wrote, I was no longer in a position to be a member of it. I then packed my bag and left, never to return.

I also wrote a letter to the Empress, revealing all the sad improprieties of the organization. It never reached her. It must have been suppressed by her private office. Nor, as I discovered later, was my letter of complaint even preserved in the office's files. Instead, I was visited in my flat one morning by a Savak official who apparently wanted to investigate the matter. From his attitude and his remarks I could see that I was regarded as a rebel who had to be tamed. He asked me menacingly if I hadn't reflected on the significance of leaving the Empress's service in this way. The implication, he told me, was that I had been disloyal to the Empress and therefore disloyal to the regime. I was in the deepest trouble. Try as I would, I couldn't explain my position. But finally, since I couldn't possibly resume my post in the organization as a matter of principle, I saw no alternative but to promise him that I would not refuse another state office if it were offered to me. If I had not done so, Savak would have made it impossible for me to work even in the private sector, or to study at a university. They had the power, I knew, to make me persona non grata in my own country.

At first I had thought that Savak would be pleased to see that someone was defending the social ideals of the Empress. But sadly I had learnt that they thought quite differently. Instead of combating corruption itself in order to counteract the increasing dissatisfaction among the people and to ensure the continuity of the Shah's regime and therefore of the monarchy, they tried to use suppression of the truth and cunning short-term interventions. Without realizing it, they were digging the Shah's grave.

The incident which had shocked and angered me so much was of course not unique, and probably constituted only petty theft compared to other cases of embezzlement – there were many influential people who lined their pockets at the expense of the innocent and deserving. I remember a day in the bitterly cold winter of 1975, watching needy people sitting in the waiting rooms or queuing in the corridors of the Ministry for Social Welfare. One wanted to obtain official permission to bring his old, sick mother to a state hospital for an operation. Another had heard that the Ministry would supply invalids with free crutches and had come to see if he could have a pair for his brother, who had lost both legs in a building site accident. Others had seen the pitiful hovels in southern Tehran that they called homes washed away in the winter floods, and were awaiting an official decision on their future. As there were no storm drains in Tehran, winter rainwater simply flowed down from the rich suburbs of the north to the slums of the south.

In the Minister's own waiting room warmly dressed officials were waiting to see him on various state and social errands. But even they had to wait. While a secretary invented excuses and covered up for her boss, he was in fact ensconced with two close friends and a couple of girls in the sauna and Turkish baths which he had had constructed behind his office in the Ministry.

But the conversion of the Ministry for Social Welfare into the Ministry for Private Welfare was not his only misdemeanour against his fellow human beings. His particular speciality was the importation and sale of drugs and medicines which had been withdrawn in European countries because of their dangerous side-effects. Three years later he would be one of the first to be arrested by the Islamic revolutionaries and sent to the notorious Evin prison. His possessions were confiscated by the Revolutionary Court. Today he plays a new role in Iran acting as a front-line military surgeon in the war with Iraq.

During the course of my increasing disillusionment with the

discrepancy between the pretensions of my job as head of public relations of the children's organization, and the feasibility of the aims I had set myself, I felt I had to do something about restoring my self-respect, which was at a very low ebb. I decided to do something for myself. Since I had always been interested in literature, particularly German literature, I signed on at the University of Melli. As I had been educated abroad, and to allow for my professional commitments, the arts faculty agreed that I need not attend all the relevant lectures, but I would have to complete the written work required each term and sit all the examinations along with the rest of the students. This intellectual involvement was a godsend to me now, for after my interview with Savak six months were to pass before I was offered another state post. But one thing was certain. I stood firmly by my resignation, a resignation which was an abandonment not of the Empress but of a corrupt organization which used her protection for its own selfish ends.

8

The Golden Age of the Pahlavis

My resignation in 1976 coincided with the peak of Pahlavi domination, with all its splendour and extravagance. The light around the newly reaffirmed Peacock Throne was initially sufficient to dazzle the rest of the world, and above all to blind the ruling caste themselves. But was this splendid display the actual core of what the Shah himself had claimed was the rebirth of Persia? Was this really the Golden Age of the Pahlavis?

During the three years I had spent at the Empress's children's organization, much had been happening on the social and political fronts in Iran. The first year, 1973, had been a decisive one for me: I had moved from the diplomatic service into the 'humanitarian' sphere of activity of the Empress, and had at the same time registered as a university student. But it was also a decisive year for Iran and the whole industrialized world. It was a year which held out the prospect of an unprecedented shift of power. On 31 December 1973, following an extraordinary session of OPEC, His Majesty Mohammed Reza Pahlavi, the King of Kings, the Light of the Aryans, announced to the world a further considerable increase in the price of mineral oil, and demanded that the rich industrial nations should put an end to their wasteful consumption of energy and should from now on make more cost-effective use of oil. His aim was to represent himself as the Messiah of the industrialized world, and his proclamation was based on the astronomical profits made from the first increase in oil prices, earlier in 1973, which inspired him to his vision of being able to raise Iran to the level of a fifth world power within the next twenty years.

This was not the first time that the Shah had demonstrated his power. Two years previously he had invited heads of state and other political leaders from every country to the notorious celebrations in Persepolis. Above all, the Shah could boast of the military supremacy of his country in the Middle East, which he had ensured by means of huge orders of sophisticated weapons from America.

The price increases of 1973 were to raise the mineral oil income of his country from $5 billion to $20 billion. From this point onwards the Shah wanted the speed of technological development to be four times greater, before the oil ran out. He enjoyed the new leading role which he could play on the world stage. Within a year his country had become one of the richest nations in the world, but it was still a developing country, more than half of whose population was illiterate. My work had brought me into direct contact with the poverty and the many other social flaws of Iran, and I could not imagine how wealth alone would be able to remedy these deeply rooted problems.

Although we at the Organization for the Protection of Children renewed our efforts for social welfare every day – despite the obstacles placed in our way – and we could enumerate our achievements with pride in our annual reports, it seemed to me and to many of my colleagues that we were only solving surface difficulties and in the short term, without being able to intervene in the real roots and causes of this deplorable state of affairs. We gradually became more and more pessimistic and came to the view that conditions could not be changed after all.

Religious faith was as strong as ever among the poor and uneducated majority. On a visit to the Shia Holy Mausoleum in Mashhad I experienced this staunch faith with my own eyes. Hundreds of sick people, including lepers, stood or sat in the courtyard, waiting to be admitted to the sacred interior of the shrine. At the monument itself I encountered a further dense crowd of men, women and children, all seriously ill or diseased, wailing and sobbing as they tried to get close to the relics in the shrine to beseech Imam Reza for recovery. They were convinced that if they could touch the grille surrounding the reliquary they would be cured.

It was an uncanny experience and I felt quite shaken for several days. Was there any hope at all for the good intentions of us modernists, who were clearly in a minority? The more I saw of such scenes, the more powerless we seemed to be. Perhaps there were other ways of integrating Islamic ethics with modern knowledge?

According to the rules of the Shia sect of Islam, every true believer has to have a mullah as his counsellor, whom he is to consult in all matters of daily life and whose advice and recommendations are considered to be divine commands. The number of his followers determines the ranking of a mullah in their hierarchy and his position of power in the religious community of the country. These religious leaders had already resisted Reza Shah's first modernization projects, modelled on the Western pattern, in the 1930s. They were particularly angry about the abolition of the *chador*, or veil, for women. Their resentment was then transferred from Reza Shah to his son, our Shah, whom they accused of completely Westernizing Iran. While our Shah was now increasingly suppressing the influence of the clergy with the aid of his security police, they in their turn were using every opportunity to scare their followers away from all innovations by branding everything new as *haram* – harmful, and forbidden by Islamic law. In this way religion had become a political weapon against the Shah. Our greatest hurdle was not material poverty, nor ignorance, nor illiteracy, but the distrust with which the simple and deeply religious bulk of the population regarded the Western-oriented modernists.

The Organization for the Protection of Children had set up a clinic in the south of Tehran in 1974. Its services were supposed to be available free of charge to the families from this slum quarter of the city. Many more mentally handicapped children were brought into the world in such families than in those living in better conditions. In the majority of cases the handicap resulted from parental ignorance about childcare, the treatment of diseases and the dangers of marriage between blood relations. While the babies were being examined by medical specialists, their mothers had the opportunity of listening to lectures and watching films about childcare, personal hygiene and birth control.

The women who came to us were all very poor and could not even read and write. I could not imagine, for example, that they would ever be persuaded to exchange their all-enveloping Islamic dress and black veil for simple, practical Western clothes. How could these women, who comprised the majority of the female population, identify with us and take our advice about how they should lead their lives? They merely looked at us with distrust. We dressed differently, spoke differently and behaved differently. The cultural contrast between the women of the lower classes and those of the middle and upper classes of Iran was far too pronounced, and I could not see any chance of this huge gulf ever being narrowed.

What seemed to me to be most incongruous was the way the Empress dressed when she appeared in public. Earlier, during the first few years of her marriage to the Shah, she had dressed much more simply, much more appropriately for the people of a developing country. But the more powerful the Shah became, the more his millions piled up, the more opulent and showy the Empress's wardrobe became. Astronomical sums were spent on a wardrobe which was kept constantly up-to-date by famous designers from all over the world. In spite of her efforts in other directions, the Empress was increasingly losing credibility by never being seen twice in the same outfit.

After our clinic had been operating for some time an official opening by the Empress was arranged. How strange she must have seemed to the veiled women of south Tehran, in her black and white haute couture ensemble with matching hat and gloves! The visit was of course reported in Iran's media, which wanted to portray her as humanitarian. Pictures of the opening were shown on television the same evening, but despite Savak's censorship of a conversation which had taken place between the Empress and a local woman it was not possible for them to conceal the discrepancy between the splendour which Farah radiated and the simplicity of the ordinary people whom she met. The Empress had been right in front of me at the time of the censored conversation, and I had heard it all.

'How are things with you at home?' the Empress enquired. 'Are you and your children in better health since you have been coming to the clinic? Are you following the instructions that you are given here?'

The timid answer was spoken in a rustic accent: 'We should like to, but our husbands are against it. They asked the mullah if we could use baby cream and baby powder. He said it was un-Islamic and a sin. The mullah knows better than we do, so we threw them away. We had to throw away the tins of food we were given, and the vitamins. But otherwise we are following the programme.'

The Empress was amazed and could not think of anything to say, so we led her away rather awkwardly. A few moments later everyone had forgotten what the 'stupid' woman had said.

No one had any idea at that time, of course, that this poor woman had made an emblematic and historic statement. Its true meaning and natural consequence were to be found in the Islamic Revolution of 1978, when the masses replaced the strongly Western-oriented Pahlavi Empire by a seemingly simple and popular regime of the mullahs. The veiled woman from south Tehran obviously trusted the Islamic priest, who with his plain robe, his popular way of speaking and his modest lifestyle was much closer to her reality than the chic, perfumed Empress. Everything about the Empress was foreign and incomprehensible to the majority of the population, while everything about the mullahs was familiar. That peasant woman, like thousands of others, had taken part in the mass exodus from the villages into the cities, and had brought her Islamic views, rooted in tradition, with her into the modern urban civilization.

The flight from the land, which reached a peak in the mid-1970s, made our social welfare efforts more difficult, since we were never in a position to fulfil all the growing needs. The situation had become increasingly more involved and complex. The state itself, which had precipitated the exodus through neglecting agriculture, gave us very little support. The pressure of overpopulation in the cities indicated that the Shah's land reform programme had been a complete failure. And the state was even incapable of solving the accommodation problem in the cities, let alone of dealing with the social antagonism arising from the new economic system.

While on a visit to a village in the north of the country I came across the backwardness which existed on the periphery of modern industrialized Iran. The village consisted of wretched little huts made of mud and straw, without any kind of sanitation or running water. The narrow streets were choked with mud and the solitary food shop was shabby and fly-blown. Just one part of the village was supplied with electricity, and only a dirt road led to the place. The threadbare clothing of the villagers and the extremely sparse furnishings in their huts – worn rugs, a few old cushions strewn on the floor, and tattered blankets – bore further witness to their sad existence. The primary school, which was shown to me by a student who had set it up himself, had obviously been equipped at minimum cost. The Shah's social reforms had provided for the creation of an education corps, which students could join instead of doing military service and act as teachers in village schools. 'Look,' he said, 'this village does not have a public bath, nor any kind of sanitation, nor a first aid post – but, as you'll have noticed, it does have a new cultural centre for its children!'

The centre to which he cynically referred was one of the many superfluous undertakings set up to promote culture and education, and which had been introduced all over the country by the Organization for the Intellectual Development of Children and Young People. This organization was strongly supported by the Empress; one of her closest friends, Lily Amirarjomand, who had been trained as a librarian in America, was its director. Many young artists, writers, film producers and child psychologists were paid high salaries by the organization to be responsible for selecting and purchasing books, films, games and other leisure equipment for children and young people. The great majority of these employees were Western-oriented pseudo-intellectuals from well-to-do families. They had no idea of the psychological structure and needs of the population.

'On the one hand we have to fight for months with the authorities about essential items, such as the heating costs for our school,' complained the student, 'while on the other hand millions are being spent on such futile projects. These children,' he continued, 'need clothes, better living conditions, better food and simple instruction in line with their psychological situation!' He said that the children had used the cultural centre once or twice, but that the books and games were too sophisticated for them. They were also expected to help their parents at home and in the fields after school. He went on to tell me – in confidence, as he was afraid of Savak who had become much more unscrupulous during this period – how disappointed he was at the whole course of events in the country. He had begun his work in this village with great enthusiasm, and had even given up studying medicine in order to do so.

With the help of people in the village he was now trying to build a public bath for them. He showed me the site, for which he had so far received not a penny from the state. In the evenings he held classes for the older villagers, who had never before tried to read and write. He made house calls twice a week and helped families to learn the basic principles of health and hygiene. 'Every time I travel to Tehran,' he said, 'mostly to beg in vain for some money for my modest development projects, I become increasingly aware of my own naïvety, especially when I see what they are spending on industrial schemes and how the upper class lives.'

I had met this student in the city of Rasht, in the office of the director of a children's home which I was visiting. The young man was trying to find accommodation in the home for a child from his village who was an invalid and whose mother had died of jaundice. The director had turned him down on the pretext that they did not have a single place left. The student, who knew that I had been sent to make an inspection from the headquarters of the Organization for the Protection of Children, asked me to persuade the director to take the child. Afraid that I might write an adverse report on him when I returned to Tehran, the director did not hesitate.

The student was grateful, and pleased when I said I would like to see his village. Afterwards I wanted to explain to him that I really did understand his problems and worries, but for him I was probably just another representative of the Imperial Court, who, in his opinion, was not affected at all by what she had just seen and who had managed to achieve something for him by means of knowing the right people. But I had recognized just what was needed to develop our country and, just as he did, I found the lack of support and of understanding on the part of the Shah's administration very hard to accept.

I was planning to adopt a more honest approach, for example, in our weekly journal and in other publications, which only presented a positive, trouble-free picture of our activities for the welfare of children, and to publish for the first time an analytical account of the current state of affairs. My trips into the provinces, where we had active branches, would, I hoped, provide me with accurate and detailed information based on personal observation. But after only two official trips I met resistance from the director of the organization and from many other members of staff who did not want to see our inefficiency and professional problems revealed. They feared that the Empress might punish them by sacking them from their highly paid posts, which, in addition to allowing them to control considerable funds, guaranteed them power and prestige in Iran. I, on the other hand, was of the opinion that we had to point out the truth to the Empress and to the public. My research trips were sabotaged and discontinued, and my boss, Dr Aligholi Loghman-Adham, gave me precise guidelines as to how I was to report the organization's activities.

I did not have the psychological and physical qualities required for political rebellion against the regime, but I could easily imagine the path which might lead that student, and many others like him who worked for the education corps, from charitable idealism to revolution. The regime was not even capable of satisfying the intellectuals, who were in favour of the Shah and his social reforms, and was alienating them to an increasing extent.

The most powerful opposition to the Shah's regime, both in Iran and abroad, had always come from the students. Since the *coup* of 1953, when the Shah was restored to power mainly with American support, there had been many protest campaigns, some involving bloodshed, at the University of Tehran, but they had always been suppressed by the security police. The Shah had already escaped an assassination attempt at Tehran University on 4 February 1949 when a young man disguised as a photographer shot him five times. He was also amazingly lucky to escape four other attempts on his life. One such attempt occurred on 10 April 1965 when a soldier of the Imperial Guard tried to shoot him down at the

Marble Palace. Only one bullet found its target, hitting the Shah's left ear. Savak maintained constant checks on all aspects of academic life; most importantly, it prescribed what was and was not to be taught, and any contraventions by academic staff or students were at once detected by its agents and denounced. These repressive measures left no framework for intellectual individualism or free expression of ideas and opinions or of criticism. While the academics constituted a passive opposition, the students often organized public campaigns. During the economic boom of the 1970s the opposition at the universities became more vociferous and more open, in spite of the enormous financial aid granted to students by the state. The students expressed their dissatisfaction and frustration in protest actions, strikes and demonstrations, and caused general chaos and disorder. In this decade there were only very few intellectuals who were able to take the regime seriously.

In June 1975 I witnessed a confrontation at the University of Melli between the security forces and a group of student protesters who had organized a strike. The strike was meant to last a week, and no one was supposed to attend lectures or examinations. At that time I was taking a number of examinations and wanted at all costs to avoid them being postponed for a year. On one particular day when I had an examination to sit there was an unusual silence hanging over the hilly university campus, famous for its beautiful setting and idyllic gardens. I was just going up the steps to the arts faculty when I noticed that the statue of the Shah by the entrance – in the centre of a square surrounded by flowerbeds – was covered with a white cloth. Later I discovered that the students had beheaded it. In the German department, our director of studies and her colleagues were having a meeting to decide whether they should hold the examination or postpone it. Three of my fellow students, sitting in a waiting room, told me about the threats which had been received by the various departments from the striking students. Savak had advised the departments not to be intimidated by these threats and to follow the normal timetable.

After an hour it was decided to hold the written part of the examination – but in the department itself rather than in one of the public lecture rooms, so that we should not make ourselves too conspicuous. The papers had hardly been distributed when we heard shouting and the noise of breaking glass in the faculty rooms. We locked the door and remained silently in our seats. The battle lasted for over an hour, and through the window we could see how the troublemakers were being violently beaten up by security forces and then taken away. Nevertheless we continued with our examination, which went on late into the evening.

The next day there was not a trace of the chaos caused by the students, apart from the beheaded statue of the Shah. During the night all the broken windowpanes had been replaced and order had been restored. But the university was still without its usual life and bustle. It was the first time that the University of Melli, which was considered to be an academic institution for the privileged, had experienced such unrest.

Student protests were, however, the order of the day at the University of Tehran, where everybody was now wondering if the degree ceremony, which was to take place the following week, would still be held in the university amphitheatre. In due course an announcement was made that there would be no academic graduation ceremony that year.

Usually the Shah himself took part in this ceremony. In 1974, presumably for security reasons, the Empress had come to the university in place of her husband, and I too had received an invitation. She wore a black gown to express her respect for the academic environment, and on her arrival in the amphitheatre the entire audience of students and staff rose to give her a standing ovation, indicating that, in contrast to her husband, she still enjoyed a certain amount of popularity among intellectuals. The vice-chancellor spoke about the achievements and aims of the university, and expressed the gratitude of the students for the generous financial assistance which had been granted them by His Imperial Majesty. There was no mention in his speech of any problems or conflicts; he made it sound as if everything at the university was running smoothly and peacefully. He was of course worried about his position, like every other person who held an important post in Iran; university vice-chancellors were nominated by the Shah himself.

In August 1974 the Shah's cultural adviser, Dr Mohammed Baheri, one of the few Court officials who had a good reputation, had the courage to report to the Shah, his ministers and the education authorities the truth about the atmosphere in the universities. He did this during a conference on education, whose proceedings were televised. Everyone who watched the programme was amazed, for previously only hypocrisy could have been expected from an adviser of the Shah. He told the Shah that the students were of the opinion that the state was trying to bribe them with its financial support, so that they would not cause any unrest.

'Is that really true?' asked the Shah in real or affected surprise. 'We thought that they would be glad to be able to pursue their studies without any financial problems, so that they could then serve their country in a more positive frame of mind. Isn't it unjust to make this kind of accusation?' No one answered the Shah's question, however, and after an embarrassing silence other educational matters were discussed. I knew Dr Baheri well, and was in professional contact with him. He was famous for his interest in launching intellectuals and liked to move in academic and artistic circles. On New Year's Day 1976 I was to have an unforgettable encounter with him.

Due to the increasing resentment at the universities the Shah no longer wanted to take part in any of their official functions, and so it had been arranged instead that outstanding students from Iranian universities should be presented to him at the Golestan Palace in Tehran on that day – he was not to be seen as having totally lost touch with academic life. I found myself among the fifty men and women from various academic fields who were chosen for this occasion – having first all been checked by Savak. We were accompanied by the deans of our faculties and by Dr Baheri – the man whose daring remark at the conference had won him particular popularity among the students.

The Golestan or Rose Garden Palace, used only for imperial receptions on New Year's Day and on the Shah's birthday, was built in the nineteenth century, when Tehran was a provincial town, and stands in a magnificent garden surrounded by tile-decorated walls. The interior is equally magnificent with halls of mirrors, stalactite vaults and large reception rooms filled with exquisite silk carpets and paintings.

There were many other groups of people in the garden – cabinet ministers in their official, gold-embroidered uniforms, court aides in ceremonial dress, and army generals resplendent in their medals and decorations. As we entered the lower great hall we met members of the diplomatic corps who had already greeted the Shah and were about to leave the Palace. Our audience had been fixed for 10.30. At twenty past ten we were led up the side staircase into the vestibule, where a group of members of Parliament was also waiting to be admitted. Court adjutants stood at attention in elaborate uniforms hung with sheathed daggers.

Soon a door opened and the Shah's Master of Ceremonies appeared in full Court dress. Imperiously he ordered us and the members of Parliament to enter the reception hall in absolute silence and in single file. The hall was not as large as the other rooms, and there were altogether about a hundred of us who had to stand in a row forming a circle and exactly five centimetres apart, as instructed by the Master of Ceremonies. It was practically impossible to do so, however, since the room was far too small for so many people. In our attempts at least to stay in line we created a soft murmur, for which the Master of Ceremonies could not forgive us as he was responsible for complete observance of protocol. The Shah was waiting in a side room for the signal that everything was now ready for him to enter and receive us. In a rage, the impatient Master of Ceremonies ordered his assistant to throw us out of the hall without seeing the Shah, and to let in the next group instead. We were driven out like cattle, forced down the staircase and out of the door. Confused, offended and downcast, we stood around in the garden wondering what to do.

After about ten minutes the members of Parliament, who had managed to be received by the Shah, came out and expressed their sympathy over the way we had been treated. Immediately after that we saw Dr Baheri approaching us, accompanied by the Minister for Higher Education. Both were very sorry for us but could not advise us on what action we should now take. The original intention had been that we should each receive a medal from the Shah, and we had been looking forward to this very much – what a disappointment, especially for those who had travelled from the provinces.

As we were standing around I suddenly had an idea, which I passed on to Dr Baheri. I took him on one side, as I did not want the other students to know that I too worked for the Court. 'Do you think we could arrange for the students to be introduced to the Empress this afternoon at the Niavaran Palace?' I asked. I knew that the Empress held public audiences for various groups of people between two and six o'clock on New Year's Day, since I myself was supposed to be going to a reception at 4.15 that afternoon with my colleagues from work. The Shah's cultural adviser liked the idea and said he would telephone the Palace straightaway. Before he went he asked me to look after the student group until he returned; when I looked round at them again I noticed that the deans of faculties had already gone, deeply offended. I was well aware what dangerous consequences this ill-considered incident could cause in the universities, so I did my best to keep my fellow students together and to soothe their tempers. A few moments later we heard that the Empress would receive us at three o'clock. On her orders, tables had been reserved at the Hotel Vanak, where we were to dine later as guests of the Imperial Court.

Although we were tired by the events of the day, the Empress's gesture encouraged us to keep going through the further strain that lay ahead. The Niavaran Palace, the imperial couple's residence, lay in northern Tehran at the foot of the mountains. The square outside was crawling with American and European cars, uniformed chauffeurs at the wheel, taking their prominent occupants to be set down at the gate of the imperial Palace. It was as if we were taking part in some gigantic fashion show at which all the world's famous designers and jewellers were presenting their latest masterpieces. On this beautiful spring day – the sun was shining, it was warm, there was a gentle breeze, the colourful tulips in the square were smiling and the sparrows were twittering on the brand-new twigs of the plane trees – the Empress was receiving the élite of Tehran to accept their best wishes for the New Year. The soldiers of the Imperial Guard allowed the guests to enter without suspicion.

A long, wide drive led through delightful grounds with lawns, flowerbeds, fountains, ancient cypresses and plane trees to the colonnaded, rococo-style imperial residence, built in the mid-nineteenth century. The entrance doors stood open: guests who had already been in to see the Empress were continually coming out, while others went in.

The ground-floor rooms consisted of huge halls with magnificent stucco ceilings and marble floors. They had been built on various levels, so that one went up or down wide staircases from one hall to another. Immediately I realized that the pomp and splendour of the interior had quite overwhelmed my fellow students: indescribable wealth was amassed here in the form of antique furniture, huge chandeliers, baroque-style mirrors in magnificent gilt frames, marvellous oil paintings and fine silk carpets. The anachronistic ceremonial uniforms of the Court employees, imitating the style of Louis XIV at Versailles, also contributed to the theatrical atmosphere of the interior of the Palace.

The students were all the more confused when they realized that the Shah's Master of Ceremonies, Hormoz Gharib, the man who had thrown us out of the Golestan Palace, was also present. He was walking up and down in the halls, issuing orders with great self-assurance. When it was our turn to go into the audience chamber he acted as if he was now seeing us for the first time.

The Empress was wearing a white lace dress, with her lovely dark hair hanging loose on her shoulders. Around her throat were three rows of pearls and on her fingers she wore a single ring set with a huge diamond. Behind her stood the director of her private office and the vice-chancellors of the universities of Tehran and Melli. Our New Year speech was given by a student of philosophy. It had originally been intended for the Shah, and had now undergone appropriate modifications. Although the student had been told not to mention our unpleasant experience in the Golestan Palace, her tone became facetious when she thanked the Empress for her generosity in having received us in spite of her fully booked day. The Empress regally shook hands with each one of us, in a way that struck me as somewhat vain, and gave each of us a gift of a small bag made of blue material and containing a gold coin embossed with her own portrait. The bags were handed to her from a velvet-covered tray by the Master of Ceremonies. It was extremely ironical. That morning he had thrown us out of one palace like riff-raff, and now here he was standing in another, quite unabashed, handing out gold coins.

The size of coin received on New Year's Day from the hand of the Shah or Empress corresponded to the rank of the recipient. In view of the number of people we had seen in the two palaces, several hundred gold coins must already have been given away. Indeed, later that day, in my capacity as head of public relations in the Empress's Organization for the Protection of Children, I attended another such ceremony and received a second gold coin!

The Empress only spoke to one of us students, and he was asked a few questions about his plans for the future. The whole audience did not last more than seven minutes at the most. It was a great anti-climax for us all and quite different from the day we had envisaged. What was the function of the two vice-chancellors behind the Empress? Pure formality, of course. How they would have pleased us if they had introduced us in person to the Empress and had told her in a few words something about our specific subjects and our achievements. In that way they could have assured us that our country really needed people like us and that our efforts were appreciated. Instead, we left the Shah's magnificent palace clutching a psychologically worthless gold coin. It could not compensate for our disappointment. In the evening we read the report in the newspaper: 'His Imperial Majesty the Shahanshah this morning bestowed his favour on the best students of the year during the New Year ceremony at the Golestan Palace.'

If both the broad masses of the poor and the ranks of the educated had been so completely alienated from the regime, which groups in society were the true beneficiaries of the unprecedented mineral oil wealth? Who was receiving the real gold in the Golden Age of the Pahlavis? It was not the professional middle classes. It was not the villagers who had come to the cities in search of their fortunes. No, those who benefited were the former great landowners who had now become industrialists, the unscrupulous businessmen and land speculators, the members of the more important state authorities, and, naturally, the Imperial Family itself!

When land reform was introduced in 1960 it was done in a rush, without any systematic short- or long-term planning. The right means of achieving reform in a country such as Iran were not properly thought out and researched, and this was the case with every other development project. Needless bureaucracy – too many self-important functionaries in too many plush offices, achieving absolutely nothing – had struck me forcibly when I was job-hunting around the ministries on my return from school in Switzerland in 1967. Although the reform measures were simply a shrewd political move on the Shah's part, designed to win over the peasants and to prevent a revolution by them, these changes could have been a real success if efficient, honest, intelligent administrators had been available.

The first phase was the groundwork for the transition from a rural feudal system to a modern capitalist economy. This transition took place very rapidly, and it was thought that the new system could function on the basis of land distribution alone. But the peasants, who were sold or were lent money to purchase plots of nationalized land as members of co-operatives, still remained dependent on the state for machinery, pesticides and other technical aids. Before the reforms they had had to submit to the feudal lords, who took away most of their harvest; now they were slaves of the complex bureaucracy of a state which was incapable of putting together an effective plan for this transition. The real problem lay in the peasants' ignorance, which on the one hand intensified their lack of independence, and on the other made the whole process of modernization of the land a doubtful proposition from the outset. Little was done to educate the peasantry, so 'reform' was doomed.

Modern methods of agricultural production demand technical expertise – the ability to use machinery, an understanding of fertilizers and pesticides, and a knowledge of up-to-date methods of animal breeding and husbandry. This was not taken into consideration at all. Trained technicians did not want to work in the provinces when they were offered much more interesting prospects in urban industry, and the state itself was neither able nor willing to instruct the new peasant landowners in the techniques of modern agriculture. Although the farmers received a certain amount of support from the state through their village

Iran in revolt. Below: The Shah's troops police the riot (Camera Press).

Above left: Prime Minister Bakhtiar, installed in desperation by the Shah (Camera Press).

Above right: Prime Minister Hoveyda (Camera Press).

Below left: Mohammad Mossadegh (Camera Press)

Below right: Princess Ashraf, twin sister of the Shah (Camera Press).

Above left: Farah Diba shortly after her marriage (Camera Press).

Above right: Empress Farah impeccably westernised before the revolution (Camera Press).

Below: The Shah and the Empress leave Iran forever (Associated Press).

The Shah in exile in Marrakesh (Camera Press).

co-operatives, productivity increasingly declined due to inefficiency and lack of up-to-date knowledge. Moreover, the fragmentation of land holdings as a result of reform created a vast number of economically non-viable units. As a result, by the beginning of the 1970s Iran, previously self-sufficient, became dependent on imports for all kinds of foodstuffs. And maximum agricultural efficiency is of course particularly necessary for an arid, infertile country such as Iran.

While agriculture sank further into decline and village life increasingly stagnated, factories and large industrial complexes mushroomed around all the cities and acted like magnets on the frustrated ambitions of the peasants. The Aryamehr steelworks and petrochemicals refinery in Esfahan, the electrotechnical industry in Shiraz, mechanical engineering in Tabriz and Arak, and the automobile industry in Tehran were only a few examples of the rapid growth in these fields. More than a century after most of Europe, Iran was experiencing its own industrial revolution, along with most of its adverse effects but only a few of the benefits. It looked as if the state had given up its hope of agriculture becoming more profitable, and was now concentrating completely on industry and commerce.

Right at the beginning of the land reform programme thousands of disillusioned agricultural workers who, unlike the peasant farmers, had not been able to purchase any land of their own, had already migrated to the cities to seek employment. They were gradually followed by the farmers, whose conditions had also hardly improved at all and who wanted at least to give their children a better education in the cities. Urban life offered the additional lure of cinemas, television, restaurants, parks and department stores. Shabby shanty towns started to grow up on the edge of the cities, creating a volatile mass of restless workers who would later be tinder to the sparks of revolution.

The former great landowners had predominantly invested their capital – the money which they had received in compensation for their estates – in large industrial enterprises and banks, while the sons of the traditional bazaar shopkeepers had gone over to lucrative businesses such as importing food, luxury articles, electrical household appliances and spare parts for industry and technology. Some of them invested in clothing or other consumer goods manufacture, in supermarkets, hotels, restaurants, night-clubs, boutiques and luxury sports and recreational clubs, while others put their money into land speculation and the construction industry.

Members of the Imperial Family were involved in most of these industries and businesses. With the exception of a few industries, profits from these enterprises went only to them and to the upper classes. They in turn kept these businesses afloat because they could afford to buy the expensive imported foods, to spend money like water in their nightclubs and to fill their houses to bursting with upmarket consumer goods. Everyone wanted to 'get rich quick', and to show off ostentatiously once they had got there. To do so they did not have to exert themselves in the free market economy, which received sustained support from the Shah, since initiative and competition – the most important factors in a capitalist economy – played no part in this economic system. Only with the right contacts could one's capital be increased many times over in a few months. The *laisser-faire* economy was monopolized by a few large and influential owners of capital, their agents and, as always, members of the Imperial Family, who were all interested only in short-term, quick-profit deals. It was all too easy to gain access to these circles through cunning, bribery and pimping, and to pave the way for big transactions which were mostly illegal and fraudulent.

Once, sitting with a friend at a fashionable Tehran café, a man sitting at a corner table with a woman was pointed out to me. I looked over and saw an attractive, tanned, athletic-looking man in his mid-forties, talking to a beautiful Persian girl in a strapless summer dress. He was one of the Shah's Court adjutants, and I had often seen him at the New Year ceremonies at the imperial Palace. My friend asked me if I knew what he had done before. Apparently he had been a bit-part actor in a small Tehran theatre until one day he met the Minister of Court.

'Why ever did they give an actor that job?' I asked, puzzled.

'Because he's so good-looking,' she explained. 'You know how important it is at Court to be seen in the company of beautiful young men and women!'

'Do you really mean to say that it's enough just to have a pretty face?' I asked.

'Not for men,' she replied somewhat ambiguously. 'Good-looking men bring pretty girls with them.' It was apparently the ex-actor's task to organize Court parties to which he invited beautiful women, like the one he was currently escorting, whom Court officials and influential business people could then get to know a little better. 'Pimping's certainly one way of earning your money!' she finished up.

Kish island, just off the coast of the Persian Gulf, had become a secluded business haven for the Shah and his family and the nouveaux riches. The man in charge of the island was Mahmoud Monsef, who called himself an engineer; he was the nephew of Assadollah Alam, the Shah's Minister of Court. All international transactions with the oil-rich Arab states and the Far East that were carried out from this business and pleasure base were entirely private and occurred outside Iranian jurisdiction or the grasp of the Iranian treasury. Thus all taxes and import duties could be evaded and illegal traffic in drugs, pornography and prostitution could take place without fear of retribution. Ordinary Iranians were not allowed to set foot there. My father even told me once of a priceless archaeological site on the island, to which the museum had no access and from which antiquities were taken to be sold abroad.

I was once a delegate at an educational conference which was held there. The island was indeed extraordinarily beautiful, especially as we had left behind a Tehran in the grip of winter, but it was marred by the knowledge of all the degeneracy and corruption that took place there. A fellow delegate with whom I had struck up an acquaintance knew Mahmoud Monsef, and he invited us both to a party at his villa. I was not keen, and kept on procrastinating, and in the end my colleague went alone. When I next saw her, several hours later, she told me how disappointed she felt. She had had to come back earlier than anticipated, she explained, because smoking opium always made her start shaking. She had therefore missed seeing the Shah, who was expected at the party later.

The unscrupulous commercial attitude of the new bourgeoisie, which was based purely on maximizing their own profit, allowed corruption to blossom at all social levels. 'Cram your pockets with money' became the unwritten national motto. In the ministries and other state organizations, which received huge subsidies for their absurd industrial projects, embezzlement was rife. Bribes were accepted by high state officials for obtaining the Shah's approval of a contract from abroad.

During the boom years the hotels in Tehran were always fully booked with speculative foreign businessmen who did not want to miss any of the great investment opportunities offered by what seemed a politically and economically stable country. In the mornings they had meetings with influential gentlemen from both public and private sectors, and in the evenings they enjoyed the entertainments of the capital. In the many smart restaurants, bars and nightclubs of north Tehran they were able to see the glitter and ostentation of the Iranian bourgeoisie for themselves and to admire the looks of the wealthy Iranian women. These women spent most of their time in beauty salons, boutiques and hairdressers or at coffee mornings, to which they usually invited a fortune teller to reveal their husbands' love affairs or to dream up new lovers for themselves. Every time I met this sort of woman I remembered the Empress's idea of the role of educated women in Iran – the idea which she had expressed during our first meeting in St Moritz.

Were these privileged, rich women familiar with the problems of their country, and did they recognize their own social role in it? I thought not. They were involved in the modernization process of their country only insofar as they imitated the superficial manifestations: they drank too much, dressed in exhibitionist clothes, danced and flirted in the most vulgar manner in the nightclubs, and changed their lovers from one day to the next. The foreign visitors who witnessed this must have asked themselves if they really were in an Islamic country, for the members of these social circles showed no sign of adhering to the tenets of Islam.

One of the most lucrative areas in this period was showbusiness and pop music. Pop singers of both sexes and showbusiness names received huge fees for a brief appearance in a hotel or in the private home of one of the many Tehran millionaires. The nightclubs were swarming with pretty dancers who charged large sums for private engagements with influential capitalists and their agents, at which they indulged in the world's oldest profession.

Within a few years the new élite had had magnificent villas built in the most attractive parts of northern Tehran, and these properties vied with each other in size, style, extravagance of interior decoration and the number of rare and exotic trees and flowers. Some members of the urban proletariat were able to earn quite a lot in these years, too; the workers in the booming building industry, based on speculation, were particularly well paid. But in general enormous social contrasts had been created in Iran, and increased the people's dissatisfaction.

In 1975, wages in twenty-one of the country's leading industries went up by 30 per cent on the Shah's orders. The workers even received an extra month's pay as a New Year's gift in 1976. But the pay rises did not greatly improve the lot of people at this level of society. They still endured bad living conditions, partly because they had large families to feed, partly because they did not want to give up their lifestyle for religious reasons, and partly because the state did not provide the necessary inexpensive housing.

The modernization of Iran had one single effect on their lives: each of these families owned a television set and a Peykan car, which could be bought on hire purchase. The Tehran traffic was drastically affected by the sales of these locally built vehicles. For the working population it was quite normal to spend three to four hours a day sitting at the wheel in city centre traffic jams, waiting in vain for some divine miracle to get the traffic moving again. In addition to ignoring the traffic regulations, like all Iranians, most of these drivers were inexperienced novices.

Various other factors contributed to the daily traffic chaos. There was a lack of qualified personnel at the Transport Ministry. A public transport system of any sort was still only in its infancy and there was no proper plan to extend it. Furthermore, the absence of an effective sewage system made the construction of an underground railway practically impossible in Tehran – French experts had been racking their brains about it for several years without producing any satisfactory results. A real disaster occurred whenever it rained heavily in Tehran; then the poor people's houses in the south were flooded with sewage. How on earth the

Shah was hoping to turn Iran into a twentieth-century welfare state I could not visualize by any stretch of the imagination.

The car industry had been founded in 1962, on the orders of the Shah, by a self-made man from the bazaar who had accumulated capital through various businesses such as car washes and Mercedes-Benz dealerships. Initially, Irannational built buses, minibuses and small trucks with technical assistance from Mercedes-Benz. Later its production was extended to cars, reaching a peak in the 1970s. Soon Ahmad Khayami, the head of the industry, became one of the richest and most powerful men in the country. His palace on one of the northern hills of Tehran, where his grand receptions and parties were attented by the Tehran élite and members of the Imperial Family, was an empire in itself. He was one of the many nouveaux riches who had become close friends with the Shah's relations as a result of his business dealings with them. His daughter's wedding had been the talk of the town. Delicacies for 1500 guests had been flown in direct from Paris. The bride herself had received a Maserati, a villa in Beverly Hills and a set of diamond jewellery as engagement presents, and compensation of $1¾ million had been agreed for her in the event of a divorce. And indeed, just a week after the magnificent reception the bridegroom did divorce her – he had, it seems, fallen for someone else. Ordinary people were shocked both by the sheer waste and by the superficiality of relationships among the upper classes. While these people lived in extravagant style in the pure air of fashionable northern Tehran, the city itself was choking in the chaos of overpopulation, uncontrolled traffic and atmospheric pollution.

Overpopulation was not only the consequence of the enormous exodus from the villages. The new industries also required skilled workers, who could not be found among the Iranian population. The country had therefore become a massive importer of labour from India, Pakistan, Afghanistan, the Philippines and South Korea. All these people needed housing, social welfare, doctors, hospitals and food, and their children needed education. The ministries were crowded out with people seeking assistance. But how could a system which was inept and over-bureaucratic to start with hope to deal with these additional problems?

At the peak of the Iranian economic boom there was not even an orderly banking system. To make a simple transaction such as withdrawing money it was necessary to go to at least four different counters and frequently to spend half the day at the bank – only to be asked to return the following day. And the Shah wanted to turn Tehran into a world financial centre! For me, life in Tehran was becoming increasingly unbearable. I felt as though I were living in Bertolt Brecht's fictional city of Mahogonny, his symbol of American capitalism which blossomed on immorality like a town in the gold rush, only to be destroyed by criminal elements. There were plenty of signs of the upward advance, but somehow there was also a feeling that at some stage we would experience a fall. Everyone sensed this volatile atmosphere.

Since so much money had been in circulation and had been pumped into the arteries of the Iranian economy, prices had risen by leaps and bounds. Property and rents were most rapidly affected by this overheated economy and became the target of unscrupulous land speculation. New buildings mushroomed out of the ground wherever a little bit of space remained. Ugly, shoddy, jerry-built apartment blocks and houses sprang up in every city, especially Tehran. The inhuman and irresponsible actions of these profit-seeking property speculators were constantly escalating.

All countries consider their airports to be the shop windows from which foreign visitors will gain their first impressions. In developing countries an airline and an international airport are the symbol of their link with the modern technological world. On the occasion of the 2500th jubilee of Cyrus the Great the Shah had had a grand marble arch erected on a huge square in western Tehran, at the approach to the wide boulevard which led to the airport. Modelled on the arches of ancient Persia, it had been designed by a local architect and was supposed to symbolize modern Iran under the Pahlavis, whose power was commensurate with that of the great kings of the Persian Empire. This spectacular Shahyad monument really did impress visitors, whose journey from the airport always took them past it, but the Shah was not satisfied yet.

He also aspired to a new airport building, which was to have a similar effect on foreigners. Tenders were invited and the greedy construction firms swooped down like vultures. In this case, as in winter's day in 1975, passengers waiting for their flights to Europe in the vast marble halls of the newly opened Mehrabad airport heard strange noises like chunks of ice falling down. But before they could work out what was happening a huge crack opened up above their heads and the roof collapsed on to them. Hundreds of people were killed. Only a few survived, and they had serious injuries.

The fateful alliance between the imperial house and the nouveaux riches caused a fresh and justified popular outcry after this disaster. The corrupt building contractors had deliberately not complied with the building regulations, in order to divert a considerable sum of money into their own pockets and into those of their imperial clients. There were other events which similarly characterized the rampant corruption in Iran. The public took note of them, and their anger mounted.

—9—

In the Empress's Private Office

After 1976, when I left my job as head of the secretarial and public relations department of the Empress's Organization for the Protection of Children, I would have preferred to retire altogether from public service and lead a more peaceful life. I had gained my first degree, in German literature, at the University of Melli and was preparing a thesis for a master's degree at the University of Tehran. In my spare time I also wrote articles for a television magazine called *Tamasha*, translated short stories and took part in a monthly television programme entitled *Books and Opinions*, which had been launched by a university professor. It dealt mainly with reviews of classical and modern world literature. I was trying to forget the frustrations and disappointments of the previous nine years, first in the service of the Shah at the Iranian Embassy in Berne, and subsequently in the service of the Empress.

The threat from Savak after I had resigned from the children's organization began to seem distant and empty. Four months had passed without my having been offered a new post. They had warned me not to refuse such an offer, or else I would be made to suffer. But since I had heard nothing further from them I had the feeling that they must have dropped the whole thing: intimidation was, after all, one of Savak's standard weapons. Their warning, I told myself, was probably intended to remind me once again of their omnipresence in the country.

But they had not forgotten me. One morning I received a telephone call from the Empress's private office and was told that

Dr Hushang Nahavandi, the recently appointed head of the private office, wanted to see me the following week. He had been vice-chancellor of the University of Tehran for several years, and his nomination had resulted in sharp criticism in academic circles, which were hostile to the Court and regarded the appointment as degrading and hypocritical. Although, due to her commitment to social welfare, the Empress was not condemned to the same extent as the other members of the Imperial Family, her private office was regarded as part of the Court Ministry, which had such a poor reputation. However, everyone knew how the vice-chancellor had attracted attention to himself. In the same year, 1976, the Shah had directed him to arrange for the preparation of a 7000-word interpretation of the philosophy of the Revolution of the Shah and His People. This infallible document presented the Shah as a wise father of the nation. It was published in booklet form, went on sale, and was also used in schools as a textbook, rather like Mao Tse-tung's Little Red Book. Intellectuals hated it, but afterwards the vice-chancellor was appointed head of the Empress's private office.

With the aid of his closest colleagues, he had succeeded in defining the role and position of the monarch within the Iranian political system. The Shah, he had written, was not only the political but also the spiritual leader and teacher of the nation. He, the Shah, had developed the idea of the Revolution in his mind and had transferred it by means of the mystical bond existing between him and the people. Thus he – the enlightened monarch – was to his people as a father to a son, a relationship which requires no intermediaries. This document, a confirmation and justification of the absolute power of the Shah, disputed the basic principles of the constitution of 1906, which restricted the powers of the monarch and delegated them to Parliament. It represented the people as no more than the subjects of the Shah, dictated to by the Shah and unable to act on their own initiative.

The call from the private office at this time did not come completely out of the blue, for I had recently been told in confidence of its likelihood. A member of the board of trustees of the Organization for the Protection of Children, which in recent times had also taken over the administration of the secretarial office of Madame Diba, the Empress's mother, had apparently been instructed by Savak to find a job for me. After I had not seen my former colleague for six months, she rang me quite suddenly and told me that the new head of the private office was looking for an experienced assistant, particularly one who knew English and French, and that she had put forward my name to him. My earlier conversations with Savak left me no choice: I knew it was more than my life was worth to decline any new appointment.

The appointments procedure at the Court Ministry normally took about three months – the time it took for the person concerned to be thoroughly vetted by Savak. Once again I was an exception. After an interview lasting half an hour the head of the private office introduced me to the directors of the various departments and then led me into a small room on the same floor, where his own office was. 'Please sit down at your desk,' he said. 'I should like you to begin work today.' My first thought was: 'At last they accept that I'm harmless!' But that was just another illusion. A few minutes later I was visited by the security chief of the private office, who handed me a ten-page form to be completed in triplicate within the next three days and returned to him with twelve new passport photographs.

That was the third time I had been checked out by the security services, because I had moved from one institution to another. At the beginning of my career, in the Foreign Ministry, I had had to complete a similar form. The second time, the check had been necessary for my post in the charitable organization. But this time the procedure took much longer. Not until I had been working in the private office for fifteen months did I receive security clearance from Savak. Then I was appointed head of the international section. In the meantime I had been fighting constantly with feelings of uncertainty and humiliation, for it was not only the security chief and his assistant who knew of the delay; the whole office seemed to be in the picture.

I was puzzled about the reason for this delay. Was it because I had resigned from my last post? Had I said something at the university that I should not have said? Was there something wrong with my friends and acquaintances, about whom I had had to report in detail on the form? Or had my articles in *Tamasha* contained something counter to the ideology of the Shah's regime? Why didn't they leave me in peace? On the one hand they forced a privileged post on me, while on the other they held up official confirmation of my appointment once I had taken it. The delay became all the more worrying when I learned that other employees of the office had only had to wait a maximum of three months for their approval from Savak.

In spite of this humiliation and intimidation, I was convinced that I had done the right thing in leaving my previous post: I had rebelled against corruption, injustice and hypocrisy, and I had dared to state in my letter of resignation why the realities of that organization were impossible to reconcile with the noble aims which had been postulated by the Empress. I am sure that, besides myself, there were other loyal but worried employees of the Empress who resisted corruption, but whose views did not reach the imperial ears.

My greatest wish, now that I was working in her private office, was that I might at some time be able to talk to the Empress alone, and to tell her of my worries. I never got a chance to do so: the office was run in such a way that I only met the Empress at official functions, at the opening of museums, at concerts and at New Year ceremonies, to shake her hand and to bow briefly to her. Some people thought that the Shah's family was so deeply involved in corruption that the problems must be attacked from above, which the Shah would obviously resist. But the Empress was different, wasn't she? I was certain she was not involved in the immoral dealings of the members of the Imperial Family. If she knew about them she was probably unable to do anything about them, either. But even though she hoped to create a different image for herself by her social and cultural activities, unfortunately she was embroiled by her friends and advisers in such grandiose and irrational projects that she, too, gradually became divorced from reality. For instance, she gave her support to arts centres with lavish facilities which only the bourgeoisie could enjoy. She didn't seem to realize what the ordinary people needed, in the same way that she seemed unable to see how her high-fashion European clothes offended and alienated them.

In 1958, one year after the foundation of Savak, the Shah had formed an independent supervisory body called the imperial inspectorate; it had so far been headed by two different people – both generals and among the Shah's closest advisers. One of them, General Fardoust, was a former schoolfriend. Amazingly enough, he was the first general to betray the Shah and support Ayatollah Khomeini's Revolution. Today he is the head of Khomeini's secret service, Savama, which replaced Savak. He was not the only one of the Shah's advisers to have collaborated with the regime's opposition for many years.

The role of the imperial inspectorate was to pursue corruption, incompetence and possible disloyalty among ministers and high state officials, and also any injustices perpetrated by them, and to report to the Shah. In practice, however, the inspections which were carried out from time to time were no more than laconic dabbles. Properly and wholeheartedly run, it could have been massively effective.

After I had been employed in the private office for some time I heard to my amazement that the inspectorate had begun comprehensive investigations of the account books of the Organization for the Protection of Children. I couldn't imagine who had tipped off the inspectorate about the deplorable state of affairs there! The enquiries lasted for two months, during which time my former boss, Dr Aligholi Loghman-Adham, the head of the organization, died suddenly of a heart attack. Everyone said he had died of fear, because he knew what the results of the investigation would be. However, these results – that is, the detection of his embezzlements – were never made public and the people whom I considered had been his accomplices kept their jobs. The fact that no changes had been made showed that the inspectorate did not, in fact, even report such cases to the Shah and the Empress, or that they dismissed the findings and accepted such irregularities as normal.

This inspectorate proved in any case to be no more than a cosmetic device. In its entire twenty years' existence it only revealed three cases, all connected: three air marshals were dismissed for falsifying requisitions for the purchase of spare parts for aircraft. Why, therefore, did the Shah not require the inspectorate and Savak to pursue this consuming disease of corruption more vigorously? The answer lay in the Shah's ambivalent position.

Whilst he knew that for the country's public and international image there had to be some evidence that corruption was under control, it was not in his private and domestic interests to have his secret service delve too deeply. The fact was that he himself and the members of his family were quite happy to see their own business interests satisfied ahead of any other competitors for state contracts. It was another example of the failure of the Eastern mentality to distinguish between private interest and public good. Wherever conflict might arise, family interests came first.

It is in this deeper sense that, for the Shah, the state was, as for Louis XIV of France, an extension of himself. He truly operated on the principle of '*L'état c'est moi*'. After 1973 he had said that he wanted to raise the status and standards of Iran to those of France. How ironic this statement sounded, since both Court life and the conditions of the peasantry bore a striking resemblance to those in the France of a later king, Louis XVI, in the 1780s. The Shah's Palace, with its gilded mirrors, silk carpets and eighteenth-century furniture, was like a latter-day Versailles, and his people, too, were in the mood for a change . . .

Now that I had ended up in the private office of the Empress herself I felt as though I had been pensioned off, or kicked upstairs. The powers that be were obviously not prepared to allow me to be dynamic or critical, or to show honest commitment. The regime had succeeded in turning me into a bureaucrat. My responsibilities were pure office work – translations, writing letters and suchlike. No social activity or decision-making were required of me.

The private office consisted of fifty people, mainly women. At the beginning of the 1960s the office had only employed three people, a private secretary and two assistants, but as time went on, and especially as a result of the increase in the Empress's responsibilities, the office had expanded considerably. Her purely personal correspondence – letters to friends and acquaintances – and the organization of her daily timetable and audiences were taken care of by her private secretary. This secretary had five assistants, all daughters of serving or retired generals or of high-ranking diplomats. The general secretariat was divided into a home department and an international department. The home department was presided over by an elderly former functionary in the Foreign

Ministry, who had been in that job for nineteen years. The international department was eventually entrusted to me. The private office also encompassed departments dealing with personnel, finance, public relations, culture, building and architecture. A further department was concerned exclusively with matters relating to the forty cultural and social organizations of which the Empress was patron. The administration of these organizations and of all the museums and centres for art and culture had been assigned by the Empress to old schoolfriends and relations.

This group saw its task as the creation of a cultural identity for modern industrialized Iran by building a bridge between Iran and Western culture. Since 1973 they had been receiving large subsidies for the realization of this ambitious but imperfectly conceived aim. The money was intended for international art and film festivals, new museums and cultural centres, the repurchase of objects of Iranian art in European salerooms, exhibitions of works by European painters and sculptors, the staging of European plays, the opening of a large, Western-style opera house and the invitation to Tehran of famous international ballet and opera companies. It was very well meant, but it was only addressed to a certain social stratum, the Western-oriented upper élite and the new bourgeoisie, who would supposedly be able to identify with it; however, the great majority were not really bothered, and though they attended such cultural functions they did so merely to be seen. There was a great similarity between the organizers of these events – the opportunistic intellectual entourage of the Empress – and their consumers, the nouveaux riches and the upper echelons of the Shah's administration. Neither had any real interest in the ordinary people, and could only reflect their own tastes and preferences in the work they were doing.

The educated élite surrounding the Empress now believed it had found a formula which could unite the adopted Western technology with the traditional values of the country. An élitist avant-garde with far-reaching aims was created. Among other things this avant-garde became a fanatical patron of modern art, which, it was anticipated, would be able to represent the fusion of old and new. An exhibition of modern Islamic calligraphy by contemporary artists – mainly imitations of the Cubist style – was a vivid example of the kind of artistic effort which the avant-garde applauded. Was it supposed to encourage the people to understand Western art?

What was ironical was that the assimilation of Western values had not taken place even among the Western-oriented élite, who were now supposed to transmit these ideas to the people. Despite their clothes and consumer possessions, their basic attitudes had not changed. They were far removed from the most important characteristics of the nations of the West: rational thinking and a sense of duty and social responsibility. What these intellectuals did not want to understand was that the needs of the common people, although they were deeply religious Moslems, could not be fulfilled by displays of modern Islamic calligraphy. The people could not even identify with their own political leaders, let alone with modern Western ideology. While the Shah was fantasizing over the vision of a highly industrialized Iran, the Empress was busy with the problems of retaining old traditions and reconciling them with modern values, and the mass of the population was living in its own very different world.

Was there no sensible formula for the development of an Eastern democracy in Iran? Although I had become alienated from Islam as a result of my education in the West, I thought it was wrong, and in the long term impossible, for the Western view of life to be forced upon a whole nation. One compromise could have been modernization without Westernization, with consideration being given to Islamic values and to the maintenance of ancient traditions and customs, in conjunction with free rein for the formation and expression of opinions; but then those responsible would have had to be much more modest and realistic than the Shah and the Empress. This formula might have prevented the emergence of extremist opposition both from the left and from the religious side.

The Empress's private office was, in principle, supposed to form a link between her and the people, to pass on the messages and requests of the people to her and to carry out her orders. In practice, however, the office functioned quite differently. The petitions were handled by us in the office, without her knowing anything about them: in the first place she was occupied with much more 'important' questions connected with Iranian culture, and secondly the director of her office, who was always chosen from the higher echelons of the administration by the Shah himself, blocked every path to her, like a goalkeeper saving penalties. Not only the people, but we, her own employees, were kept at bay. We saw her only rarely, for she never appeared in her private office to see what we were doing, what sort of people we were and how her office functioned. It was common knowledge that access to the Shah was extremely difficult, since Court etiquette forbade it. But it was said that the Empress, not unnaturally, had free access to the Shah and dared to speak quite openly to him about various problems in the country. But how could she describe reality to her husband when she herself had lost her links with the people, and when increasingly restrictive Court etiquette was making access to her almost as difficult as it was to the Shah? We all knew, for example, that the Court Master of Ceremonies, Hormoz Gharib, took large fees in return for arranging an audience with the Shah for his ministers. This official's huge palace in Elahieh, the district of Tehran where all the wealthy people lived, graphically demonstrated his power and his huge fortune.

Access to the Shah and to the Empress was, then, the highest privilege that could be had in our country. It was the way to gain control over all spheres of life. No wonder that those few people who enjoyed the privilege wanted to keep it for themselves. It is true, of course, that even in Europe the present-day royal Courts have their own eitquette and protocol, and that it is not easy to obtain an audience with the Queen of England or the King of Belgium. But those rulers have no active political involvement in their countries. In Iran, on the other hand, everything functioned only on the orders of the Shah and the Empress, who were absolute monarchs. Therefore the Imperial Court and its executive bodies – the private offices – possessed tremendous power. The officials of the Court, depending on their role, had developed a special sphere of influence which distinguished them from the other functionaries of the state.

The most influential and most privileged of all, the one who had absolute carte blanche, was the Court Minister, Assadollah Alam. He even, very occasionally, represented the Shah in public if it was thought necessary. He had held his post for several years, was an old friend of the Shah and the biggest landowner in the country. He was reputed to be the only landowner who had remained unaffected by the land reform measures.

Since his bitter experience in the 1950s with his Prime Minister, Mossadegh, the Shah only trusted those few employees whom he had selected himself. That same experience had led him to use Savak to suppress all political parties which had come into being during Mossadegh's time. At the heads of the only two legal parties, Melliyoun (Nationalist) and Mardom (People's), he had conveniently installed two of his most faithful servants.

At the start of the social reforms in 1960, the Shah, as a token of his new liberal attitude, appointed Dr Ali Amini as Prime Minister. He had been Finance Minister in Mossadegh's cabinet. However, when Amini began to counter corruption, the Shah once again felt threatened and, in 1962, replaced him with his friend Assadollah Alam. Alam in turn passed on the Premiership in 1965 to Amir Abbas Hoveyda and himself became Court Minister. It was at this time that the Shah consolidated his absolute monarchy. Parliament also became a servant of the Shah, instead of a servant of the people, and the Shah placed at its head another of his closest colleagues, Abdollah Riazi. Yet another favourite, Sharif-Emami, was made President of the Senate.

As was the case in the NIOC, the National Iranian Oil Company, which was run by another friend of the Imperial Family, Dr Manutschehr Eghbal, key positions in both civil and military spheres were held only by people who accepted the Shah as absolute ruler and who were prepared to kiss his hand and be subservient. The husbands of the Shah's sisters, for example, held such posts: General Mohammed Khatami, who was married to Princess Fatemeh, was commander of the Imperial air force, while Mehrdad Pahlbod, Princess Shams's husband, became Minister of Culture and Arts after his wedding. General Khatami was the pilot who had flown the Shah and Queen Soraya to Rome when they were exiled by Mossadegh in 1953. To modern Western ears the terminology of their relationship with the Shah sounds quite extraordinary. They addressed him as Khodaygan (All-Powerful), Shahanshah (King of Kings), Aryamehr (Light of the Aryans) and Alahazrat Homayouni (Illustrious Majesty), while they referred to themselves self-depracatingly in the third person as *bandeh* (subject), *tschaker* (humble servant) and *gholam* (slave). They were of course all products of the Shah's obsession with power, and since they enjoyed the great privileges of absolute power, with their obsequiousness they drove their master further and further in the direction of *folie de grandeur*. These figures had played an important role in the 1967 coronation ceremonies, the 1971 Persepolis festivities and other grandiose schemes. From all this the Shah somehow developed his curious vision of being able to raise Iran from its present position to the level of the highly advanced civilizations of his ancient ancestors, whilst simultaneously acquiring Western sophistication, too. As the wife of the illustrious Emperor and the first lady of the land, Her Majesty the Shahbanou of Iran, as the Empress was officially named, was idolized and fawned over just as much as her husband, particularly after the Shah appointed her his regent.

To the Shah, the Empress and the Imperial Family, the chosen flunkeys behaved like the most abject servants, but in Iranian society they wielded an alarming amount of power and this disturbed the people. In order to reinforce their power these functionaries followed the principle of divide and rule, and were constantly engaged in internecine scheming. Each of them therefore had his own group of toadies and favourites, who formed a faction around him and vied with the other factions.

This struggle for power excluded any co-operation between ministers and state bodies. Unless you were a Hoveydaist, an Eghbalist, an Alamist or a Sharif-Emamist, or belonged to their most intimate circle, it was impossible to reach a high official position. In Iran, as I had discovered when looking for my first job in 1967, it was only the very low-level positions in the public and private sectors and at universities that were advertised. All the respected and important posts were filled either by direct nomination by the Shah or through connections with his favourites.

The Empress's private office was, after that of the Shah, the most important within the Court Ministry. The mother of the Shah and his brothers and sisters also each had a private office, a private secretary and numerous employees at their disposal. The Court Minister bore the overall responsibility for these offices and received an annual subsidy for their expenses equivalent to $50 million. Only the Court Minister, the private secretaries, the Court adjutants and the Master of Ceremonies were paid high salaries; the other officials were paid in accordance with the state wages scale, with allowances for age, qualifications and number of years of service. My monthly salary, for example, was a fairly good 90,000 Rials (£750), but the director of the private office, as far as I know, earned 700,000 Rials (£6500). In addition he received many bonus payments. To put this in perspective a domestically manufactured Hillman Hunter or Peykan cost £3750, an ordinary meal in a restaurant about £3.50 and a pair of tights £1.75.

The high public subsidies for the imperial private offices were only part of the total funds and capital assets of the Imperial Family which were accumulated in the Pahlavi Foundation. Outwardly a charitable, non-profitmaking organization, it had been set up in 1958 by the Shah to camouflage the imperial riches. The public income of the Pahlavi family flowed into the coffers of the foundation and was then intensively reinvested. This was the Shah's method of laundering the billions drawn by his family from profits on the sale of mineral oil. Although the Foundation assisted Iranian students abroad, financed a few homes for the blind, the deaf and dumb, and orphans, and distributed food and clothing to the needy on religious holidays, its true function and its main interest was to multiply the capital of the Pahlavi family by means of investment. In the 1970s the annual subsidies for the charitable activities of the Foundation alone fluctuated between $200 and $250 million. The main investments were in stocks and shares, cement works, sugar refineries, insurance, banking, merchant shipping, hotels, gambling casinos and nightclubs. In addition, the Shah's brothers, sisters and nephews had interests in large commercial and industrial concerns.

The board of the Pahlavi Foundation consisted of the Prime Minister, the Court Minister, the President of the Senate, the head of Parliament and the President of the High Court of Justice, together with five other administrators, also selected by the Shah, who each received an annual percentage of the net income of the foundation as a bonus. The omnipresence of the Pahlavi Foundation in all spheres of public life in Iran demonstrated the extent of the interconnections between the Shah's family and the economy of the country.

Surprisingly enough, however, the Empress's private office was housed in an inhospitable four-storey building in Iranshahr Avenue, in the busy city centre. The rooms were small and modestly furnished, and nothing of the pomp and luxury of the Imperial Court was discernible. For security reasons there was not even an official sign at the entrance, so that it looked just like all the other ugly grey office buildings in that street. More fashionable office complexes were at this time under construction in a magnificent park opposite the imperial Palace in Niavaran, and we were set to move in there when they were completed. We were all looking forward to that day, for it was planned to provide office accommodation for the Empress herself and we would then be able to see her more often. But this project was never to be realized.

My room in the private office was a small, windowless cell and boasted only a tiny desk, a chair and a large portrait of the Empress which covered practically the whole of one wall. I felt like a prisoner in there – in some ways quite appropriately. Every morning a thick bundle of letters addressed to Empress Farah from all over the world would arrive on my desk, and I had to answer them. Some asked the Shahbanou for financial assistance; others praised her for her social and cultural undertakings. Some people sent her little presents; others expressed their concern about the treatment of the Shah's political opponents in Iranian prisons. Some simply asked for tourist information about our country; some were from mothers writing to ask for an amnesty for their sons who had been arrested in Iran for drug dealing. Some contained complaints against Iranian firms or public authorities which had not met their obligations, and asked the Empress to intervene. Some protested against the extravagance of the regime, some against its repressive measures. The latter petitions had to be passed on immediately to Savak, who put their writers' names on the blacklist that was circulated to overseas embassies; these foreigners would never be given a visa to enter Iran. Many of the letter writers requested autographed photographs or an audience with the Empress, which demonstrated her popularity in the outside world – quite a contrast to the criticism to which the Shah found himself subjected.

Only personal letters or those from world-famous personalities, together with a selection of her Iranian correspondence – predominantly questions of finance for new cultural undertakings, or reports on projects already in existence, or requests from prominent Iranian or foreign diplomats – were taken once a week, by the head of the private office, to the Niavaran Palace, to be shown to the Empress. She then passed on her instructions to him. He was the only person in the private office who regularly saw the Empress and had direct contact with her.

Her private secretary, Farideh Mirbabai, whose office was next door to mine, was a former schoolfriend of hers. But even she went rarely to the Palace and only spoke to the Empress on the telephone when necessary, mostly to confirm her daily timetable and to inform her of changes and postponements. Although the private secretary ranked below the head of the private office in the hierarchy, she regarded herself as the head of the office for all practical purposes and adopted an extremely authoritarian, often almost offensive, attitude to her colleagues. By virtue of her position she often interfered in the affairs of other departments, and when she entered other offices she expected everyone to stand up as a mark of respect. From my very first day I sensed that we should come into conflict with each other. Although I did nothing to provoke her – on the contrary, I always tried to make her understand that I was not ambitious and that she need not feel threatened by me – she was continually at pains to demonstrate her authority to me.

She tirelessly reminded us that it was a great honour to be permitted to work for the Empress. Once, from my office, I overheard her declaiming in her customary imperious tones to the five secretaries who worked in her department: 'You people should never forget for a minute that you have been granted a great honour in being permitted to work for Her Majesty. We are all her servants! You should therefore not imagine that any kind of work is beneath your dignity. Even if you were asked to clean the floor of the private office every morning, you should consider it an honour.' Ironically, she herself expected to be treated like the

Empress! Later I was to recognize that her authoritarian manner had only been skin-deep. The harrowing effects of the revolution wiped it away, leaving an approachable, warm-hearted woman.

There were many arrogant personalities of this kind in the Empress's entourage. The whole atmosphere in the private office was one of fear. We did not dare speak openly and had to exercise constant self-censorship. In this repressive environment, the rival directors of the various departments shamelessly vied with each other to gain the confidence of the head of the private office and to be allowed to do just as they liked. Intrigues and plots were the order of the day. One typical incident was the quarrel which flared up one afternoon between the private secretary and one of the departmental directors. It was about an important letter which had been signed by the Empress and brought back from the Palace but had then got lost somewhere in the private office. The private secretary claimed that the departmental head had been the last person to have it. He was equally convinced that he had handed the letter on to her. The quarrel became more and more violent and the participants accused each other of intrigue and theft. The letter never came to light, but the private secretary achieved what she had wanted: the departmental director concerned, with whom she had never got on, lost his boss's favour as a result of this contretemps and was soon replaced. Luckily, I did not have to have much to do with Farideh Mirbabai, and although she often tried to set me against the other directors and win me over to her side I kept a certain distance between us.

My work often brought me into contact with Mahmoud Mosleh, an elderly gentleman who ran the administration of the home department of the Empress's secretariat, since many of the requests from abroad had to be passed on to the other ministries for appropriate action. Now and then he showed me letters of complaint from ordinary Iranians containing appalling revelations of social injustices. Since, in spite of all efforts at modernization, neither social security nor a real system of legal protection existed in Iran, the people were forced to notify the Shah or the Empress directly of their troubles and beg them for help. The ministries responsible were unable to do anything because of their inefficiency and indifference.

A peasant farmer, for example, had written to say that the agents of an influential man in the province had forcibly driven him and his family off the land which he had received as a result of the Shah's land reform. He had filed a complaint in the local court, but had been told that his title deeds did not give the precise position of his land in relation to the neighbouring property; he would therefore have no chance of getting his land back by taking legal proceedings.

'Tell me, are letters like this ever passed on to the Empress?' I asked my colleague. He laughed without mirth, patted me on the shoulder in a fatherly way and told me that I was a naïve idealist. 'Are you still not familiar with the system?' He lowered his voice and locked his door, so that no one could eavesdrop. 'Do you know how many petitions like that are received here every day? If we were to send them all to the Empress she would be reading letters all day long! And anyway,' he continued, 'as far as this farmer is concerned the man whose agents took his land away from him is the business partner of one of the Shah's brothers. So what can we do?' He shrugged his shoulders. 'It's just a vicious circle!'

I had nothing more to say and left his room, feeling depressed. Then I remembered a letter written to the Empress in French by a student who thought that by doing so his message and his request for an audience would be more likely to reach her. He had a lot to tell her about the true events and political developments in Iran, he wrote, all information that was of urgent interest to the regime. I had shown the letter to the head of the private office and he had actually tried to arrange a meeting with the student. But when I asked his secretary what had emerged from their conversation he said with a smile: 'Nothing – the boss just thinks he's crazy!'

Chaos and disorder were rampant and could be witnessed at all levels of daily life in the overpopulated cities. No one took their work seriously. It was only the increasingly bureaucratic machine, the pointless correspondence among themselves about the petitions received, which kept the state authorities constantly busy. The junior officials were just as dissatisfied as the petitioners with the hopeless bottleneck into which the country had got itself. On top of all this, there was constant Savak repression in the form of censorship of the press, the universities, authors and artists. On occasions the naked power of Savak came glaringly into the limelight. Perhaps the most horrifying incident started harmlessly in a Charles Jourdan shoeshop. A husband had been helping his wife to choose a pair of shoes when a second customer had entered and demanded instant attention. And no sooner had she received this attention, to the annoyance of those being served, than she had accused the husband of stealing her purse. Even as he stood up to protest, her bodyguard, who had been lurking in the doorway, shot him down in cold blood. Nothing was ever done about this murder: the instigator had been the wife of a high Savak official. Savak was, after all, the highest repository of justice in the country!

Admittedly during the first few months of 1975 the Shah had already acknowledged that his political programme was facing great problems. In March he proclaimed the formation of a single party, Rastakhiz (Resurrection), as a substitute for the two existing state parties. All Iranians who were loyal to the monarchy and to the principles of the Revolution of the Shah and His People were now to join this party. Those who did not want to join would be quite free to make themselves known; the state would then issue them with passports so that they could leave the country. With this decision to introduce a one-party system the Shah could no longer keep up the pretence of having a parliamentary political system – and pretence it had been, for control of Parliament was in the hands of Savak and its members were not freely elected.

The new party was to conduct debates on topics of popular interest in Parliament – but naturally only those which fell within the framework of the ideology of the regime. Important problems such as freedom of opinion, freedom of the press, corruption in the upper classes, the national budget, and defence or oil policies, were ignored; only such matters as education, traffic, housing, health, market prices and commodity speculation were acceptable. The main aim of the party was to restore the now missing mystical link between the Shah and the people. The speeches of the party leaders and the cabinet ministers were therefore coloured with a combination of almost unbearable pathos and exuberant nationalism. The party also attempted to motivate all Iranians to participate in the development of their country, a process which was nearing stagnation as a result of their passivity and dissatisfaction. But how could the Shah expect the people to believe in this showy political manoeuvre?

An enormous registration book was circulated in all workplaces, and everyone was expected to enter his or her name and join the party. Non-employed people were requested to go to the local Rastakhiz branch to enrol. Within a few months the party had gained enormous weight in the everyday politics of the country, but without enjoying any popular support. It was only a group of political opportunists who had flocked into Rastakhiz to draw up and carry through the guidelines of the party programme and to praise the Shah for his great deeds.

The dissatisfaction of the people and their disgust for demagogic propaganda must have produced great disquiet in the religious community, since, for the very first time, a mullah had the courage to stand up in public to draw the Shah's attention to the general malaise. The occasion was the annual ceremony organized by the Imperial Court in one of the great mosques of Tehran to celebrate the Islamic festival of Ide-Fetre that took place after the fasting month of Ramadan. These functions were obviously intended to demonstrate the respect of the Imperial Family for Islam, and for this reason they were televised live and in their entirety.

After the religious ceremony was finished, the preacher began to inform the Shah, who was sitting in front of him flanked by his close associates, of growing social conflicts. This hazardous undertaking elicited utter amazement all over the country. He told the Shah that injustices were being suffered by the ordinary people, and that corruption was rife, particularly among the Shah's own entourage. He urged the Shah to do something about the situation. Interestingly enough, while the preacher was speaking the television cameras were focused on the faces of those sitting with the Shah. The monarch himself only shook his head in concern.

Afterwards some people said that the whole scene had been engineered by Savak to give the impression that the Shah had become more liberal and could take constructive criticism. No one could know for sure whether the sermon had been spontaneous or contrived, but a sudden adoption of religious subjects in the

Empress's range of cultural activities seemed, even though superficial, to mark an important turning point.

This new awareness was expressed at the beginning of 1977, at the opening of a vast modern cultural centre called Farhangsara, or the House of Culture, in the middle of a park opposite the imperial Palace in Niavaran. About two hundred prominent people from all over the country were present, and the Empress's staff also attended. In the presence of the Empress, an open-air dance was performed by dervishes. A mystical atmosphere had been created by the dancers with their rhythmical chanting of the name of the Shia Moslem Imam Ali. The words 'dervish' and 'Sufi' sometimes appear interchangeably in Farsi. Sufism itself is synonymous with Islamic mysticism, which first emerged in Baghdad in the ninth century. Sufis live a contemplative, ascetic life and believe in the unity of being, constantly seeking inner truth through meditation and invocation of the divine name. The dance of the dervishes begins with a journey from the multiplicity of the visible, material world to the unity of the invisible. They continue dancing in this fashion until that ecstatic state is attained in which the human soul is united with the divine essence, from which it is believed to emanate. It was in the twelfth century that, regardless of the growing antagonism between the Sunni and Shia factions of Islam, the Sufis began to form fraternity sects known in Iran as dervish orders. These mystics reject orthodox Islam and, above all, orthodox Shiism.

On this occasion the Empress had decided not to sit and watch the performance on the chair reserved for her, but came and sat, quite modestly and naturally, on the ground with the rest of us. She was obviously moved and overcome by the ecstatic incantations of the dervishes. The Shah had also been supposed to attend this opening, and everything had been arranged with this in mind. The Empress surprised us by turning up all alone, looking tired, sad, and wearing an ordinary summer dress and hardly any make-up. It was almost as if she had suddenly realized what difficult times lay ahead for us all. I was sitting only a few feet away from the Empress and could see tears in her eyes. When I asked a colleague sitting next to me if she had noticed them, too, she said she had. At this moment I knew that I still had deep feelings of admiration and loyalty for the Empress. She was an idealist who acted in good faith. If only she had not been cut off from reality by her self-seeking advisers!

In June 1977, two months before the opening of this cultural centre, three leading members of the illegal National Front opposition party – Shapour Bakhtiar, Karim Sanjabi and Daryoush Frouhar – had addressed an open letter to the Shah in which they expressly described his regime as dictatorial, immoral, corrupt and repressive, and demanded in the name of the Iranian nation that he should cease to exercise absolute power. 'The principles of the Iranian constitution and the universal declaration of human rights have been violated to an incomparable extent in this country,' the letter stated. 'Police brutality has reached a peak, while national dignity has been completely destroyed by the all-embracing spread of corruption, immorality and subservience.' The country was, they claimed, on the brink of economic, social, political and cultural disaster. The only way to save the situation was to restore individual freedoms and to end totalitarian rule. In other words, the Shah's liberal opponents were demanding that the leadership of Iran should be transferred to Parliament and the government, as provided for in the constitution. The authors of the open letter were former colleagues and followers of Mossadegh, forming the National Front Party in support of his constitutional concepts.

This letter, which was freely circulated in intellectual circles throughout the country, reached the Emperor six months after Jimmy Carter had won the presidential election in the United States. Immediately after Carter had taken office he had called upon the Shah, on the basis of the declaration of human rights which he had adopted as his main political platform, to carry out a wide-ranging programme of liberalization in Iran. But it was not until he had seen this open letter that the Shah felt obliged to make concessions. In August 1977 he had a kind of cabinet reshuffle, as if he were playing chess, but nothing really changed.

Amir Abbas Hoveyda, who had served him as Prime Minister since 1965, was replaced by Jamschid Amouzegar, the Interior Minister and the Shah's representative in OPEC. Hoveyda was, naturally, associated with the political, social and economic developments of the 1960s and 1970s. The Shah did not dismiss him, but made him his interim Court Minister. Assadollah Alam had been seriously ill for some time and had no objection to withdrawing from the post, which he had held for several years. Hoveyda had been able to retain his post as Prime Minister for such a long time because, unlike certain of his predecessors, he had not acted against the Shah but had carried out his orders without question. He was an ideal servant as far as the Shah was concerned; loyal and submissive, with an intuitive flair for politics. With these changes at the top the Shah intended to give the impression of turning in a new direction, so that later on he could make Hoveyda the fall guy for all the errors perpetrated by his regime. In October of the same year Amouzegar was also elected General Secretary of Rastakhiz; he had thus risen to the position of the second most important figure in Iranian politics. The Shah remained, as before, the political, military and spiritual leader of the nation. He seemed to think that, once political debates were permitted in Rastakhiz, the required liberalization had been put into effect. Amouzegar claimed to be a liberal and appeared to believe in healthy, moderate growth. He saw his role as one of damping down the severely overheated economy and saving the country from its present impasse. That was not an easy undertaking, for the whole economic situation was out of control.

The Shah's total lack of appreciation of the incompetence of his regime was demonstrated clearly and ironically when the then Chancellor of the Federal Republic of Germany, Helmut Schmidt, came to visit him in Tehran in November 1975. The counsellor from the German Embassy, who was present during their talks, told me afterwards that the Shah had warned Herr Schmidt of the imminent downfall of West Germany. He had claimed that German society had become unstable, and that inflation and recession pointed to a hazardous future. We might wonder today if he was not perhaps obliquely referring to his own country, for in September 1974 the Shah had purchased 25 per cent of the shares in the Krupp steelworks, and a year after the conversation with Helmut Schmidt he became the owner of a further 25 per cent of the entire Krupp Foundation. The inconsistency of his stance towards the West, which obviously regarded him as its closest ally in the Middle East – this having followed the oil price increase –

stood out clearly in all his interviews with Western journalists during this period. The impertinence of his remarks to Helmut Schmidt was an extreme example of his inability to make political judgements.

After Jimmy Carter's demands for reform in Iran, no changes were made in the activities of the Empress. On the contrary, these really got into top gear, for she was, after all, only concerned with humanitarian aims. The Empress's advisers saw the role which she had so far played as the best chance of improving Iran's image abroad. Discreet contacts were made, for example, with various foreign universities, and hints were made that the conferring of an honorary doctorate on the Empress in recognition of her humanitarian work would strengthen mutual friendly relations and would contribute to world peace. The result was a series of invitations from various universities, including some in Czechoslovakia, Romania and the United States. Even the Shah had previously been awarded a degree from Harvard.

This all meant more work for me. Each degree ceremony required a speech by the Empress stressing the specific relations between Iran and the country in question. An Iranian political scientist wrote the draft texts, which he then completed and translated with my help. The purpose of all these speeches was to emphasize the Empress's contribution to the welfare of her people and simultaneously to point out in a subtle fashion that the government of Iran still stood on a secure and firm foundation, thanks to the Empress and her sound thinking and actions. It was an attempt to counterbalance the shattered image of the Shah abroad. The frequent trips made by the Empress in 1977 were not restricted to universities; she also visited international organizations concerned with the problems of the developing countries. At least fifteen speeches were written and delivered that year. In the meantime the Shah remained at home, having abandoned even his beloved winter visits to St Moritz. The Empress, however, continued to go there for skiing holidays with the children.

We heard repeatedly that the Shah's health was deteriorating and that he was undergoing regular treatment by foreign specialists who were flown in to Tehran, but the fact that he was suffering from cancer of the spleen was known only in Court circles. He had become thin and pale and had lost his upright, confident bearing. He no longer officially opened new projects, not even industrial ones – here, too, his role was being completely taken over by the Empress. Military parades were the only ceremonies which the Shah still attended. There were good reasons for this: first, he had in recent years equipped the Iranian armed forces with the latest and most expensive weapon systems, bought from the West; and secondly, he probably wanted to make a few appearances still in order to play down his poor state of health, both for his own benefit and for that of the public. But even when making these rare public speeches he was incoherent.

In spite of the pretence of strength and stability in our country, the Shah must have been aware that it was not in fact West Germany but Iran which had run into very serious difficulties. He appeared to need more than ever America's assurance of full support. His Ambassador in Washington, Ardeshir Zahedi, organized a state visit for the imperial couple in November 1977, but events turned out rather differently from the way they had been planned. The Shah and the Empress arrived at the White House to be met with a large anti-Shah demonstration by Iranian nationals living in America. It quickly escalated into a full-blown riot, at which point the American police intervened. As Jimmy Carter and his wife were welcoming the Shah and the Empress on the steps of the White House, clouds of tear gas wafted over the two couples. The exchange of welcoming speeches, transmitted by all the television networks, had a somewhat peculiar effect as a result of their watering eyes. The demonstrations continued throughout America for the duration of their visit.

In the meantime, in the Empress's private office in Tehran we received a very odd leaflet whose origins we were unable to discover. It must have come from some opposition group in America and it contained an account, with photographs, of the distribution to Iranian students of bribes initiated by the Shah's Ambassador. They were apparently being asked to neutralize the anti-Shah demonstrations on the arrival of the imperial couple in Washington by shouting pro-Shah slogans. One of the photographs showed a diplomat with an open briefcase, crammed with banknotes, which were being handed out to a circle of Iranians standing by him. The leaflet also alleged that various excesses and acts of financial corruption had been committed by Zahedi. Furthermore it claimed that Zahedi had turned the Iranian Ambassador's residence in Washington into a den of iniquity, inviting American politicians to be entertained by high-class call girls and to indulge in caviar, champagne and opium. The so-called Persian Room, with its mirrored walls and ceiling, silk carpets and Oriental floor cushions, was said to be the scene of these lavish parties.

On the return of the imperial couple a long report from a well-respected American public relations firm, addressed to the Empress, landed on my desk. In view of its importance I translated the whole thing into Persian and passed it to the director of the private office for immediate submission to the Empress. The report contained a thorough analysis of the causes of the Shah's unpopularity abroad. Blame was laid in particular on his foreign representatives, and special mention was made of the Ambassador in Washington, whose irresponsible, thoughtless behaviour, in conjunction with his complete political ignorance, had had a highly detrimental effect on the image of Iran and its leader. It was high time, the report concluded, for steps to be taken to ensure that other countries were made aware also of the positive side of the regime and its work in the field of welfare. The firm added that it was prepared to undertake this task of enlightenment on the Shah's behalf. The last time I saw that report it was in the hands of my boss. Normally I would have received it back in due course with personal notes written by the Empress, and I would then have carried out her orders. Whether the report was suppressed, or whether it was sent somewhere else, I shall never know.

At the end of December 1977 President Carter and his wife came to Tehran. The fact that this return visit took place only six weeks after the Shah had been to Washington strongly underlined the importance of Iran for the USA; such a rapid succession of state visits is most unusual. Obviously Carter had also felt that at this decisive time the Shah should receive assurance, for all the world to see, of America's support.

A magnificent banquet, attended by the Shah's closest Iranian and American advisers and their wives, was held on the Western

New Year's Eve, 31 December. The beginning of the festivities, with the Shah and President Carter exchanging their official speeches, was shown live on Iranian television. The President praised the Shah for his long years of effort for the welfare of his people and congratulated him on his achievements, which had turned Iran into an 'island of stability' in the middle of the most conflict-ridden region in the world. This had all happened, so he said, thanks to the trust which the Iranian nation placed in its leader. As a sign of friendship, the two heads of state raised their crystal glasses of French champagne to drink to the indissoluble union between the USA and Iran, and to the New Year.

The two leaders seemed totally unaware that the Iranian people do not celebrate the Western New Year and that, in the Islamic faith, the consumption of alcohol is forbidden. However, the year now beginning was to be the last one in which such cultural inconsistencies could occur. By December 1978 Iran was torn by radical political changes of shattering proportions.

10

The Revolution

As early as 1975 – hardly two years after the oil price increase and the associated acceleration of the economic boom – social discontent had become really noticeable. The thousands of workers who had settled in the cities during the 1960s and 1970s, to earn more money and gain better living conditions, found themselves culturally alienated. Even their relatively high earnings had not been much use to them: continually rising prices and rents forced most of them to send their families back to the villages while the workers lived alone in the ghettos of the cities. These workers, predominantly men with unsophisticated religious notions, had formed a new social class, the dissatisfied industrial proletariat; they could very easily be swayed by the equally dissatisfied mullahs, themselves the victims of discrimination.

Students were another important disaffected faction in the cities. Their numbers had increased many times over during these years, because the opening throughout the country of several new state-subsidized universities and research centres had attracted more and more young people of both sexes. These institutions in themselves were the result of the Shah's introduction after 1973 of free schooling and higher education.

The majority of these new students came from modest, deeply religious families and were quite unable to approve the pomp and luxury of the lifestyle of the Shah's family and the urban upper classes. One of their fundamental demands was academic freedom, something that the regime did not want to grant. All academic institutions were subject to Savak's brutal repression, and the Shah was horrified by the very idea of autonomous universities. Certainly he had recognized the need for an educated workforce to administer modern, industrialized Iran, but he failed to appreciate that true academic life is impossible without freedom of thought. He seemed to think that the universities were production lines for manufacturing technocrats.

The university terms of 1977 were particularly affected by student unrest – strikes, boycotts and sit-ins in lecture rooms. But the real agitation did not begin until 1978, when army tanks rumbled on to the campuses. At this time I was attending seminars on German literature at the University of Tehran and still working for my master's degree, as well as being employed in the Empress's private office. Our seminars were often interrupted by the troubled events of that year.

The university complex lies in the busy Shah Reza Avenue in the heart of Tehran. This long road, which runs through the whole city from east to west is one of the most important thoroughfares in Tehran. I was usually able to walk to the university from the private office in Iranshahr Street; it made no difference what time of day I went along Shah Reza Avenue – I always saw noisy crowds and heavy traffic. Whatever were so many people doing all the time on the streets, I wondered. Had they given up their jobs? Why was there nothing for them to do in their spare time? I was bemused. But a state which is not even capable of solving its acute housing problem would never be able to take care of the leisure needs of its citizens.

There was a horrible tension in the streets. Any trivial incident could flare up into an altercation. Dissatisfaction and frustration could be read clearly on people's faces. These masses frightened me, since I could see in them no social solidarity, no consideration and no sympathy. Yet my job in the Empress's private office seemed unreal and detached in comparison with what I was experiencing at the university and in the streets.

Every day I saw evidence that the link between the regime and the people no longer existed. People were now daring enough to grumble about the regime in public and to criticize the Shah's family for their immorality and corruption. The mounting disgust of ordinary people such as bakers, greengrocers, domestic servants, labourers and, indeed, the students and university lecturers with whom I came into daily contact made my position as someone who worked for the Imperial Court more and more problematical and paradoxical. On the one hand I understood perfectly how this situation had been created and felt deep sympathy with my compatriots, yet on the other hand, as a functionary of the regime and an employee of the Empress, I felt I ought not to let my loyalty be affected by outside events. But since the beginning of 1978 I had carefully refrained from revealing the nature of my job to many of the academics and students I met at the university.

Even the activities of the private office were not immune from the spirit of the moment. The ministries, which had as a rule reacted very quickly to our instructions about petitions from the people, now appeared not to take us very seriously. This resulted in confusion, which gradually degenerated into actual disobedience. The instructions of those in charge were no longer carried out immediately by their subordinates. Obviously even the employees of the Court Ministry had begun to question their positions.

As early as mid-1977, when the open letter to the Shah was circulating throughout Iran, a new political climate was perceptible. It seemed that all Iranians who had in some way been disappointed by the Shah's regime and felt that they were being victimized took this opportunity of speaking out. Whether the Shah liked it or not, liberalization could not be put off any longer. Further open letters and telegrams were addressed to the Shah and the Prime Minister from various groups. Some well-known authors and artists signed a letter of protest and demanded that the Shah should put an end to censorship. Progressive lawyers sent a telegram insisting on the autonomy of the legal system, which was in the power of the government and unable to take proceedings against corruption.

But none of these protests resulted in any measures being put in hand by the government. Instead, the hypocrites advising the Shah aggravated a delicate situation and rocked his throne more and more. Then, an irrevocable provocation of the religious sensibilities of the people, which finally opened the floodgates to bloody revolution, resulted from a leading article published in the newspaper *Keyhan* in January 1978 on the instructions of the Shah's

Minister of Information and spokesman for Rastakhiz. In this article Ayatollah Khomeini, then in exile in Iraq, was accused of being a British agent of Indian, not Iranian, origin. He was also charged quite openly with immorality. In the resultant violent disturbances about thirty people were killed in Qom, the holy pilgrimage city of the Shias, where the Ayatollah had lived until his expulsion from the country in 1965 and where he had taught at the theological college. The Revolution had started. Public insurrection broke out when theology students there were shot by the regime's security police as they protested in the seminary grounds. Demonstrations and impassioned funeral processions followed in Qom and other cities in memory of the religious martyrs.

Since the mid-1970s Khomeini had been announcing to the orthodox sections of the population, on inflammatory, smuggled tapes, his religious teachings and his hate for the Shah, but it was not until after the publication of this misguided and provocative article that he was raised to the rank of the saviour who was to free the Shia people from their sufferings. As a protest the Tehran bazaar, the commercial centre of the capital which simultaneously represented the religious community, remained closed for several days. The old-established Iranian traders all came from the bazaar, which was still based on old commercial and business principles and had not allowed itself to be taken over by the modern economy. The protest by the religious bazaaris against the offensive article in *Keyhan* and against the deaths in Qom was not merely restricted to the closing of their shops. They also played an important part in the initial stages of the revolution. Their greatest contribution was the financial support of the families of the victims of street battles, and those of striking workers and public employees.

In the private office, I was an eye witness to the gradual dissolution of the Shah's absolute power. This could be clearly observed in the changed behaviour of those who held power. The haughty, authoritarian private secretary to the Empress had become much more democratic and treated the rest of us in a noticeably more humane fashion. She, too, had realized that it was time to make concessions. But this about-turn came too late. The few personal concessions made by the Shah also seemed comical and useless. The court distributed to all the ministries and public organizations, for example, a large photograph showing him in the long white robe of a pilgrim to Mecca. These photographs were also put up in all the public squares. Shortly after this the Shah and the Empress, flanked by their closest entourage, visited Imam Reza's mausoleum in the holy city of Mashhad. This visit, reported in full on Iranian television, showed the Empress wearing a long black *chador* – the Islamic veil – and no make-up. However, her veil was made of fine, expensive lace, and the effect, more erotic than pious, was the subject of much public criticism. Religion in a subdued form, and insofar as it remained aloof from the political life of the country, was always used by the Shah as a mere prop for state sovereignty.

As a symbol of protest, the *chador* played a decisive part in the whole process of the Revolution. Veiled working-class women, whose young sons had been killed in street battles, marched in huge demonstrations. In chorus with their menfolk they shouted slogans against the regime and condemned the Shah and his family. But these women were now joined in sympathy by veiled women students, housewives, professional women and other Westernized, educated Iranian women from the middle classes. They showed incredible courage and uncompromising determination which could only induce admiration. Their strong presence in the demonstrations allowed them to form a sort of protective barrier for the male demonstrators. And from the time that these women joined it, the Revolution gained increasingly in religious fervour.

The open letters of the democratic liberals who opposed the absolute power of the Shah but accepted him in principle as a constitutional monarch – in other words, they only wanted concessions from him – had opened up the path to much wider horizons. Political opposition to the Shah had been suppressed by Savak since 1953; in the present climate it was suddenly unleashed, at home and abroad. From September onwards many anti-regime intellectuals living in exile returned to Iran without fear of arrest. These opponents of the Shah did not, however, all tend towards Islamic fundamentalism; there were also Marxists, Maoists, socialists and members of the democratic National Front party.

Up to this time the strongest opposition had been formed by the exiled Marxists; in 1960 they had founded the Confederation of Iranian Students Abroad, whose publications I had come across in Switzerland in the early sixties and whose membership had risen to over fifty thousand by 1977. The original founders belonged to Tudeh, the illegal Iranian Communist party, and their early leadership was soon threatened because of its close relationship with the Soviet Union. In addition, Savak was reputed to have smuggled highly paid spies into Tudeh. In the late 1960s the Confederation had become very radical, and followed the ideological doctrines of Maoism and Trotskyism. Its political programme for Iran would doubtless have involved the elimination of the Pahlavi regime and the creation of a communist political system. Now this group had begun to intensify its links with students in Iran and to mobilize them for the political battles ahead.

Even more radical were the two underground guerilla organizations – Fedayin, who were Marxist, and Mujahidin, of Islamic-socialist persuasion. They had first appeared at the beginning of 1970, engaging in terrorist campaigns in the villages of the north and assassinating leading Savak and American military officials throughout the country. The relaxation of repression at the end of 1977 enabled them to become involved in more open political activities all over Iran. Their public meetings on the Tehran University campus, which were attended by hundreds of people from all levels of society, were a clear indication of this; that campus had in any case become a centre of free political discussion and speechmaking. Iran had certainly become politicized: I saw it all at the university as I was going to my seminars.

A hitherto unwonted political awareness had suddenly developed among the ordinary men and women of Iran, even among the schoolchildren. Factory hands, small shopkeepers and construction workers held discussions on the kind of family and social problems with which they were confronted. Numerous other groups met in mosques to pray together and to hear the highly politicized speeches of the Islamic clergy. Iranian television continued to comply with Savak's censorship regulations, while the state-controlled daily newspapers, *Keyhan* and *Ettelaat*, had started printing editorials and reports which were severely critical of the regime's home and foreign policies. The 'dummy' Parliament and the Shah's single party, Rastakhiz, continued to lose power and influence.

On 29 March 1978, a few days after the Persian New Year, a peaceful and well-organized opposition demonstration took place in Tehran, with a hundred thousand people participating and demanding for the first time the abdication of the Shah. The demonstrators included academics, lawyers, teachers, state officials, students, traders from the bazaar – in short, representatives of the educated strata of Tehran society. A week previously, on 21 March, the Shah and the Empress, dressed, as every year, in grand ceremonial robes, were to have received representatives from the various sections of the population for the New Year greetings ceremony in the Golestan Palace. On the afternoon of that day women's groups, the administrators of organizations under the patronage of the Empress and the members of her private office, would have been received by her in the Niavaran Palace. But just a few hours before, we were informed by the Shah's Master of Ceremonies that the reception would not take place. This news produced an atmosphere of worry and foreboding in the private office; many of us had begun to feel that the throne was seriously in danger, but we did not dare to talk about the consequences of the riots.

If only the Shah would agree to withdraw from the political arena, become a constitutional monarch and put an end to absolutism. If only he would announce immediate free elections, so that the various opposition groups could be represented in Parliament. Why was he holding back? Was it really that hard for him to give up absolute power? Weren't his advisers telling him how entrenched the opposition already was in the country?

During this period the letters addressed to the Empress from all over the world which landed on my desk bore witness to the fact that the foreign media had taken the political unrest in Iran much more seriously than had the Shah and his security police. Journalists at home, however, under pressure from Savak, concealed the truth about the turbulent events in all parts of the country. During the whole of 1978 the only source of information about the unrest was the radio news transmitted each evening in Farsi by the BBC. Many Iranians listened in; for fear of being detected by Savak, families collected in one room and locked the door behind them. With the World Service sound turned down almost to a murmur we crowded around the set and listened to the latest, and increasingly terrible, news from our native country. In the letters and telegrams we received at the private office foreigners, predominantly Europeans, expressed their concern about the future of Iran. Every week I put together a selection of these letters which were then handed to the Empress by the head of the private office. This represented a definite change of course, for until then 95 per cent of all the correspondence had been dealt with by the private office direct, and the Empress had known nothing about it.

In April 1978, when Western journalists asked the Shah what he thought about the increasing volume of protest among his people, he described the unrest as the result of the 'unholy alliance between the black and the red'. He was referring to the Islamic clergy and to his Marxist opponents, who in his opinion no longer wished to see a stable Iran. The peaceful mass demonstrations at the end of March in Tehran led to bloody street battles in Tabriz, Mashhad and other cities between May and July. The Shah's military forces had begun to shoot at unarmed demonstrators. Each evening the BBC reported these riots and gave the numbers of demonstrators. Police stations, hotels, cinemas, banks, Savak vehicles and lorries transporting alcoholic drinks were set on fire.

Similar clashes had also taken place in some parts of the capital. I had to drive from my home in the northern suburbs to the centre every morning. Realizing that it was not practical for me to share his flat, my father had got me one of my own not far from where he and my stepmother lived. It became a refuge for me, where I could meet my relatives and friends from my childhood. That summer I ran into signs of unrest on the streets nearly every day – demonstrations which held up the traffic, shoot-outs, fire-raising, stone-throwing and many other disquieting scenes. But I still had no idea that I would see far more shocking and bloody street battles, let alone hundreds of dead and grotesquely mutilated bodies lining the roads.

On 5 August, Constitution Day, the Shah addressed the nation in a message in which he announced his willingness to hold free elections during the next election year and to recognize other political parties besides Rastakhiz. But the Iranians had lost all faith in him, and the rebellions continued. The Shah still seemed unable to understand that his people were demanding action, not empty promises, and that they blamed him and his family for the havoc that the country was now experiencing.

At the very last reception at the Imperial Court, on 20 August 1978, I was able to observe for myself the total lack of realism, bordering on schizophrenia, of our monarch in these last tragic months of his reign. The reception was held in Saadabad, in a Palace belonging to the Shah's mother. Rumours were circulating at the Court that it had been the old lady's idea to hold a garden party at her Palace to mark the annual commemoration of the Shah's return from exile in 1953 and the fall of the Mossadegh government, since the usual public celebrations could not take place that year as a result of all the unrest. Ironically, 20 August had been declared by the Shah the Day of National Uprising, for, twenty-five years previously, his friends had financed pro-Shah demonstrations which had helped bring him back to the throne. The opposition, on the other hand, regarded his return to power as a *coup d'état* organized by the CIA.

The top military and civilian crust of the country had been invited to the garden party: cabinet ministers, the presidents of the Senate and the National Assembly, members of Parliament, members of the Court, party leaders, army generals, newspaper editors, television and radio directors and high judiciary officials. Security was intense, and the Palace gardens were crawling with soldiers of the Imperial Guard.

August is the hottest month in Tehran, when daytime temperatures can soar to 40–42°C. The evenings are a little more bearable, but air-conditioning is still usually necessary. The imperial palaces were situated in Shemiran – the cool, wooded, fashionable northern district at the foot of the Elburz mountains. Thanks to the tall old planes and pines and to the beautiful mountain air it was very difficult to believe, on that evening, that it was in fact the red-hot Tehran high summer. By 7 p.m. the women, all in long evening dresses, most of them very low-cut, needed something around their shoulders to keep them warm. Although the invitations had specifically prescribed long evening dresses for the women and dinner jackets for the men the Empress was wearing a short, very décolleté summer dress of organza with a bold, colourful flower design.

The entire Imperial Family was sitting on the Palace veranda in baroque-style armchairs: the Shah's mother, Empress Farah with her four children and the Shah's brothers and sisters. We all sat down on garden chairs and watched a number of European dance groups who were to provide the evening's entertainment. From my seat, only a few yards from the imperial party, I could observe every movement they made. The Shah, sitting next to his mother, looked downcast, worn out and much older than usual. He had lost a lot of weight since I had last seen him in person. He also appeared to be totally preoccupied.

While the Empress and the other members of the Imperial Family nodded their heads occasionally as a sign of welcome to the guests, the Shah seemed quite indifferent, occasionally whispering something into his mother's ear. I was appalled to see, epitomized in him, the decline of the monarchy and the end of an era. It was depressing to see the powerful Shahanshah, the King of Kings, the leader of the nation, the man with such great ambitions for his country, so broken. Perhaps the rumours that he had cancer were true? The whole evening he did not move from his seat for a second and stuck close to his mother like a helpless child. When dinner was served, everyone except the Shah and his mother came down from the veranda and actually helped themselves from the buffet of Persian and European delicacies. The Shah and his mother, meanwhile, were served with food by two Court waiters.

After dinner we returned to our seats to watch the finale. When the lights went out we saw a spectacular programme of acrobatic dances, performed by dancers wearing fluorescent costumes and waving glittering sparklers in the air. However, before this extraordinary show there had been a strange moment, disquieting for everyone. The Prime Minister, Amouzegar, who had been absent from the reception, suddenly appeared on the veranda and whispered something in the Shah's ear. Whatever it was that he said, it made the Shah so angry that he pushed his Prime Minister violently away from him. Amouzegar left the Palace immediately. The next day it was rumoured that he had resigned and left the country. Many people thought he had flown to the USA after having informed the Shah of the American government's wish that he, the Shah, should step down.

Only a few days after the reception at his mother's Palace, as popular aggression increased further, the Shah nominated the President of the Senate, Jafar Sharif-Emami, as the new Prime Minister. The grandson of a well-known religious leader, Sharif-Emami was instructed by the Shah to form a 'government of national reconciliation'. He set up a new ministry which was to be concerned exclusively with religious matters, and he quickly had all the nightclubs and gambling casinos closed down. While the bloody demonstrations against the regime continued as before, the parliamentary debates of the new government, which were shown live on television, consisted of a war of words between ministers and high-ranking public figures in the Shah's administration, who accused each other of treason, theft and financial and moral corruption. The overall situation was, of course, unchanged.

Dr Nahavandi, the head of the Empress's private office and my boss, was now made Minister for Higher Education in the Sharif-Emami cabinet, and his post in the private office was taken over by Dr Seyd Hossein Nasr, a scholar of Islamic art and culture and a Harvard graduate. Two years previously Dr Nasr had organized an exhibition of Islamic art, science and technology at the Hayward Gallery in London. Opened by Empress Farah, it included original manuscripts of the Koran and priceless bronze and copper engravings. In addition, Dr Nasr had represented Iran at the International Islamic Conference which took place concurrently in London. Interestingly enough, that conference dealt with topics such as Islam and human rights, the moral and social teachings of Islam, the definition of an Islamic country, Islam and nationalism, women in Islam, the economic system in Islam, Islam and the modern world and the conflict between Islam and Western technology.

It was at this time that I was asked to make an urgent translation by the editor of the television magazine *Tamasha*, for which I was still working; apparently it was on the orders of the Empress. The article I was to translate was an extremely long one entitled 'Le Développement et l'Environnement', and had been published in a

French scientific journal by a writer called Ignacy Sachs. In the experience of the author, who was studying the problems of the Third World from a sociological standpoint, imitation and assimilation of Western technology was an impossibility for these countries. He had reached the conclusion that such nations now had no choice but either to design new development models based on their specific cultural reality, or to stop development completely. He was also of the opinion that the West should cease exploiting the natural resources of these countries, which were already dwindling anyway. Ignacy Sachs thus held out the prospect of an age of anti-development, not only for the developing nations, but also for the highly industrialized states of the world. The Empress was clearly concerned about the problems of culture and development in our country. But still no real measures were yet being taken with regard to Islam as the national cultural focus or to the slowing down of mechanization. The theory put forward by the author of that article, however, was soon to be proven in practice by the Islamic Revolution in Iran, whose hostility was directed not only against the Pahlavis, but also against the West and against progress.

For this reason the appointment of Dr Nasr, a recognized authority on Islamic culture, as the head of the Empress's private office was regarded as mere window dressing, and he himself lost his academic prestige when he accepted the post. Also, due to the unrest, the office's activities had considerably lessened, and our new boss's audiences with the Empress were gradually reduced to two a month. Furthermore, the daily drive for his staff through the increasingly fierce street demonstrations became more and more difficult, especially since we had to pass through the very heart of the city, where battles were taking place between demonstrators and the military. The Shah and the Empress no longer left their Palace in Niavaran, and the Imperial Guard had set up barricades around the whole area.

By the beginning of September the uproar in the Tehran streets had reached a peak and we had to telephone Colonel Madani, the security chief of the private office, every day to ask whether we should still risk driving to the office. But the message was always the same: 'Her Imperial Majesty wishes her office to remain open as always and her staff to perform their official duties.' This meant that we risked our lives daily in order not to disappoint the Empress. I felt it was no longer safe to drive my own car and took a taxi every morning, provided I could find one; otherwise I walked the six or seven miles. Several times I was wedged in between the revolutionaries and the military forces in the middle of a street battle, and only escaped being killed by pure luck. My colleagues at the private office also experienced dreadful scenes every day and risked their lives again and again. Our shared fears created a bond which had not existed before. Many had vanished, but those of us who remained maintained our ground. In a way it seemed the safest thing to do. From the private office building we could see what was happening both behind in Shah Reza Avenue and in front in Iranshahr Street; when we heard shooting we all lay down on the floor. The demonstrators were not armed: they threw stones or set parked cars on fire. The biggest mass demonstrations took place in Shah Reza Avenue. It was particularly alarming for us to hear the fierce cries and chanted slogans of the united masses against the Shah and his family – they were so close that they seemed directed against us, as employees of the Imperial Court.

The religious aspect of the Revolution was especially noticeable in the month of fasting, Ramadan, which in that year lasted from 4 August to 4 September, when the masses of the faithful mourned the martyrs' deaths of the revolutionaries. Together they chanted: 'If you want justice and you believe in the martyrdom of Imam Hossein, if you are men of God, unite to strengthen your religion and to destroy the Pahlavis!' On 4 September, the festival of Ide-Fetre at the end of Ramadan, two hundred thousand people assembled in the streets of Tabriz and Mashhad. They all wore long white robes to symbolize the Islamic shroud, and they were demonstrating that they were prepared to sacrifice their lives for religion and for the annihilation of the Shah's regime.

The government of Sharif-Emami had obviously not been capable of bringing about a national consensus and restoring order, and as a result on 7 September martial law was declared by General Gholamali Oveissi, the Commander of the ground forces. One of the toughest of the Shah's military men, he was called 'The Butcher' by the people. But the opposition was already so strongly mobilized that it no longer feared such measures. In spite of the announcement of a state of emergency, we at the Court Ministry still had to turn up every morning in our departments just as if the country were at peace.

On 8 September, Black Friday, troops opened fire on unarmed civilians who had organized a mass demonstration in southern Tehran. Jaleh Square became the scene of an atrocious bloodbath in which at least a thousand men, women and children were killed, the victims of a monstrous act of inhumanity for which the Shah could never be forgiven. Immediately strikes were declared in various public organizations, ministries and banks. But the most effective strike was that by workers throughout the oil industry, which paralyzed the economy. Oil revenues dried up; petrol disappeared from the pumps; public transport seized up and there was no heating in this exceptionally cold winter. Conditions were impossible.

Meanwhile, the street battles became increasingly violent. The demonstrators, constantly under fire, now defended themselves with petrol bombs which they threw at the Shah's troops. 'Down with the military, the enemy of its own people!' they shouted. 'Down with the Shah! God come to our aid!' It seemed very odd to me that, although the Shah had equipped his army with the most modern, expensive weapons of war, which could have been used against a foreign army, he was surprisingly lacking in the means which had been developed in the USA and Europe in the 1960s for dispersing rioters. Water cannon, tear gas, riot shields, protective masks and all the other paraphernalia which may be deployed against unarmed demonstrators are horrible things, but the Shah might have utilized them at the beginning of the unrest. Now, of course, it was too late anyway.

I simply could not understand how the military could shoot so brutally at demonstrators who were only proclaiming their political demands. At work we now did nothing but discuss for hours on end the political situation in the country and our own position. The new boss came into the office only very rarely, contacting us by telephone from his home to pass on the Empress's gratitude for our steadfastness. By November we were among the few public employees who were still loyal; the rest had made the country's economy grind to a halt by joining the general strike as a means of expressing their solidarity with the masses. In the evenings we worked with paraffin lamps, now that workers at power stations were also involved in the strike. In this ominous darkness, the nights punctuated from time to time by gunfire, we waited in desperation for a solution. But the time for reconciliation had long since passed.

The Shah now replaced Sharif-Emami's civilian government with a military one under General Azhari, the sixty-one-year-old Chief-of-Staff and another of his hard-liners, and he became completely dependent on the army for his protection. This action only served to emphasize his weakness. He simultaneously sent his former Prime Minister Hoveyda, and all of his colleagues who had represented the absolutism of the Shah, among them General Nassiri, the head of Savak, to prison. My former boss in the Empress's private office, Dr Hushang Nahavandi, was also imprisoned because he was the author of the Shah's political ideology, as was the former Minister of Information, Daryoush Homayoun, who had published the defamatory article about Ayatollah Khomeini and who was now regarded by the Shah as a catalyst of the Revolution. And so he turned against his own closest advisers and used them as scapegoats.

This move not only further weakened his extremely shaky credibility in the eyes of the people, but also made the rest of his close advisers and the entire entourage of the imperial couple very nervous. Gradually and discreetly they gave up their jobs and fled the country, few of them empty-handed, and most with wealth enough for the rest of their lives. My new boss in the private office, Dr Nasr, also disappeared and we never heard from him again. His private secretary told us that he had been asked by the Empress to attend an art exhibition in Japan, but nobody believed it. Everyone knew that he was never going to come back. The National Bank of Iran then published a long list of all the well-known, influential persons who had fled abroad with their funds and showed details of the amounts involved in their transactions, none of which was below £2 million.

Ayatollah Khomeini had been expelled in October that year from Iraq, where he had been in exile. The Shah, now politically on good terms with Iraq, had persuaded the Iraqis to deport him because of the unceasing torrent of religious and political propaganda he was smuggling in over the border. Once settled in Paris, the Ayatollah had the media of the West at his disposal and was able to publicize to the whole world his uncompromising demands regarding the abdication of the Shah. All the major opponents of the Monarch living abroad, with their wide range of political viewpoints, surrounded this old man, this oracle, with whom they had only one interest in common: the overthrow of the Shah's regime.

When the Shah put together a military government in November, all public services such as transport, electricity, water, banks, customs and industries such as oil had already been put out of operation by strikes encouraged by Khomeini from abroad and by the National Front within Iran. During this hard winter the inhabitants of Tehran had to queue for hours in the snow for petrol. From France, the Ayatollah urged the troops not to shoot at their own brothers and to join the people in opposing the Shah. The disintegration of the army had already begun at the horrifying Black Friday battle in Jaleh Square; many soldiers deserted and many more refused to obey their officers. The house of cards was beginning to topple.

On 7 November the Shah turned imploringly to his people in a television broadcast and made these historic admissions:

> As your monarch, who has taken an oath to protect national unity and the Shia religion, I renew my oath before the Iranian nation and promise no longer to tolerate the mistakes that have been made, the unlawful actions, suppression and corruption, and to see that the nation is compensated. I have heard your revolutionary message, the message of the people, the Iranian people. I am the guardian of the constitutional monarchy, which is a gift of God entrusted to the Shah by the people. I guarantee the protection of everything which you have achieved by your sacrifices. I guarantee that in future the Iranian government will distance itself from tyranny and violence, and will act in accordance with the constitution and with social justice.

It was not the once all-powerful Shah who spoke but a weak, ill and broken man who had aged very quickly. For the first time he referred to himself in the first person and did not use the royal 'we'. But it was too late.

It was not only the corruption of his regime which had resulted in such fierce opposition, it was also the fact that he had made the country increasingly dependent on the West with his ill-considered plans for modernization and mechanization. The number of American technicians and experts in the country, and above all in the army, led to great resentment among the masses and especially in academic student circles, who described the Shah as a puppet of the Americans representing the interests of the West, and particularly of the United States. Khomeini seemed the exact opposite of the Shah. He demanded that the country should be made independent of all foreign influences, a very attractive proposition for educated and uneducated Iranians alike, and particularly for the groups organizing opposition from all political directions.

The military government seemed indifferent to the promises made to his citizens by the Shah, for immediately after his emotional television address to the nation shots were fired at unarmed students from the tanks posted on the University of Tehran campus. In order to get a grip on the revolt the military government had closed this university, the centre of political gatherings. On that November day students stormed on to the campus and protested against the presence of armed forces there; the soldiers immediately began to fire at them, an appalling scene which was shown live on television. It was the first time since the outbreak of the Revolution that the television station had been bold enough to show a scene of this sort as it happened, and revealed that there was now a split in the media, too. The power of the Shah's regime had quite clearly reached the brink of the abyss.

A Court adjutant, who had been sent to the Empress's private office from the Court Ministry because certain measures were apparently to be taken to ensure our safety, informed us that for some time now the Shah and the Empress had been going on to the flat roof of their Palace in Niavaran in the evenings to watch the rioting. Despite the curfew, in the evenings thousands of people shouting '*Allah Akbar!*' (God is mighty) and '*Khomeini Rahbar!*'

(Our leader is Khomeini) would rush into the streets or go up on to their flat roofs to show their support for the demonstrators. It is almost incredible to imagine the Emperor and his Empress calmly watching the destruction of their capital as if it was yet another firework spectacle for their entertainment. One is reminded of Nero at the end of his days as Roman Emperor.

According to this Court employee, who had access to the Palace, the first time they had viewed the spectacle the Shah had said to the Empress: 'Is that really my people who are rebelling against me? I thought my people loved me!' Such naïvety at this point was astounding. It speaks volumes for the destruction of the Peacock Throne. In order to see for himself how serious the situation was, soon afterwards the Shah went up in a helicopter to observe the street demonstrations in daylight.

After this visit the Court adjutant never came to the private office again, and the security measures which he had mentioned were also completely forgotten. As before, we continued to be exposed to great danger. At the beginning of December we were eye witnesses to the greatest mass demonstration seen in Shah Reza Avenue since the outbreak of the Revolution. Over a million people from the various opposition groups – among them thousands of women, mostly veiled – marched peacefully and in amazingly good order for several miles through the avenues of Tehran and voiced their final demands: 'We want Khomeini! We want Khomeini! We want an Islamic Republic! Down with the Shah! Down with all the Pahlavis!'

This was the very last peaceful demonstration we saw in Tehran. Shortly afterwards, when the Shah was seen to be still resisting and not prepared to step down, the demonstrators resorted to mob violence. Large groups of them broke into the offices of ministries and public organizations, and also those of private firms who had not joined in the general strike, and smashed everything in sight. We in the Empress's private office were not immune from their attentions.

I shall never forget that dreadful experience. It happened at three o'clock in the afternoon one day in mid-December 1978. The personnel director, Bijan Shahrais, the private secretary, Farideh Mirbabai, and I were sitting together in one of the offices on the fifth floor, discussing the events of the Revolution and the still open question of the Shah's abdication.

'I'm convinced,' said the private secretary, 'that His Imperial Majesty won't give up his country so easily. We mustn't let ourselves get demoralized because of this rebellion.'

'You can hardly call it a rebellion still,' I replied. 'It's a total collapse of the social system. Even the military government hasn't been able to restore order.' I asked the personnel chief where Mr Shirakh, the Empress's financial director, was. I hadn't seen him for several days. His son, too, who worked as a secretary in the office, had not been to work for some time.

'Haven't you heard?' was the sarcastic response. 'Our two colleagues have flown to America with their whole family!'

'How many of us are still coming to work, then?' I asked.

'About thirty-five,' he answered.

'Her Majesty the Empress was very downcast on the telephone today,' sighed the private secretary. 'She's deeply disappointed that her most trusted employees have left their jobs in such a hurry. Even her cousin, Madame Khoseimeh Alam – the one who used to run the carpet museum – has fled the country with her husband.'

I reminded them of another turncoat colleague of ours, a man called Firouz Shirvanlou, director of Farhangsara, the House of Culture, the largest such centre in Iran. 'He declared his solidarity with the people two weeks ago in the daily paper, and then renamed the centre after Nima Yushidj, a poet who broke all the traditions. Aren't they a load of opportunists? He of all people, the great sycophant who enjoyed so many privileges and was still kissing the Empress's hand only a few weeks ago!'

'Do you know how many tax-free Mercedes he's imported for himself since he took office?' asked the personnel director, who then answered his own question. 'Four! And now he's a revolutionary, if you please!'

Suddenly our desultory conversation was interrupted by the crash of breaking windows and a hubbub on the lower floors of the building, followed by screams. We all rushed out on to the stairs, where we found the rest of the staff had also taken refuge. We could hear the security chief of the private office, Colonel Madani, arguing downstairs with the attackers, who seemed to be armed with long sticks.

'What do you want here? We're just a trading company,' claimed the colonel.

'That's not true!' the attackers screamed. 'You barefaced liar! Do you think we don't know you're one of the biggest branches of Savak? Come on, comrades – let's clean up the scum here!'

As the colonel still barred their way, they said: 'If you don't work for Savak, then show us your office letterhead with your firm's name on it!'

The director of the building and architecture department, Mr Iranpour, said he thought we were crazy just to stand there and wait to be killed. 'Come on – the colonel once told me there's a secret door hidden behind the wall on the third floor! It's an emergency escape route!' Everyone followed him to the third floor, where we tried to smash through the wall with two large hammers. But we had no success. 'Dammit!' he shouted. 'That bastard lied! There is no door!'

Then there was a dreadful commotion on the stairs and the revolutionaries were racing up to get us. 'Look at these women,' they cried sarcastically. 'Get up there, quickly, you dirty servants of the Pahlavis!' They were a group of about forty bearded young men who might have been students. Some of our women colleagues screamed and begged for mercy. They promised to cover their heads and become good Moslems. The private secretary, three other secretaries and I dashed upstairs, rather pointlessly, to lock our desks and filing cabinets. Instinct and training led us to protect the documents. It seems extraordinary now that we took such care over essentially trivial and banal scraps of paper. The private secretary rang the Empress at the Palace. 'Your Majesty!' she blurted. 'We've been attacked by the mob. They're carrying sticks and are only on the second floor at the moment – soon they'll be up here, though. But we've made sure that the files are safe!' As she hung up she gasped: 'Her Majesty thinks we should ring Savak straightaway!' There was no reply. Then the rioters burst into the room and we were their prisoners.

After three hours without knowing what would befall us we women were set free by the students. We had to promise not to come to the office any more. The men were still under guard there. Outside, by the entrance, a number of revolutionaries had assembled to cheer on the attack. When they saw us they began to shout insults: we were filthy agents of Savak, and degenerate lackeys of the Pahlavis. A few steps further on we were besieged by a vast crowd of demonstrators who forced us to sing anti-Shah slogans with them: 'Say, "Down with the Shah!" Say, "Death to the Pahlavis!"' That evening the demonstrators set fire to all the vehicles in the streets, and many office buildings were in flames as I stumbled past them on my way home. The military had given up shooting.

Next morning I received a telephone call at home from the Empress's private secretary. Apparently the Empress had ordered the contents of our offices, including papers and files, to be evacuated in army trucks and transported to the Reza Abbassi cultural centre in the old Shemiran Street in northern Tehran. I think I was supposed to breathe a sigh of relief. She added that we were now all to come to the centre immediately and await Her Majesty's orders.

I went, for I was frightened to stay on my own and sought the relative safety of company. The modern centre was mainly used for art exhibitions, and we found it full of Iranian surrealist paintings and modern sculpture. We had no idea what the Shah and the Empress were planning. Why on earth did the Empress insist at all costs on the continued existence of her private office when all the institutions in the country had been torn apart? Every day we heard contradictory reports about the Shah leaving the country. Once we heard that His Majesty was going but that the Empress was staying. Another time it was said that there were disagreements between the imperial couple: the Empress was to stay, along with the Crown Prince, but the Shah was against it. Then people thought that they had both left the country. All these reports from the Palace showed how undecided the question of the Shah's abdication still was. We heard, for example, that General Gholam-Ali Oveissi, who commanded the ground forces, had told the Shah: 'To suppress the revolution is a matter of a million.' He proposed the bombing of the holy city of Qom, the Shia Moslem powerbase, killing a million people, in the belief that this would stun the religious leaders and their followers into abandoning the Revolution and effectively obliterate the Shah's main opposition. The Shah refused. Oveissi left for France, where he was murdered by Khomeini's agents in 1984.

On 30 December the Shah dissolved the military government and appointed as Prime Minister his long-time political opponent, Shapour Bakhtiar, one of the leaders of the National Front party who had sent the first open letter of protest to him. His colleagues expelled him from the party immediately, because they had already allied themselves with Khomeini in Paris and did not want to enter into any compromises with the Shah. Bakhtiar was a Western-trained democrat who believed that he would be able to save the country's constitution, which was very progressively conceived and in which the principles of parliamentary democracy were firmly anchored. He thought, at this time of crisis, that he could preserve the country from a victory by the radical mullahs. His conditions were that the Shah should grant him authority over the whole administration, and that the Imperial Family should go abroad until the situation had returned to normal. Apart from the Shah and the Empress and their children, all other members of the imperial house had long since left the country. Thus from 30 December 1978 until 11 January 1979, when the Shah and the Empress took their leave of Iran, uncertainty persisted.

On the day before their departure we were told that the Empress wanted to receive us all at the Palace. But immediately afterwards, when her private secretary had spoken to her on the telephone, she told us with great regret that the Shahbanou was not feeling at all well and had therefore asked only to receive her, the private secretary.

On 11 January, when the Shah and the Empress finally got on to a gigantic empty Iranian airline Boeing at Tehran airport and were about to fly out of the country, the private secretary distributed personal notes of thanks from the Empress and gave each of us a gold coin bearing her portrait. I often think about that empty plane and wonder why Her Majesty, who could arrange for the rescue of her trunks, correspondence and files, could not arrange for us to fill some of those empty seats. The Empress had begged the secretary, she told us, with tears in her eyes, to pass on her gratitude. She also wished us to be told not to give up hope and to wait for her, for she was sure to be back again soon. . . .

11

An Islamic Interrogation

Despite the Empress's optimism, the Shah must have known that they would never return to Iran. His sad face, the tears rolling down his cheeks at the airport, and his express wish to take with him a spadeful of his home country's soil were all clear indicators of that.

The people were jubilant at his departure. For three days they danced and celebrated in the streets of Tehran, pulling down the few still intact statues of the Shah and the Crown Prince, driving with their headlights blazing and shouting: 'The Shah has gone! The Shah has gone! We've done it! We've done it!'

But what was to become of us who had remained loyal to the Empress to the bitter end and continued to go to our workplaces? The Empress had escaped from danger and left us, in the midst of a nightmare civil war, with a letter of thanks and a gold coin. She had been shattered to see how friends from her schooldays and her own relatives had left their jobs, even in the early phases of the Revolution, and fled. These were people who owed to her their immeasurable privileges and wealth. Perhaps this was why the Empress, deeply disappointed, had decided not to grant us a last farewell audience. Her disappointment can hardly have exceeded our terror, however, abandoned as we were to the whims of the retaliating revolutionaries.

Now we became fully aware of the gravity of our own situation. What would happen if Prime Minister Bakhtiar, whose call for temporary withdrawal the Shah had finally accepted, did not succeed in bringing the country under his control? Bakhtiar pitched straight in, dissolved Savak, thus ending repression, and then tried to win for his own government the support of the deeply divided army and the media. To prevent the return of Khomeini he closed all airports and borders.

But the strike continued, and further massive street demonstrations showed that the people didn't want the new Prime Minister either. They called for him to resign and shouted for Khomeini. Bakhtiar tried to reach a compromise with the moderate religious circles in order to protect the constitution and prevent things moving in an extreme direction. But the faithful millions were waiting for Ayatollah Khomeini, whom they now called Imam Khomeini. He was their saviour, the hidden twelfth Imam of the Shias who, by his resurrection, would liberate the world from injustices. Bakhtiar, on the other hand, was supported only by a handful of middle-class Iranians. A demonstration in Tehran organized by his supporters, a mere two thousand men and women dressed in fashionable Western clothes, itself showed the hopelessness of his attempts.

Bakhtiar's government, which in the final analysis had been called to power by the Shah himself as his last concession, was identified by the opposition with trying to save the Shah's regime and was associated by them with Iran's dependence upon the USA. The arrival of General Heusser, second-in-command in NATO, to hold consultations with the Shah's generals in Tehran immediately before the imperial couple departed, confirmed people's distrust of Bakhtiar. 'Our way is neither East nor West!' and 'An Islamic Republic is our goal!' were the slogans proclaimed by the people as they were now formed into Islamic revolutionary committees by mullahs from the mosques.

It was high time that the thirty of us who still remained in the office decided upon our future. Bakhtiar's chances seemed hopeless. Tehran airport was still closed. The country was gripped in a fever. A military putsch was in the air. But what sort of putsch it might be we couldn't tell, because the army was split between royalists and revolutionaries. There were rumours of a new 'army of the people'. For us there were only two possibilities: either to go into hiding until we could escape from the country, or to stick together and await our fate.

After a lot of discussion we chose the second alternative. The reasons were obvious. Since Savak had been dissolved, hundreds of fearful secret agents had gone under cover, hoping to escape the vengeance of the enraged population. We didn't want to be counted among them as they were discovered one after another, day by day, beaten up and finally hauled before revolutionary committees. The feelings of hatred for the Shah were now released in the purest desire for revenge.

Bakhtiar did not suspect that Ayatollah Khomeini would become a political as well as a religious leader, and hoped for reconciliation. He could no longer resist the stubborn demands of the people, and on 1 February he reopened the airport to allow the Ayatollah to return from Paris. Iranian television, still under Bakhtiar's control, broadcast the arrival of the spiritual leader live, but only for a few moments. A tall, dignified, bearded old man dressed in a turban and long robe descended, as if from the heavens, from a giant Air France jumbo jet. A uniformed airline official assisted him down the steps. Before the transmission had begun the Shah's portrait had been flashed up on the screen, accompanied by the Iranian national anthem, but immediately after it we saw a picture of the Ayatollah, accompanied by a song specially written for his return:

> Khomeini, Khomeini, you are our Imam!
> Khomeini, you are the leader of the Revolution!
> We welcome you!

This bizarre sequence of events was the result of divided loyalty among the television staff. But the remainder of the Ayatollah's triumphant return, which seemed to have brought practically everyone in Tehran to the airport to greet their religious leader, was not televised. Bakhtiar, still fighting for the existence of his government, had suppressed it as it would only have added to the Ayatollah's already enormous popularity. Above all, he wanted to try to prevent the army withdrawing its support from him. It was not until three days later that the 'converted' camera crew had the courage to broadcast the entire film of Khomeini's return: surrounded by some two million wildly excited people, his car drove to Shahyad Square, now renamed Freedom Square. From here he continued towards Beheshte-Zahra, the Tehran cemetery. The scene showed how the firm, unbending will of the masses could destroy even one of the world's most powerful governments. It illustrated the extraordinary intensity of religious belief in Iran, a phenomenon which the Shah and his advisers could never accept.

At the cemetery the Ayatollah expressed his gratitude to all the martyrs of the Islamic Revolution, a revolution for which much blood had been shed and whose spirit must be preserved at all costs. 'The struggle is not over,' he warned. 'It must be pursued until we have stamped out the very last vestiges of the Pahlavi regime! Islam has been with us! Islam will be with us!'

A second broadcast showed where the Ayatollah was to live. His supporters had taken him to a school in a poor area of south Tehran, which then became a place of holy pilgrimage. Every day many groups of people from all over Iran arrived at this school building to be blessed by their leader. It was from here that the Imam now led the Islamic revolutionary committees throughout the land: in high contrast to the Shah, he would sit on the ground with his back against a cushion, eating only modest portions of bread and yoghurt or boiled potatoes. Ironically, the Ayatollah nominated an old National Front party colleague of Bakhtiar's, Mehdi Bazargan, as the legal head of the country's government.

In his speeches the Ayatollah laid careful emphasis on the words 'Islamic Revolution' and 'Islamic Republic'. In this way the Ayatollah, now assured of massive support from the people, sought quite consciously to exclude all other forms of government – the forms of government, in other words, which the various other opposition groups that had played a decisive role in the revolution were proposing.

The country's political situation remained extremely tense. We now had two governments – one led by Bakhtiar from the Prime Minister's office, and one over which Bazargan presided from a schoolhouse in the slums of south Tehran. In theory Bakhtiar was still in charge of the army and the media; but Bazargan enjoyed the support of the masses and, indeed, of part of the armed forces.

On 9 February, precisely a week after Khomeini's return, armed revolutionary guards stormed our office. We had been talking nervously when they burst in, holding guns. Two colleagues and I tried to escape from the third floor through the emergency exit, which led down into the rear yard. But down below two bearded men dressed in green guerilla uniforms were waiting for us, and we were seized and driven back into the building. They locked us all into a narrow vestibule in the lower basement, taking it in turns to keep watch over us. It was incredibly crowded and stuffy. I could see from the pale faces of my colleagues, male and female alike, that they felt as frightened as I did. For three hours we sat on the floor waiting, without exchanging a word, dreading the thought of what the guards might have in mind for us. The young man watching us kept playing with his rifle. At four o'clock his companions came down and ordered us to go upstairs. Petrified, we just stared at one another, assuming that the end had come. They led us to the reception hall on the first floor, where we could look out of the many windows into the front courtyard and beyond into the street. We were to remain here under guard until instructions had been received from the revolutionary headquarters – from the schoolhouse where the Ayatollah and his advisers were living.

Towards evening, when the guards brought us bread, boiled eggs and water, it became clear that we were going to have to spend the night there. Two new guards took over the watch while the others patrolled the rest of the building – we could see them now and again in the courtyard. Suddenly the nerves of one of my colleagues, Mehri Kazemi, gave way and she broke down in tears: 'For God's sake just tell us what you want of us! What are you waiting for? Stick us against that wall and shoot us. I can't stand it any more!'

The guards remained silent. We held our breath. At that very moment machine guns started firing outside and one explosion after another shook the city. Shelling started. Was it the beginning of a military putsch? We clutched at one another, believing that the end of our world was near. Tehran shook and we were quivering. Our guards had sprung up and positioned themselves beside the exit, ready to shoot. 'The Imperial Guard has attacked the air force barracks! Air force cadets loyal to the Ayatollah and the Revolution have opened the arsenal to the people,' shouted one of them in triumph. 'Now the people are armed and can protect the Revolution!'

Our guards divided us into two groups for the night. The men were led back into the basement, while we women remained upstairs in the reception hall. Then they brought us army blankets. It was a horrible night: dogs barked incessantly, and shots were fired. It was quite impossible to get any sleep.

The next morning the armed people's militia stormed the imperial palaces, the Parliament building and the Prime Minister's office. We could see them from the window of the cultural centre, riding past on tanks and lorries. 'Bakhtiar has gone!' we heard; our hope of being freed had vanished. But it did seem as if the Imperial Guard was continuing to fight, because the shooting went on unceasingly. Gradually, we felt able to start talking to one another. The Empress's cousin, Mina Sadegh, the head of the arts department, thought when she looked at the guards that she would undoubtedly be the first to be killed. On the other hand the Empress's private secretary, Farideh Mirbabai, still seemed to believe that the Imperial Guard would win. For my part I said that I thought we were all finished. In the midst of this turmoil the victorious crowds also opened all the prisons releasing prisoners held by Savak on political grounds. In the excitement they also unwittingly freed the city's criminals and the ministers whom the Shah had just imprisoned in his belated attempt to place the blame for what had gone wrong on a group of his close advisors. With the exception of the Shah's former Prime Minister, Amir Abbas Hoveyda, they all fled to the West. Hoveyda decided that he must stay to prove his innocence to the Iranian people before the revolutionary court. This moral stance proved to be a fatal error since he was found guilty and executed by firing squad in 1979.

That evening, when salvos began to ring out very close to us and the whole city started to shake again, the private secretary's eyes began to glitter, for she thought that a *coup d'état* leading to the return of the imperial couple had begun. She was, of course, completely wrong, because an hour later one of our guards informed us that he had learnt from his companions down in the street that the television and radio station had been occupied by the revolutionaries. They turned on their transistor radios and we heard: 'This is the voice of the Islamic Revolution. In the name of Almighty God we pronounce the end of the dictatorial regime of the Shah.' This was followed by recitations from the Koran.

The next morning the door opened and three men in civilian clothes led into the room our male colleagues who had been left in the basement. They declared that they had been sent from revolutionary headquarters to question us. To my amazement the head of security in the private office, who had escaped during the first attack on our office in Iranshahr Street, was among the prisoners.

The questions which Ayatollah Khomeini's emissaries wanted to ask us lasted for over a week, during which time we were given very little to eat and had to endure minimal washing facilites. We all felt extremely uncomfortable.

To begin with they handed each of us a sheet of paper. 'You have one hour in which to answer briefly and clearly two questions which I am going to ask you. One: Explain why you worked for the Court of Mohammed Reza Pahlavi. Two: What is your view of the Islamic Revolution?' I was filled with an intense sense of horror. We were surrounded by young revolutionary guards passionately believing in their sacred cause and with loaded guns pointing towards us. A trigger-happy guard could have shot us on the spot or we could have been ordered outside for instantaneous execution in the yard. So tense were my nerves that I felt as though I were floating, hypnotized, like a puppet, ready to accept whatever fate had in store. But the emissaries left the room and we had to begin to answer the questions which would decide whether we lived or died. I wrote:

> I worked for Empress Farah because I believed fundamentally in her objectives and in her attempts to alter the social conditions in Iran. She appeared to me to be a person of honesty. By working for her I wanted to achieve something useful and constructive for my country, but the more the true nature of the Shah's system became evident to me the more hopeless and absurd my own efforts appeared. The two occasions on which I resigned from the service bear testimony to my view of the Shah's regime, but I was recalled each time. My last post in the Empress's private office consisted of dealing with her foreign correspondence.

I looked up and glanced for a moment at the faces of my colleagues, contorted by their efforts to justify why they had worked for the Imperial Court and what they had done there.

But I had only filled half my sheet of paper. The second question still awaited me: What is your view of the Islamic Revolution? I took a deep breath and tried to collect my thoughts. 'An impressive Revolution,' read my first phrase, 'in which women, men and children from all social levels in our country have participated and shown their constancy, sense of sacrifice and solidarity. It is my hope and the hope of all Iranians who love their country that the new government will be based upon social justice and democracy.'

What the others wrote, I was never to learn. The answers were sent back to the headquarters of the Revolution for a decision. We then waited a further twenty-four hours for Ayatollah Khomeini's instructions. Finally, our investigatory judges appeared. They were four strict-looking young men of threatening countenance, and their curt behaviour indicated immediately their merciless attitude. The interrogation began.

Our names were called out from an alphabetical list and we were sent one after the other to the third floor. There in a small room sat two inquisitors at a desk, as I found when it was finally my turn to be summoned.

'We are both Islamic scholars of the law,' explained one of them. 'We want to know about your past,' he continued. 'It is in your own interests to tell the truth!'

'In the name of Almighty God,' said the two in unison, looking downwards because I was unveiled and my naked head was an offence in their eyes.

Then the older of the two opened a file and asked: 'In your personal papers it is stated that you organized the journeys to Switzerland of Mohammed Reza and Farah Pahlavi while working at the Embassy in Berne. Is that true?

'Yes.' So they had broken open the filing cabinets and knew everything about our past careers. In all probability they knew more than we did ourselves. Their questions plainly suggested that they had also got hold of Savak's secret reports. The interrogation continued:

'Your task required you at that time to maintain a close relationship with the Swiss secret police. Is that true?'

'Yes.'

'Why did you, and not someone else, have charge of such a task?'

'Because I grew up in Switzerland and could speak the languages of the country.'

'You mean you did not work for Savak?'

'No. On the contrary. From the moment I entered the state service I was under constant Savak surveillance. My criticism of what went on in my areas of activity caused them to be permanently suspicious of me.'

'Why did you leave your post as public relations director of Farah's charity organization?'

'Because I was asked, together with the other directors, to sign a document which would sanction the import of a substandard milk powder to be fed to mentally handicapped children. In Sweden, this powder was used only as cattle food.'

'Explain how you came to hold this post in Farah's private office.'

'I received a telephone call from Madame Diba's secretary. She was also a member of the charitable organization's board of trustees. She told me that she had recommended me to the new head of the private office, who needed an assistant with foreign languages. I was then telephoned by the head of the office himself. It was fear of Savak that made me accept this post.'

'Your career suggests that, despite what you have told us, you had great sympathy for Farah. Why?'

'Because of her social ideals. Because she herself told me, when I met her for the first time in Switzerland, that she wanted to help needy people in our country. And then she was a warm-hearted and honest person – not like the other members of the Court.'

At that moment I thought to myself that the next question would surely be: 'What did you think of the Shah?' But to my amazement it was never put to me. Yet I had mentally prepared an answer – I was going to say that I disliked him and his family for the damage they had done to my homeland, and did not consider him to be an appropriate ruler for a developing country. But the questioning took another direction.

'Why didn't you import a duty-free Mercedes like all the other members of the private office?' The judge was leafing through papers lying on the desk in front of him.

'I don't like large cars.'

'How do you explain the fact that you had no interest-free loans?'

'I hate having debts.'

'But why did the others have such high loans?'

'Did they?' I was being disingenuous at this moment.

'Yes. Two million Toman. Three million Toman. Four million Toman.' This was £100,000, £150,000 and £200,000.

'I don't know why.'

'Because they were running businesses on the side! Of course you knew about it!'

'No,' I protested.

'What do you know about the gold coins in the private office safe?'

'I know there's a collection of specially minted gold coins for ceremonial occasions, which are sometimes brought out for particular annual events and given by the Empress to foreign and Iranian dignitaries.' I was of course fully aware that there was a store of gold coins, stamped with the portrait of the Empress and worth millions of pounds, in the safe in the finance department. The largest coin of all was 15 centimetres in diameter and a whole centimetre thick.

'But the safe is empty. Do you know who kept the key?'

'Only the director of finance and the head of the private office.'

'Where are these "gentlemen"?'

'I haven't seen either of them for two months.'

'Then you know that they have fled the country?'

'No, I didn't know.'

And that was the last question. A revolutionary guard led me downstairs to join the others in the hall. From the window I could see heavily armed, bearded young men clambering into the Mercedes parked in the courtyard and driving off. I felt terribly weak and could barely talk to my colleagues.

One by one they were led upstairs. The interrogation continued on its merciless course, but not everyone came back – many were taken away from the centre. The trial lasted for several days. There was only one thing that we could read, as a way of feverishly passing the time, but it was something horrible: newly printed copies of *Keyhan*. The paper published long lists of ministers and generals who had been executed, illustrated by horrific photographs of the grotesquely distorted faces of hanged men, dangling with broken necks from rows of ropes. One was the chief of Savak.

Suddenly, after many days, I heard my name called. They took me upstairs again. My destiny was in the balance. I entered the little room where the two Islamic judges were still sitting. Sentence had been passed; I could return home – if I still had one – on condition that I reported every other day until further notice to Niavaran Palace and had my identity card, which they now handed me, stamped. Totally exhausted, I dragged myself home.

This was certainly the most critical moment in my life and I badly needed my father. But he had died the year before – in February 1978 – of a sudden heart attack. Since my return to Iran in 1973 from my post in Berne I had found constant consolation from all the frustrations of my work by talking to my father. He knew the Iranian system far better than I. Now I ruefully remembered the day twelve years earlier when he had wanted me to join an international organization and not the Shah's civil service. In a sense he had been right. I had not been able to make the necessary adjustments to fit in with the Shah's administration. The system had not absorbed me, nor had I been able to adapt myself to its values. The only person to whom I could now turn was my stepmother. Although we both felt profound grief that my father had gone, we were somehow glad that he had not been destined to experience these terrifying days.

Life went on, but as in a vacuum. In accordance with the orders of the Islamic revolutionaries, the day after my return I visited Niavaran Palace, which until a few weeks before had still been the splendid residence of the imperial couple. The iron gates, once kept tightly shut and patrolled by imperial guards armed with machine guns, were standing wide open. Above them hung a gigantic portrait of Ayatollah Khomeini. How often I had visited this Palace under different circumstances. Now you could enter the great antechamber without being stopped. And what a scene awaited me: ripped oil paintings were hanging at crazy angles from the walls. There had been looting – not for wealth or gain, but simply for the sake of destruction. The great gilt-framed mirrors, which had once reflected the elegance of the Court, lay on the marble floor in jagged slivers. The giant cut-glass chandeliers had been smashed to smithereens. The portraits of the Shah and the Empress had been stamped upon and thrown into the corners. Exquisite Louis XV furniture lay in broken piles across the floor. Of the valuable silk carpets there was no sign whatsoever. These alone might have been stolen by dealers. A few decapitated statues remained in their niches, but above them had been smeared in heavy red letters the slogan: 'Long live the Islamic Republic!' The glorious empire of the Pahlavis had finally and irrevocably vanished. And it had not merely vanished, but had been mocked, destroyed and defiled.

Did it have to be this way, I asked myself, pulling my black veil deeper across my forehead and showing my identity card to a mullah who was sitting behind a simple desk. Could the Western values of material well-being and individual freedom ever have rooted themselves in this Islamic culture? Even the Shah, who had been so influenced by the West, had respected only material wealth and not the West's respect for freedom. The Revolution showed that the Iranian people were concerned not with materialism but with honouring their ancient faith. But could the Shah still have prevented the Revolution if he had shown more respect for Islam and led a less extravagant life? His ultimate mistake had been to turn a blind eye to the colossal corruption of his entourage. And he had failed to act against that corruption, not because Savak had succeeded in concealing it from him, but because he and his own family had been profoundly involved in corruption themselves.

Western political democracy, upon which the 1906 constitution was based, quite simply failed. The majority of the Iranian people had not rejected a national leader. Far from it: they need a strong and charismatic figurehead and one to whom they can offer respect and devotion. But the Shah, in abusing their loyalty, failed them in this. It remains to be seen if Khomeini will succeed.

I left the Niavaran Palace, once the scene of the Shah's glory and now of his fall. Filled with confusion, I sought my way outside. I had worked for a regime which had misused my energies, while I could not succeed in explaining to the new rulers that I had always wanted to work for the people. They branded me as one of the followers of the Shah's regime.

Outside, it was spring.

Epilogue

Seven years ago I was dragged into one of the few true revolutions to have occurred in world history. *Coups d'état*, in which power is simply seized by a new ruler within an existing system of government, have been innumerable. But a true revolution happens when an entire system so loses touch with the mass of its population that the people rise up in an explosion of spontaneous and devastating discontent. Such was the French Revolution, that put an end to the absolute rule of the monarchy in France; such was the Russian Revolution that destroyed the tsars; and such too was that Iranian Revolution of 1978–79. The Shah, like the French kings and the Russian tsars before him, had attempted to rule his people as an absolute monarch.

Returned to power in 1953 by a *coup d'état* engineered from outside, Mohammed Reza Pahlavi had tried to create a national identity through his ideology of the 'true Iran', the Iran of the ancient Persian kings of the pre-Islamic period. But it was an artificial creation of intellectuals, a romantic idea whose only reality was in the magnificence of costume and ceremony. No social cohesion followed. On the contrary, cohesion had to be increasingly provided by the secret police, whose sinister role of unending surveillance and repression I grew to know only too well. And behind the surface glamour, behind the Peacock Throne, lurked the unscrupulous channelling of public wealth into private pockets, that fundamental confusion of state service and personal reward which is known as corruption.

The regime systematically suppressed all dissenting voices. Yet resistance to the Shah had become overwhelming by the autumn of

1978, when all shades of opposition united in a single, mighty and unpremeditated street protest. Opponents of all kinds were in the streets, and I knew many of them – students, teachers and lecturers, civil servants, doctors, lawyers, both men and women, and of course mullahs and vast numbers of industrial workers who had streamed to the cities from the impoverished countryside in search of their fortune.

With hindsight it is plain that Ayatollah Khomeini and his supporters never had any intention of creating a pluralistic society to accommodate the Marxists and the Western liberals who had joined the infuriated masses. From the outset they intended to establish an Islamic Republic, probably the world's only state ruled exclusively by priests as God's representatives on earth. But two events of major significance hastened that process. The first was the destruction in 1981 of the Islamic party's headquarters, which killed seventy of the country's leading mullahs, including the influential and charismatic Ayatollah Mohammed Beheshti. Beheshti thus became a martyr of the Revolution, and the party decided that the time had come to eradicate political opposition. This spelt the end of the effective presence of the Islamic Marxists, the People's Mujahidin and the People's Fedayin as many of their leading figures were then executed. The second, a still weightier event, was the invasion of Iran by Iraq in a futile attempt by the Iraqis to depose Ayatollah Khomeini. This devastating conflict, which has already lasted for as long as World War II, at first cemented the Revolution against a common enemy.

To the Western observer a holy war between two Islamic peoples may seem paradoxical. But the strength of the present regime, yet also perhaps its principal weakness, is its representation of the Shia sect. After decades and even centuries of debasement as a minority branch of Islam, the Shias felt they could stand up with pride. For the Iranian Shia élite, to rule the country of Iran is not the only and final goal. Ayatollah Khomeini has always spoken as if for the whole of the Shia religion and this includes a substantial part of the Iraqi population. But it is not that proportion that rules Iraq. Iraq's secular regime favours the Sunnis. So this long-standing war is not concerned primarily with territory, or even oil-rich territory, but is a battle for people's hearts and for power.

Khomeini has sworn not to sue for peace until Iraq, too, becomes a Shia Republic.

How many Iranians can have died in the protracted struggle? Some say 200,000, others 500,000 and some even 1,000,000. But all are martyrs and, according to the Shia faith, a martyr leaves this earth to enter Paradise. This willingness to sacrifice one's own life with no thought for self-preservation is the new element in open warfare – and a terrifying new dimension in guerilla warfare, as has been seen in the astonishing suicide attacks by young Shia men and women in the Lebanon. All over Tehran walls are daubed with the slogan: 'A nation of martyrs cannot be enslaved.' To the horror of Western eyes, sheep are sacrificed in the street to divert evil from the young war volunteers. A fountain of blood in Tehran's vast and growing cemetery spouts a grim message commemorating the unending death toll at the front.

The Western element in me is terrified by such sights, even when merely conveyed in news photographs or television film reports. But my experience of Iran tells me that ordinary people – simple and profound believers – can identify more with such a state, even at war, than with the alien pomp and ceremony of what preceded it. The fusion of politics with what was closest to the people's hearts, their religion, is a potent mixture. The hidden twelfth Imam has returned in Ayatollah Khomeini's physical form. The eternal is now present among the people. And the local mullah, who was always the wise man, counsellor, family magistrate and lawyer, is now the political deputy too. An existing, deeply rooted social network has been brought to new life.

Where then rests the weakness in this remarkable theocracy? Not in its grass-roots organization. Nor in its ideological basis. Nor in its hatred of the West and especially America, known as Satan. But it may be in the war. The German dramatist Bertolt Brecht once said, crudely but shrewdly: '*Erst kommt das Fressen, dann die Moral*' – 'Morality is fine – once your belly's full.' The deprivation caused by a debilitating war effort is growing. Simple commodities are increasingly difficult to obtain: food is in short supply; prices are rising beyond poor people's means. Martyrdom continues relentlessly. Bombing of the capital and other cities by Iraqi aircraft has added a new immediacy and horror. Will discontent return in such magnitude that a new revolution will occur in the streets of Tehran?

To whom would or could the masses turn if deprivation and suffering reach the point of explosion? What alternatives to the Islamic Republic exist? Mujahidin, Fedayin and Tudeh – the socialist Islamic, Marxist and Communist alternatives – have long been eliminated through the systematic imprisonment and execution of their members. Their surviving elements in exile are bitterly divided. Could the Crown Prince, Reza Pahlavi, return? After the Shah's death from cancer in Egypt, Empress Farah and her three younger children moved to a quiet retreat outside Boston in the USA. The Crown Prince, however, lives in Morocco and Paris. It is his sworn ambition to go back to Iran as the new Shah, and to this end he has made a pact with his father's life-long critic and that denouncer of absolutism, Shapour Bakhtiar. This ill-fated, French-trained political scientist made a last-ditch attempt to save the monarchy and the country's constitution after the Shah and Empress had fled. And quite probably in a country in which European political traditions had taken root and there were substantial numbers of influential, educated liberals he could make an admirable Prime Minister. But could the ordinary Iranian people accept this man whom they now associate with the Shah – irony of ironies – and who is so obviously Western in outlook and values? I doubt it. Could the Crown Prince, then, provide the necessary national focus in a new Iranian constitutional monarchy? Some observers say there is so much unhappiness about the war that people may be prepared to accept the Crown Prince provided he does not follow his father's ruling concepts and does not allow his father's surviving advisers and courtiers to guide him. But the return of the Crown Prince assumes that Islam would recede again as a political force; that the twelfth Imam would again disappear; that the martyrs would be forgotten; that the mullahs would give up their power in their local constituencies and villages. I cannot believe this, for the present at least.

But could women play a decisive role in such a change? After all, looking at their lot through Western eyes one sees freedoms lost, an imprisonment behind the veil in a male-dominated religion. Could mothers who have lost their children, daughters who feel locked in beneath the *chador*, form the fuse to a new uprising? Again, I do not think this at all likely. Friends whom I knew at university, as well as simple working-class women, do not feel the *chador* to be a prison. For ordinary women the veil is the way of life to which they are accustomed, while many intellectual women regard it as a symbol of liberation from the domination of Western values – and assertion of Iranian independence.

'Not East, not West, but Islam' is the saying that inspires the present regime – hence the hatred of America and Israel, and the dislike of the Soviet Union. If a change of regime were to occur, it could only be with the help of the army. But today's army is not the army of the Shah. Its generals were executed or driven out to a man. A new officer class has developed, with the solidarity won from fighting a five-year war. It is difficult to see how this could be subverted unless events took a disastrous turn for the worse. And even if they did, the army is shadowed by a second, religiously motivated fighting force, the privileged Revolutionary Guards.

Looking into the future is a dangerous occupation. But if there is any guide it has to be found in historical experience. It is possible that, if Mossadegh had been allowed to carry through his experiment thirty years ago, a moderate and conceivably pluralistic, Islamic state might have emerged. But the abuse of power by the Shah, his positively anti-Islamic stance, the cruelty of Savak, the suffering during the Revolution, and now five years of war cannot be erased. They have scarred people's memories. And the majority of those who felt happier in the West, at least in their special Iranian version of the West, have left the country. Nor can it be denied that many of those who stayed behind have discovered a new sense of self-respect. For the first time this century Iran is run by Iranians from the lower and middle classes without any open or covert dependence on foreign powers. The Shah's first task on assuming power as a young monarch had been to try to free his country from an effective occupation and partition by Soviet troops in the north and British troops in the south. It was his success here that set him on the path towards creating a new Iranian nationalism, symbolized most magnificently – and most extravagantly – in 1971 by his celebration of the 2500th jubilee of the Persian monarchy in the ancient capital, Persepolis.

But this was only surface nationalism. His third wife, Farah Diba, for whom I worked, was equally isolated in her sincere desire to improve the lot of the poor majority of Iranians and to revive the country's ancient traditions. And for all her goodwill, she, too, bore the image of Western values for all to see. Iranians wanted to return to what they felt were their real roots, not the inventions of ideologues. The Pahlavi dynasty threw away its chance of success through a belief that it could allow itself anything, much like the seventeenth- and eighteenth-century French monarchs. *They* disregarded the power of reason, while Mohammed Reza Pahlavi and his advisers disregarded the power of religion. And so in 1978 Iran witnessed the world's first revolution to turn time back, not forward.

Index